Sense and Nonsense in the Behavioral Treatment of Autism: It Has to Be Said

Autism Partnership

Ron Leaf, Ph.D.

John McEachin, Ph.D.

Mitchell Taubman, Ph.D.

with chapters co-written by:

Danielle Baker, M.S.

Andy Bondy, Ph.D.

Marlene Driscoll, M.A., LMFT

B.J. Freeman, Ph.D.

Toby Mountjoy

Doris Soluaga Murtha, M.A.

Tracee Parker, Ph.D.

David Rosteter, Ph.D.

Sandy Slater, Ph.D.

Jennifer Styzens, M.S.

Andrea Waks, J.D.

DRL Books Inc.

Sense and Nonsense in the Behavioral Treatment of Autism: It Has To Be Said

Copyright © 2008 Autism Partnership

Published by: DRL Books Inc.
                  37 East 18th Street, 10th Floor
                  New York, NY 10003
                  Phone: 212 604 9637
                  Fax: 212 206 9329

Book Layout: John Eng
Cover Art: Ramon Gil

Library of Congress Control Number: 2008927682
ISBN: 978-0-9755859-2-4

For all those who have taught, influenced and impacted me:
Ivar Lovaas, Tony Cuvo, Mrs. Adams and John Wooden;
John, Shelli, Tracee, Andi and Mitch;
Dave, Charlie and BJ;
Charlene, Cynthia and Louise;
The children, adolescents, adults and their parents;
Our critics, attorneys and bureaucrats;
My parents;
Justin, Jeremy, Cole;
And most notably Jamie!

– Ron

To my mentor, Ivar Lovaas, a true pioneer;
my wife, Julie, for all the sacrifices she has made and all the love she has given me;
and my colleagues Ron and Mitch, the most sensible people I know.

– John

To Max and Pearl,
This is for and because of you

– Mitch

About the Authors

Danielle Baker, M.S.

Danielle Baker has over 14 years experience working with children and adults with autism and other developmental disabilities. From 1993 to 1997, Ms. Baker worked with Dr. Leaf at Straight Talk Developmental Services, a comprehensive behavioral treatment program for adults with developmental disabilities which provided residential, day treatment, supported living and supported employment services. From 1994 to 2007 she worked with Dr. Leaf and Dr. McEachin at Behavior Therapy and Learning Center and Autism Partnership. Ms. Baker has provided consultation in the application of intensive behavioral intervention to families, agencies, and school districts throughout the United States and England. She earned her Bachelors degree in Psychology from California State University, Long Beach. She received her Masters Degree in Applied Behavior Analysis from St. Cloud State University.

Andy Bondy, Ph.D.

Andy Bondy has over 35 years experience working with children and adults with autism and related developmental disabilities. For more than a dozen years he served as the Director of the Statewide Delaware Autistic Program. He and his wife, Lori Frost, pioneered the development of the Picture Exchange Communication System (PECS). Based upon principles described in Skinner's *Verbal Behavior*, the system gradually moves from relatively simple yet spontaneous manding to tacting with multiple attributes. He has designed the *Pyramid Approach to Education* (with Beth Sulzer-Azaroff) as a comprehensive combination of broad-spectrum behavior analysis and functional communication strategies. This approach aims to help professionals and parents design effective educational environments for children and adults with developmental disabilities within school, community, and home settings. He is the co-founder of Pyramid Educational Consultants, Inc., an internationally based team of specialists from many fields working together to promote integration of the principles of applied behavior analysis within functional activities and an emphasis on developing functional communication skills independent of modality.

Marlene Driscoll, M.A., LMFT

Marlene Driscoll is a Licensed Marriage and Family Therapist specializing in work with families of children with autism. She is currently the Site Director for the Autism Partnership Seal Beach office and her duties include clinical supervision, counseling, program development and interventionist training and development. Ms. Driscoll began working with Drs. Leaf and McEachin in 1992 as a consultant for the Behavior Therapy and Learning Center, a center focusing on parent training for families with developmentally disabled children. She earned her Masters Degree in counseling from Loyola Marymount University in 1996. She has extensive experience in the use of Applied Behavioral Analysis and early intervention with children with autism. She has consulted with families and school districts throughout the United States and internationally.

B.J. Freeman, Ph.D.

B.J. Freeman is Professor Emerita of Medical Psychology at UCLA School of Medicine. She is Founder and past Director of the UCLA Autism Evaluation Clinic, and co-founder of UCLA's Early Childhood Partial Hospitalization Program. Dr. Freeman is considered an international authority in the diagnosis, psychological assessment and treatment of children and adults with autism and related developmental disabilities, and has published over 100 articles in scientific journals and books in the area of autism. She spends much of her professional time working with families and service organizations, presenting at parent and professional conferences and consulting with school districts to develop appropriate programs. Having recently retired after 30 years at UCLA, Dr. Freeman continues to practice in the Los Angeles area.

Ronald Leaf, Ph.D.

Ronald Leaf is a licensed psychologist who has over 35 years of experience in the field of Autism Spectrum Disorder. Dr. Leaf began his career working with Ivar Lovaas while receiving his undergraduate degree at UCLA. Subsequently he received his doctorate under the direction of Dr. Lovaas. During his years at UCLA, he served as Clinic Supervisor, Research Psychologist, Interim Director of the Autism Project and Lecturer. He was extensively involved in several research investigations, contributed to the *Me Book* and is a co-author of the *Me Book Videotapes*, a series of instructional tapes for teaching autistic children. Dr. Leaf has provided consultation to families, schools, day programs and residential facilities on a national and international basis. Ron is the Executive Director of Behavior Therapy and Learning Center, a mental health agency that consults with parents, care providers and school personnel. Dr. Leaf is a Co-Director of Autism Partnership. Ron is the co-author of *"A Work in Progress"*, a published book on Behavioral Treatment.

John McEachin, Ph.D.

John McEachin is a clinical psychologist who has been providing behavioral intervention to children with autism as well as adolescents and adults with a wide range of developmental disabilities for more than 30 years. He received his graduate training under Professor Ivar Lovaas at UCLA on the Young Autism Project. During his 11 years at UCLA, Dr. McEachin served in various roles including Clinic Supervisor, Research and Teaching Assistant, Visiting Professor and Acting Director. His research has included the long-term follow-up study of young autistic children who received intensive behavioral treatment, which was published in 1993. In 1994 he joined with Ron Leaf in forming Autism Partnership, which they co-direct and they have co-authored a widely used treatment manual, A Work in Progress. Dr. McEachin has lectured throughout the world and has helped establish treatment centers and classrooms for children with autism in North America, Australia, Asia and Europe.

Toby Mountjoy

Toby Mountjoy is the Associate Director of Autism Partnership. Mr. Mountjoy is responsible for overseeing over 100 full-time staff in the Hong Kong, Singapore and Tokyo offices. Mr. Mountjoy has been working with individuals with autism for over 12 years in a multitude of ways. He has provided direct therapy, parent training and has supervised home and clinic based ABA programs in the Asian offices. Mr. Mountjoy has also opened and overseen ABA based kindergarten programs in both Singapore and Hong Kong. In January 2007, Mr. Mountjoy established the first fully registered primary school for children with autism in Hong Kong, which has a capacity of up to 64 children. In addition, Mr. Mountjoy has also regularly consulted to agencies, school districts and families in other countries including the Phillipines, Columbia, Indonesia, Malaysia, USA, China and Vietnam.

Doris Soluaga Murtha, M.A.

Doris Soluaga Murtha has been a staff member of Autism Partnership since 1996. Her experience implementing intensive Applied Behavior Analysis programs for autistic children spans ten years. She earned her Bachelors degree in Psychology from Loyola Marymount University, Los Angeles in 1995. She earned her Masters Degree in Applied Behavior Analysis from St. Cloud University, Minnesota in 2005. Currently, Ms. Murtha is a Mentor at Autism Partnership providing advanced training and supervision to program coordinators. She has presented both nationally and internationally at conferences on Applied Behavior Analysis. In addition, she provides consultations and training to families and school districts throughout the United States, England, Asia and South America.

Tracee Parker, Ph.D.

Tracee Parker has over 25 years of treatment and research experience in the field of Autism and Developmental Disabilities and earned a Doctoral degree in Psychology from UCLA in 1990. Her training experience included five years working on the UCLA Young Autism Project directed by Dr. Ivar Lovaas. During this time, she served in the capacities of teaching and research assistant as well as Clinic Supervisor. As a research assistant, Dr. Parker was closely involved in a number of studies including the long term treatment follow-up of young autistic children and changes in self-stimulatory behavior during treatment. Dr. Parker worked 12 years at Straight Talk Clinic, Inc., a residential and day behavioral treatment program, serving adults with developmental disabilities. She served as Associate Director until 1997. Dr. Parker is currently a Clinical Associate with Autism Partnership and Associate Director for Behavior Therapy and Learning Center. Dr. Parker has presented at national and international conferences in the areas of behavioral treatment, autism and social/sexual issues and intervention. Over the past 20 years, she has provided consultation to residential and day programs, school districts, families, and other related agencies.

David Rosteter, Ph.D.

Dave Rostetter has served as a consultant to local educational agencies, state educational agencies, the U. S. Departments of Justice, Education, and Health and Human Services since leaving the U. S. Department of Education in 1986. While at the Department he served as Director of the Division of Assistance to States with responsibility for the administration of IDEA-B and relevant EDGAR requirements through review of state education plans, awarding of funds, monitoring and the provision of technical assistance to states. Since leaving the Department in 1986 he has worked in a variety of consultant and expert roles. Selected recent work experience include consulting to State Departments of Education, serving as an expert witness, and being appointed as a Monitor and Special Master to assist school districts to comply with State and Federal Laws and Regulations.

Sanford Slater, Ph.D.

Sandy Slater is a licensed psychologist who has worked with children and adults who have been diagnosed with autism and other developmental disabilities since 1981. As an undergraduate student at UCLA, he began working with Ronald Leaf, John McEachin, and O. Ivar Lovaas on the Young Autism Project. For more than two years he functioned as a Senior Therapist, Therapist, Research Assistant and Teaching Assistant on the Young Autism Project. After completing his B.A. in Psychology, Dr. Slater worked with Dr. Leaf at Straight Talk Developmental Services, a comprehensive behavioral treatment program for adults with developmental disabilities. After earning his doctorate in Clinical Psychology, he worked as the Clinical Director of Straight Talk, Inc. until 1996. Dr. Slater has worked with Dr. Leaf and Dr. McEachin at Behavior Therapy and Learning Center and Autism Partnership since 1990. He has consulted with families and school districts throughout the United States, Canada and England and he supervises treatment cases in the greater Los Angeles area. He earned his Masters Degree in General Psychology from Eastern Michigan University and a Ph.D. in Clinical and Health Psychology from the University of Florida.

Jennifer Styzens, M.S.

Jennifer Styzens has over 20 years of experience in the field of developmental disabilities and autism and received her Master's at St. Cloud State Univerisity. Formerly, she served as the Director of Client Services for Straight Talk Clinic, which provided residential and day treatment services to adults with developmental disabilities, and worked as a parent trainer for the Behavior Therapy and Learning Center, which provides training to parents of children with developmental disabilities. She has been a staff member of Autism Partnership since 1997 and has presented at national and international conferences in the areas of behavioral treatment, autism and social/sexual issues and intervention. Over the past 20 years, she has provided consultation to residential and day programs, school districts, families and other related agencies and is a special education teacher for a middle school model classroom.

Mitchell Taubman, Ph.D.

Mitch Taubman worked with Dr. Ivar Lovaas as an undergraduate at UCLA in the early 1970s, providing treatment to children with autism, ADHD, and other disorders. Subsequently, he attended the University of Kansas and studied with such founders of Applied Behavior Analysis as Dr. Donald Baer, Dr. Todd Risely, Dr. James Sherman, and his Doctoral Advisor, Montrose Wolf. Upon completing his Ph.D. at the University of Kansas, he returned to UCLA post-doctorally, where he brought Teaching Interactions, from the Kansas model, to autism treatment. At UCLA, he served as an Adjunct Assistant Professor of Psychology and as Co-Principal Investigator with Dr. Lovaas on a Federal Grant directed at autism treatment. After this post-doctoral work, he obtained his License as a Clinical Psychologist and also served as Clinical Director of Straight Talk, a program providing residential and day treatment services to adults with autism and other developmental disabilities. Dr. Taubman is currently the Associate Director of Autism Partnership, where he provides treatment oversight, training, and consultation both nationally and internationally.

Andrea Waks, J.D.

Andrea Waks is the Director of Client Services at Autism Partnership. She began working with children with autism in the late 1970s at UCLA on the Young Autism Project, where she served as a Senior Therapist, Research Assistant, and Teaching Assistant. Andi has worked with Dr. Leaf and Dr. McEachin on the Young Autism Project, the Behavior Therapy and Learning Center, Straight Talk, and Autism Partnership. She earned her Master's degree in General Psychology at Pepperdine University in 1983 and returned to school in 1993 to pursue a law degree. She practiced special education law, representing families of children with autism, before returning to Autism Partnership full-time. Her current duties include conducting behavioral assessments, IEP preparation, policy review, and classroom consultations. She consults with families and school districts both locally and nationally.

Preface

"I'm mad as hell and I'm not going to take it anymore!"
- Chayefski, 1976

The character Peter Finch made this proclamation in the film *Network*. He could no longer tolerate the insanity of network news. We too are mad as hell! Perhaps it is our mid-life crises. Perhaps it is because of our egos and arrogance. Perhaps its witnessing outstanding professionals leaving the field of autism treatment because of all the craziness. Perhaps it is because we all started in the Ivory Tower at UCLA and experienced what children could accomplish under optimal conditions and ultimately cannot reconcile anything but the best. Perhaps it's working in systems where mediocrity is not only tolerated but the standard. Perhaps it is just the insanity of the field.

It feels like every day there is more craziness. Be it the latest purported cure, or speculation on the cause of Autistic Spectrum Disorder (ASD) without a shred of evidence, or a new regulation or requirement making absolutely no sense. It is the onslaught of workshops with speakers that are using only personal charisma to sell their wares. It is service providers that pop up overnight, whose major objective is to provide treatment that will conform to the financial dictates of some bureaucracy. It includes philosophies and approaches that become the new, "in" thing. It includes groups that are fanatical adherents to dogma, wielding power over how treatment is provided to a child, without any actual consideration of the child. And it is about the victimization of parents who already have been given more to deal with than any parent deserves. Professionals are also tormented. But clearly, children and their futures are the ultimate victims! Their lives are incredibly compromised by the madness!

Hopefully this book might bring a shred of sanity to a crazy field. Perhaps this book is our catharsis, so that we can continue fighting the good fight. We love this field. It is the professionals, parents and, of course, the children, adolescents and adults that have been a continual source of inspiration. We are passionate about our work and we simply feel protective of ABA, Autism and the children! Please accept our apology for ranting, but It Has To Be Said!

Ron Leaf, John McEachin & Mitch Taubman

Table of Contents

Chapter 1 **What is ABA?** **1**

Introduction 1

ABA as an Outgrowth of Behavioral Psychology 2

ABA as a Scientific Method 3

What ABA is Not 4

Discrete Trial Teaching (DTT) 5

Avoiding Negative Side Effects of ABA 7

What is the Lovaas Method? 8

Summary 10

References 12

Chapter 2 **The UCLA Young Autism Project (YAP)** **13**

Historical Foundations of YAP 14

Description of YAP 14

Factors Affecting Generality of Results 18

    Age Considerations 19

    Role of Treatment Intensity 19

    Quality of Treatment 19

    Differences in Service Models: Workshop vs. Clinic-Run 20

    Strong Behavioral Contingencies 22

    Parent Expertise 24

    Maintaining Treatment Balance 25

    Double Therapy 25

    Quality Therapy 26

Post-YAP 27

Common Folklore Regarding YAP 28

    Myth 1: Children Received a Minimum of 40 Hours of
         Intervention Treatment 29

    Myth 2: Intervention was Exclusively One-to-One 29

    Myth 3: Intervention Occurred Exclusively at Home 30

    Myth 4: Intervention Occurred in Distraction Free Settings 30

    Myth 5: We Worked Only on Speech 32

    Myth 6: Continuous Data was Collected 32

    The Big Question: How Realistic is the Aim for "Recovery"? 33

References 36

Chapter 3   **Divergence, Convergence and Resolution?** **39**
The Emergence of Divergence 39
Style, Technique and Theory 40
Range of Discrete Trial Teaching Strategies 42
Convergence: It is Time to Evolve 43
Resolution Means Individualization 44
Autism Partnership's Evolutions 44
References 48

Chapter 4   **To BCBA or Not to B?** **49**
Who is Qualified? 49
BCBA Shortcomings 50
Might we be better off without the BCBA credential? 53
References 54

Chapter 5   **Eclecticism** **55**
The Quest for Best Practice 55
Has the Case Really Been Made for Eclecticism? 55
The Downside of Eclectic Treatment 58
References 61

Chapter 6   **Alternative Treatments for Autism Spectrum Disorders: What is the Science?** ... **63**
What is Autism Spectrum Disorder (ASD)? 64
What are CAMs? 65
    What is the Scientific Method? 66
Biological CAM Treatments 68
Table 1: Complementary & Alternative Biologically-Based Treatments 70
Nutritional Therapies 72
Secretin 73
Additional Biological CAMs 74
Non-Biological CAM Treatments 80
Table 2: Non-Biological Based Interventions 80
Sensory Treatments 83
Relationship-Based Therapies 85
Motor Therapies 87
Animal-Assisted Therapies 88
Computer-Assisted Technologies 89
Miscellaneous 91
Evaluating Treatments 92
Questions to Ask Regarding Specific Treatment 94
Conclusions 96
References 98

Chapter 7   **Critical Thinking** **105**
It's Time to Speak Out 105
Thinking Critically About Autism 106
Be Cautious! 109
Research Design 110
Multiple Interpretations 113
Correlation Does Not Equal Causation 121
Critical Eye and the Analytic Process 122
References 125

Chapter 8   **Comparing Treatment Approaches** **131**
Limited Comparative Analysis 131
ABA 132
Floor Time 135
Sensory Integration 137
TEACCH: Treatment and Education of Autistic and Related
            Communication-Handicapped Children 139
Relationship Development Intervention (RDI) 141
What is Next? 141
References 143

Chapter 9   **Home vs. School: Which Side Are You On?** **145**
Folklore 147
Autism Partnership's Position 148
References 151

Chapter 10   **Parental Resistance** **153**
"Readiness" Model 154
Priority 156
Belief that School Personnel are Incapable of Providing
            Effective Education 157
Belief that Children Cannot Learn in Groups 158
Understanding the Teacher's Perspective 159
References 160

Chapter 11   **Educational Resistance** **161**
"We Are Prepared!" 161
"We'll Take the One-Day Package" 162
"ABA is Not Effective" 163
"ABA Results Do Not Hold Up Over Time" 165
"ABA is Outdated" 166
"ABA is Disrespectful of Students" 166

"ABA is Experimental" 167
"ABA is Punitive" 168
"ABA Has Limited Age Range" 168
Not Rejection, Just Resistance 169
A Cadillac or a Chevy 170
Resolution??? 171
References 172

Chapter 12   Whose IEP Is It Anyway? **175**
How It Was Meant to Be 175
Somehow It Ended Up Like This 175
The IEP Process 178
A Unique Perspective: A Clinician Who is Also an Attorney 181
What's the IDEA? 184
ASD and the IEP 186
References 191

Chapter 13   Goals, Goals, Goals **193**
Narrowing the Scope 194
Using Targets to Teach Multiple Skills 195
The Impact of Behaviors on Selection of Curriculum 196
Sequencing 197
Pivotal Skills 197
References 200

Chapter 14   Meaningful Progress? **201**
Expectations of Progress 201
What the Law Provides 202
Paths of Progress 204
Table 1: Paths of Progress 204
Table 2: Status After Treatment 206
Recovery? 206
What is Recovery? 207
Prognostic Indicators 210
Pre-Treatment Factors Associated with Better Outcome 211
Positive Factors After the Onset of Treatment 211
What is Realistic? 212
Construct of Meaningful Progress 212
Extended School Year (ESY) 214
Arbitrary Benchmarks 214
The Individualized Decision Making Process 215
References 218

Chapter 15   Inclusion - Sense and Nonsense **221**
Introduction 221
Inclusion as a Reaction Against the Evil of Segregation 222
The Pendulum Swings Too Far: Insisting on Full Inclusion for Evryone .. 224
Finding the Middle Ground 226
Least Restrictive Environment 227
Delusions About Inclusion 228
    Delusion 1: Exposure is Sufficient 228
    Delusion 2: Inclusion Facilitates Behavioral Control 229
    Delusion 3: Inclusion Guarantees Friendships 230
    Delusion 4: Disruptive Behaviors Will be Learned if a
       Student is in Special Education 232
    Delusion 5: Modelling Must Come From Typically
       Developing Children 232
    Delusion 6: Since the Student is Progressing or at Least
       Maintaining, it is an Appropriate Placement 233
    Delusion 7: Just Because a Student is in an Inclusive Setting,
       Can We Assume it Really is Inclusion? 235
    Delusion 8: Significant and Ongoing Accommodation
       is an Effective and Appropriate Long Term
       Strategy for Inclusion 235
    The "Road Map" to Successful Integration 237
    1. Behavioral Control 237
    2. Proficiency to Learn in Groups 238
    3. Attending Skills 238
    4. Ability to Learn Observationally 239
    5. Skills Commensurate with Peers 239
    6. Interest in Peers 240
    7. Basic Social Skills 240
    8. Impact on the Classroom 241
    9. Prioritizing Content and Process: A Balancing Act 241
Philosophical & Emotional Movement 244
Research 247
A Highly Emotional Issue 249
References 250

Chapter 1

WHAT IS ABA?

By Ron Leaf, Danielle Baker & John McEachin

INTRODUCTION

Throughout this book we will refer to various models of treatment for children with Autistic Spectrum Disorder (ASD). We have chosen to start with Applied Behavior Analysis (ABA), because we consider it to be one of the most important and yet one which is likely to be unfamiliar or misunderstood by many readers. In this chapter we will explain this model in general terms and in the next chapter we will present a landmark study which has utilized this approach in the treatment of children with autism. Anyone who is familiar with our work at Autism Partnership knows that we have strong opinions about how to evaluate what works and does not work in treating this mysterious disorder. This has led to our conviction that ABA has much to offer in this field and our determination to help practitioners and parents understand how it can help them help children with ASD.

Teaching people about ABA is often not an easy task. For some it runs counter to their philosophical beliefs about the nature of parenting or about the nature of human beings and the way we should treat each other. Maybe their training has been framed as being antithetical to ABA. Or perhaps it is because of a misunderstanding of ABA itself. And, unfortunately, there has been an abundance of poor practice as well as perpetration of misinformation that has occurred not only from nonbelievers but from within the field of ABA itself. Our aim therefore is to help readers better understand what ABA is and what it is not so that they can make informed decisions about how it might help them in their daily interactions with children who have ASD.

ABA AS AN OUTGROWTH OF BEHAVIORAL PSYCHOLOGY

Applied Behavior Analysis (ABA) is a branch of psychology which utilizes principles of learning to resolve problems of mental health as well as improve how people function in everyday life (Baer, Wolf, & Risley, 1968; Baer, Wolf, & Risley, 1987; Fawcett, 1991). ABA focuses on overt behavior rather than on presumed mental states, and seeks to identify features of the environment that influence how people behave. The functional relationship between specific events that precede and follow behaviors is analyzed so that we can develop procedures to increase desired behaviors and decrease undesired behaviors. ABA is practiced in all types of settings with all types of populations and age groups and has been used to improve many behaviors including social skills (Foxx, McMorrow, & Mennemeier, 1984), job performance (Crowell, Anderson, Abel, & Sergio, 1988), language acquisition (Lovaas, Berberich, Perloff, & Schaeffer, 1966), self help (Thompson, Braam & Fuqua, 1982), and leisure skills (Wall & Gast, 1997).

ABA employs strategies that are based upon learning theory which states that learning is affected by events that precede and follow behaviors. **Operant conditioning**, a form of learning most commonly associated with B.F. Skinner, relies on systematically manipulating the consequences of behaviors to change the rate at which behaviors occur in the future. Behavior that is followed by a positive consequence (e.g., treats, praise, privileges, or money) is more likely to occur in the future. The technical term for this is "reinforcement", but in everyday language means using rewards to provide motivation. Behavior that is followed by a negative consequence (e.g., reprimand, pain, being ignored) is likely to decrease in the future (Sulzer-Azaroff & Mayer, 1991).

Respondent conditioning, first investigated by Ivan Pavlov, is another type of learning in which behavior is manipulated by altering antecedent stimuli which have eliciting properties (i.e., cues or events which precede behavior and produce involuntary responses) (Miltenberger, 2004). Learning occurs when stimuli that were previously neutral come to have eliciting properties as a result of pairing them with other powerful stimuli. Pavlov's dogs began to salivate at the sight of lab assistants, because their arrival had previously been associated with the delivery of food. Interventions which are respondent in nature include systematic desensitization (i.e., gradual exposure to a fearful situation when relaxed), flooding (exposure to fearful situation without implementing relaxation procedure), and teaching relaxation procedures such as muscle relaxation, deep breathing or guided imagery (imagining a relaxing event).

ABA also uses a variety of teaching procedures including Discrete Trial Teaching (DTT), role playing, modeling, and teaching interactions, along with behavior management techniques such as functional behavior assessment, Differential Reinforcement of Other behavior (DRO), extinction, time out, shaping, stimulus control and stimulus fading.

Individuals who study and implement strategies based upon learning theory are said to practice "behaviorism." John B. Watson is often noted as the "father" of behaviorism. Dr. Watson firmly believed that the environment was the sole determinant of behavior. He believed everyone was a *tabula rasa* or a blank slate. Here is one of his more famous quotes:

"Give me a dozen healthy infants, well-formed, and my own specified world to bring them up and I'll guarantee to take any one at random and train him to become any type of specialist I might select- doctor, lawyer, merchant-chief, and yes, even beggarman and thief, regardless of his talents, penchants, tendencies, abilities, vocations and race of his ancestors." (Watson, 1930, pg. 104)

Although behaviorists regard genetics as also playing an important role, we are mainly concerned about what happens environmentally. Behaviorism emphasizes the role of experience with the environment that influences our behavior. Since behaviorists believe behaviors can be learned, they also believe behaviors can be unlearned through environmental changes. Thus, behaviorists are quite optimistic that they can be effective as long as systematic assessment and intervention strategies are employed.

ABA AS A SCIENTIFIC METHOD

Behaviorism differs in fundamental ways from some of the other theories about human behavior (e.g., psychoanalytic, Rogerian, or Gestalt). Behaviorism utilizes an approach based on the scientific method. Behaviorists rely upon observable behaviors and attempt to remain objective by relying upon data to make treatment decisions rather than subjective interpretation. They also seek to demonstrate causal relationships through the use of experimental design which reduces the likelihood of chance or bias affecting conclusions.

It is because of its scientific foundation and insistence on objectivity that ABA can come across to parents and other professionals as cold and mechanistic. Practitioners are careful to avoid feeling words because of inherent subjectivity, instead choosing terms which are specific and clear. It is not that behaviorists disregard feelings; it is that they describe these experiences in specific and measurable ways in order to evaluate them as honestly and accurately as possible. Behavioral jargon, or the words unique to the profession, are also frequently off-putting and can make people who are unfamiliar with them feel uncomfortable or excluded. Behaviorists are also very conservative about making claims of success in treatment unless rigorous research has been performed. This puts behaviorists at a disadvantage when other treatments are promoted upon the basis of individual case results and personal testimony, or which aim to produce warm fuzzy feelings. It also puts parents at a disadvantage when faced with making treatment decisions for their children. It can be hard to be inspired by a conservative scientist as compared to a passionate and charismatic advocate of a less scientific approach.

WHAT ABA IS NOT

It is *not* abusive, cold, punitive or manipulative. It does *not* dehumanize or produce robotic children. It is *not* a simplistic approach *nor* does it have only time limited effects. It is *not* only for severely impaired children, younger students or children with ASD. When implemented properly, it is an approach that generalizes and extends well beyond a one-to-one setting.

Unfortunately, these distorted beliefs reflect the view that many have of ABA. The negative stereotype is often a result of outdated information or experience with unskilled implementation of ABA. Although many psychological approaches, teaching procedures and medical treatments have encountered resistance in their earliest days, ABA, which comes across as unglamorous, has had particular difficulty gaining acceptance. But we must remember not to throw out the baby with the bath water and not to judge an entire approach based on limited experience which has been unimpressive. Dental care, for example, has much to offer despite the fact that one might have encountered poor dental work in the past. Similarly, Catherine Maurice (1999) has pointed out that we should not reject ABA across the board based on initial unfavorable experience:

"If we allow behavioral intervention to be stomped out because some therapists are incompetent, that is tantamount to abolishing medicine because some physicians do not know what they are doing." (page 4)

DISCRETE TRIAL TEACHING (DTT)

One of the most commonly used teaching techniques employed by ABA practitioners is Discrete Trial Teaching (DTT). DTT is a specific instructional methodology based upon principles of ABA. It is a teaching process that can be used to develop a wide range of skills, including cognitive, communication, play, social, coping and self-help skills. Additionally, it is a strategy that can be used to maximize learning for all ages and populations.

DTT involves:

1. Identifying needed skills

2. Breaking complex skills into smaller parts

3. Teaching one component skill at a time until mastered

4. Allowing repeated practice within a concentrated period of time

5. Providing prompting and prompt fading as necessary

6. Using reinforcement procedures

7. Facilitating generalization of skills into the natural environment. Although not all practitioners have explicitly incorporated generalization steps, research shows that this is an important component of treatment (Stokes & Baer, 1977).

The basic teaching unit, called a **_trial_**, has a distinct beginning and end, hence the name "discrete." The trial begins with a distinct cue, which enables the student to know what is expected. In technical terms we would say it signals the availability of reinforcement if a certain behavior is exhibited. This beginning part may consist of a question ("What does a cow say?"), an instruction ("Count to 10") or an event (another child approaches, which would be the cue for initiating a social response). Next follows a time-limited opportunity to respond, typically just a few seconds. In DTT an active response is required, not just passive activity such as listening to a lecture. Consequences such as feedback or rewards are provided immediately after the child attempts to perform the skill or provides a response to the question or at the point where the time limit is exceeded. Reinforcement in the form of social praise or preferred item or activity are provided for performing the skill correctly, while corrective feedback is provided if the skill is performed incorrectly or the response is simply not reinforced.

Teaching often involves numerous trials in order to strengthen learning. The student and teacher must be active and engaged during the learning process. For example, if you are teaching a student to say the names of classmates, there should be multiple occasions where he needs to remember the name over a fairly short period of time, short enough that he will be mostly successful. Practicing saying each child's name only once each day at circle time might result in taking months to master the skill. If you are going to teach a child to tie their shoes you would first break the skill into several parts (e.g., putting the shoe on the foot, pulling up the tongue, tightening the laces, crossing one lace over the other, etc.). This is called a task analysis. Teaching begins with one subskill by itself. For shoe tying you might start with the last step which is pulling the loops tight, because that is the most reinforcing step to learn. Starting with the last step is called backward chaining. The student might need to practice this step several times a day to maximize the rate of skill acquisition. After one subskill is mastered then additional steps are introduced.

During the teaching sessions the student will receive prompts or guidance to be able to perform the target step correctly. This ensures a high rate of success which makes the learning process more tolerable for the student. Throughout the session the child receives both positive and corrective feedback according to the quality of performance so that the student learns to refine their responses or discriminate which response goes with which situation. For example, "moo" goes with cow and "quack" goes with duck. As the student demonstrates a high level of success, prompts are faded and a higher level of reinforcement is provided on trials where the student was successful without needing a prompt, or for a greater degree of independence. The goal is to eliminate prompts as quickly as possible. Finally, once the subskills are learned in the teaching session, the skill should be practiced under less structured and more natural conditions.

Coaches and instructors commonly use DTT, without knowing the terminology or being explicitly trained. For example, when learning to swim, the first objective may be for the child to just play on the steps until she feels comfortable in shallow water. Then she may practice repeatedly to placing her face into the water. After multiple opportunities (trials) and mastery, the child would proceed to the next steps, perhaps kicking on the side of the pool. Systematically and gradually the child learns more steps and doesn't proceed to the next skill until the previous step is mastered. Naturally, the lesson provides multiple opportunities for practice and good swim instructors know how to make learning fun and filled with reinforcement. They also provide assistance (prompts) as necessary and fade those prompts as quickly as possible. Through good DTT, by breaking skills down, teaching individual skills to mastery, providing prompts, giving feedback and reinforcement, and making sure that learning is fun and the child is comfortable and successful in the learning environment, the complex skill of swimming can be mastered and become a meaningful part of everyday life.

Discrete Trial Teaching can be contrasted with continuous trial or more traditional teaching methods which present large amounts of information to children without having clearly identified or defined target responses. Traditional teaching often involves delayed or minimal feedback, limited or delayed opportunity for the student to practice the skill, and infrequent occasions for the teacher to evaluate how much learning has occurred. In addition, traditional teaching does not allow for generalization of skills or measuring the use of newly acquired information in the natural environment. While this approach works for most students it is typically not effective for students with ASD.

Although it is an intensive approach, DTT involves abundant reinforcement and children quickly come to enjoy the learning process. We have found that students can not only tolerate a surprisingly large number of hours of DTT throughout the day, but actually thrive on it and come to enjoy the process of learning, provided that staff are fun, respectful, energetic and enjoy being with the children.

AVOIDING NEGATIVE SIDE EFFECTS OF ABA

Although ABA is an extremely effective approach, negative side effects can occur. Fortunately they can be overcome with adjustments to the intervention plan. Here is a list of some undesirable effects for which practioners and parents should be alert. They can be avoided by designing the treatment program in a more balanced manner.

- **Egocentricity** can result from children having their interests and preferences catered to excessively in the absence of having to give up their own preference in favor of what another person desires.

- **Attention seeking** can result from being surrounded on a continuous basis by persons who are there to give their sole attention to the child. This leads to inflated expectations about how much attention they are entitled to receive. If attention is not forthcoming for appropriate behavior, then children may resort to inappropriate means of gaining attention. Attention should be contingent on appropriate behavior, should be given in amounts that are not excessive and the child should be systematically exposed to occasions where there is a delay before attention occurs (i.e. they should have to work harder and longer before receiving attention).

■ **Dependency** can develop because adults are too quick to provide assistance and children do not have the opportunity to discover that they can do many things for themselves.

■ **Need to be correct** can result from placing too much emphasis on correct answers and not enough emphasis on effort or insufficient reward for trying things that are difficult and unlikely to be performed correctly.

■ **Inflexibility** can arise from overemphasis on routine and insufficient exposure to variation.

■ **Responding only to certain cues** comes about when instructions are routinely provided in a certain inflection and with unnecessary use of simplified language. We refer to this as "therapy talk" and it should be avoided to promote generalization.

That negative side effects can occur is not surprising given the complex nature of autism and the intensity of therapy that is required. Overly simplistic intervention and procedures that are not carried out all the way to the final phase are much more likely to cause undesirable effects. That is why we emphasize teaching in a variety of settings, to include not only 1:1, but also small group and large group instruction. It is important to teach children how to share attention with other children, for example turn taking with a toy or waiting for assistance while the instructor is interacting with another student, or cheering for a classmate who has just performed. Providing instructions using varied and natural language whenever possible helps ensure that when the psychologist, who does not use "ABA talk", probes for skills they will get the desired response, not to mention when Grandma and Grandpa come to play they too will be able to interact successfully with the child without having to become ABA specialists.

WHAT IS THE LOVAAS METHOD?

Dr. Ivar Lovaas is a psychologist who is recognized as one of the pioneers in the education and treatment of children with ASD. In the early 1960's Dr. Lovaas began investigating behavioral procedures for reducing self-injury. Children were referred for treatment who exhibited extremely dangerous behaviors such as head banging, eye gouging, eating flesh and even biting off fingers. Dr. Lovaas demonstrated that ABA was effective in reducing and often eliminating self-injury (e.g., Lovaas, Freitag, Gold & Kassorla, 1965; Lovaas & Simmons, 1969). Ignoring the detrimental behavior and providing high rates of positive reinforcement for alternative appropriate behavior proved to be effective in extinguishing the behavior in children whose behavior was being maintained by attention. However, it was a slow process and resulted in children continuing to do harm to themselves before the behavior was completely eliminated. Therefore, Dr. Lovaas investigated punishment procedures as an additional treatment component in an effort to produce more rapid suppression of self-injury. His research clearly showed that punishment combined with positive reinforcement procedures not only resulted in quicker suppression but the effects transferred to other situations and people (stimulus generalization), and resulted in the reduction of other disruptive behaviors (response generalization) such as tantrums and self-stimulation and that the treatment results were durable.

Dr. Lovaas realized that focusing solely on disruptive behaviors would be effective only as long as treatment conditions were in effect. A permanent treatment required simultaneously building in appropriate replacement behavior which could eventually be maintained through natural reinforcers. He further recognized that disruptive behaviors were not random behaviors but were actually quite understandable and generally served a specific purpose or constellation of purposes to the individual. He speculated that disruptive behaviors were, perhaps, a child's way to gain attention, communicate a desire, or avoid situations that were disliked. Therefore, in order to prevent relapse, or the emergence of new disruptive behaviors, it would be essential to teach a child new ways to achieve the same outcome, but that would not have a detrimental effect. Thus, starting in 1964, Dr. Lovaas conducted numerous studies on teaching language and other adaptive skills (e.g., Lovaas, Berberich, Perloff & Schaeffer, 1966; Lovaas, Freitag, Kinder, Rubenstein, Schaeffer & Simmons, 1966; Lovaas, Freitas, Nelson & Whalen, 1967). He showed that by using systematic teaching procedures (primarily DTT), children could learn not only language, but other important skills such as play, social and self-help.

Dr. Lovaas' research on ABA made an important contribution to improving the quality of life for children with ASD. Prior to this, most people considered autism to be a life long sentence of restricted functioning. Dr. Lovaas demonstrated that children with autistic disorders had far more potential than previously believed. He deserves to be recognized.

The use of DTT with children who have ASD is sometimes referred to as the "Lovaas Method" or "Lovaas Therapy" (not by Lovaas himself, but by others). Our belief is that it is more appropriate to use a term which is descriptive of the approach and its continuously evolving nature, rather than linking it to a specific individual. Although Dr. Lovaas was certainly one of the first to employ the principles and procedures of ABA with children with ASD on a large scale, the foundations of ABA and treatment procedures were developed prior to Dr. Lovaas. Using reinforcement, extinction and punishment to reduce behaviors as well as employing systematic teaching procedures had been used since the 1920's. Prior to Dr. Lovaas' research, ABA had also been demonstrated to be effective in the treatment of other populations.

The term "Lovaas Therapy" implies a treatment method which is defined by a single individual and which is a distinct and static procedure. Lovaas's work was never proprietary in nature and in the best tradition of scientific advancement, his work built on the research findings of those who preceded him in the field and has served as a foundation for the work of others since then. To his credit, Lovaas never claimed the approach as belonging to himself and he always encouraged his protégés to further refine the methods used to develop the skills of children with ASD. In fact the procedures that Lovaas used in the 1980's evolved and differed from those used in the 1960's. Research and clinical experience produced an ongoing evolution in treatment methods. For example, over the years punishment was eliminated as more sophisticated behavior programs were developed. Teaching techniques became less artificial and more natural. Curriculum became more comprehensive. The term "Lovaas Therapy" does not recognize the evolution of treatment. Therefore we consider it more appropriate to use the term Intensive Behavioral Treatment to describe the methods developed by Lovaas and others for the treatment of children with ASD.

SUMMARY

We, the authors of this book, have devoted our professional careers to helping children with autism and helping those who help children with autism. We believe firmly that ABA provides a clear roadmap to follow. Using the principles of ABA is more than a profession for us, it is the essence of our beliefs. ABA has been at the core of raising our children and we use it even when coaching baseball, soccer or dance (Osborne, Rudrud, & Zezoney, 1990; Luyben, Funk, Morgan, & Clark, 1986). It has even been the basis of our relationships with our friends and significant others. We adhere to an interventional, educational and developmental perspective that is guided by ABA. Our beliefs are drawn from personal and clinical experience as well as the volumes of research that have been compiled over the decades including our own small contribution. We have trained numerous parents and professionals and provided expert testimony about ABA. We admit we have strong opinions about the subject. And we believe that when others truly understand the principles of ABA, they too will become strong advocates. That is what this book is all about.

REFERENCES

Baer, D. M., Wolf, M. M., & Risley, T. R. (1968). Some current dimensions of applied behavior analysis. *Journal of Applied Behavior Analysis, 1*(1), 91-97

Baer, D. M., Wolf, M. M., & Risley, T. R. (1987). Some still-current dimensions of applied behavior analysis. *Journal of Applied Behavior Analysis, 20*(4), 313-327

Crowell, C.R., Anderson, C.D., Abel, D.M., & Sergio, J.P. (1988). Task clarification, performance feedback, and social praise: Procedures for improving the customer service of bank tellers. *Journal of Applied Behavior Analysis, 21*(1), 65-71.

Fawcett, S. B. (1991). Some values guiding community research and action. *Journal of Applied Behavior Analysis, 24*(4), 621-636

Foxx, R. M., McMorrow, M. J., & Mennemeier, M. (1984). Teaching social/vocational skills to retarded adults with a modified table game: An analysis of generalization. *Journal of Applied Behavior Analysis, 17*(3), 343-352

Lovaas, O. I. & Simmons, J. Q. (1969) Manipulation of self-destruction in three retarded children. *Journal of Applied Behavior Analysis, 2*(3), 143-157

Lovaas, O. I., Berberich, J. P., Perloff, B. F., & Schaeffer, B. (1966). Acquisition of imitative speech by schizophrenic children. *Science, 151* 701-705

Lovaas, O. I., Freitag, G., Gold, V. J., & Kassorla, I. C. (1965). Experimental studies in childhood schizophrenia: Analysis of self-destructive behavior. *Journal of Experimental Child Psychology, 2*(1), 67-84

Lovaas O. I., Freitag G., Kinder M. I., Rubenstein B. D., Schaeffer B., & Simmons J. Q. (1966). Establishment of social reinforcers in two schizophrenic children on the basis of food. *Journal of Experimental Child Psychology, 4*(2), 109–125

Lovaas O. I., Freitas L., Nelson K., & Whalen C. (1967). The establishment of imitation and its use for the development of complex behavior in schizophrenic children. *Behavior Research and Therapy, 5*(3), 171–181

Luyben, P. D., Funk, D. M., Morgan, J. K., Clark, K. A., & Delulio, D. W. (1986). Team sports for the severely retarded: training a side-of-the-foot soccer pass using a maximum-to-minimum prompt reduction strategy. *Journal of Applied Behavior Analysis, 19*(4), 431–436

Maurice, Catherine (1999). "ABA and us: One parent's reflections on partnership and persuasion." Address to Cambridge Center for Behavioral Studies Annual Board Meeting, Palm Beach, Florida, November, 1999.Maurice (1999)

Miltenberger, R. G. (2004) *Behavior modification: Principles and procedures* (3rd Ed). Pacific Grove, CA: Wadsworth.

Osborne, K., Rudrud, E. & Zezoney, F. (1990). Improved curveball hitting through the enhancement of visual cues. *Journal of Applied Behavior Analysis, 23*(3), 371–377

Sulzer-Azaroff, B., & Mayer, G. R. (1991). *Behavior analysis for lasting change.* Fort Worth, TX: Harcourt Brace.

Thompson, T. J., Braam, S. J. & Fuqua, R. W., 1982. Training and generalization of laundry skills: A multiple probe evaluation with handicapped persons. *Journal of Applied Behavior Analysis, 15*, 177-182.

Watson, J. B. (1930). *Behaviorism* (revised edition). University of Chicago Press.

Wall, M. & Gast, D., 1997. Caregivers' Use of Constant Time Delay To Teach Leisure Skills To Adolescents or Young Adults with Moderate or Severe Intellectual Disabilities. *Education and Training in Mental Retardation and Developmental Disabilities, 32*, 340-356

Chapter 2

THE UCLA YOUNG AUTISM PROJECT (YAP)

By Ron Leaf & John McEachin

The UCLA Young Autism Project (YAP) as described in Lovaas (1987) and McEachin, Smith, and Lovaas (1993) set a new standard for successful outcome in the treatment of ASD. This behaviorally based approach was slow to be recognized in the professional community, but parents soon adopted it as the gold standard. The book, *Let Me Hear Your Voice* by Catherine Maurice (1993) was instrumental in getting information about intensive early behavioral intervention into the hands of parents as well as inspiring them to take action on behalf of their children. In 1996 the New York State Department of Health completed a review of treatment methodologies for children with ASD and cited the outcome studies by Lovaas as meeting the most stringent standards for research. They concluded that this intensive behavioral treatment approach was unique in the level of evidence demonstrating its efficacy (New York State Department of Health, 1999). Also in 1999, a report from The American Surgeon General stated that behavioral treatment as implemented on the YAP is the treatment of choice (Department of Health and Human Services 1999).

Now a majority of the professional community that provides ABA treatment utilizes many of the principles and techniques that were used in the UCLA study. Yet despite the growing recognition, there is still a tremendous amount of skepticism, folklore and outright misinformation that exists regarding the YAP. In order for parents and professionals to better understand how ABA can help children with ASD, we believe it is necessary to carefully review this important research.

HISTORICAL FOUNDATIONS OF YAP

ABA is not a "new" or unproven therapeutic method. Dr. Lovaas and his associates at UCLA have been utilizing ABA for the treatment of ASD for more than four decades. Their research has convincingly demonstrated that intensive, early intervention can significantly improve the functioning of children with autism. One of the earliest comprehensive studies of ABA published in 1973 by Dr. Lovaas and his colleagues documented the results of intensive intervention for a group of children between the ages of 3 and 10 years diagnosed with autism (Lovaas, Koegel, Simmons and Long, 1973). In this study, all children received 40 hours of ABA intervention for 12 to 14 months. Intervention focused on reducing disruptive behaviors while increasing language, social and play skills. Outcome data showed substantial reductions in self-stimulation and echolalia and increases in verbal, social, and play skills. At the conclusion of the investigation, children either returned to their parents' home or to a state hospital. Follow-up measures conducted one to four years after treatment showed large differences between groups. Those children who were discharged to state institutions showed severe relapses. Disruptive behaviors returned to previous levels and appropriate skills deteriorated. Conversely, those children who went to live with parents who had received training in ABA after treatment, continued to improve. The data also showed that children who began treatment at a younger age had better outcomes.

DESCRIPTION OF YAP

Based upon the 1973 study, a new comprehensive and long term outcome study was initiated by Dr. Lovaas and his colleagues at UCLA. This study was called the Young Autism Project (YAP). Similar to the previous investigation, children in the YAP received comprehensive ABA interventions for an average of 40 hours per week. However, in order to maximize learning the following changes occurred:

· Children began treatment before four years of age

· Treatment occurred for two or more years

· All children lived with their parents

· Parents were extensively trained in ABA and were a major part of treatment

Thirty-eight children who received an independent diagnosis of autism served as subjects in YAP. Prior to the onset of treatment, extensive data and pre-treatment information were collected through parent interview, developmental testing, and behavioral observation measures.

Children were placed in either the Intensive Treatment Group or in a Control Group which did not receive intensive treatment. Due to ethical concerns regarding certain children receiving inferior treatment, selection was not based upon random assignment. Instead, assignment was based upon staff availability and was determined **prior** to referral. Detailed analysis revealed that there were no significant differences between the two groups at the onset of treatment.

The nineteen children in the intensive treatment group received an average of 40 manhours of formal ABA intervention weekly. Manhours were counted because there were sessions with two therapists, done for training purposes and to maximize the instructional time as well as permit teaching observational learning and other skills requiring a second person. The nineteen children in the control group, however, received an average of 10 hours of ABA intervention weekly as well as other intervention strategies (e.g., Speech therapy, Occupational Therapy, "traditional" educational strategies, etc.). At the end of the study a second control group was also evaluated for comparison. The children in Control Group Two did not receive intervention through YAP, but received an eclectic combination of services provided by various agencies and schools.

Intervention for children in the Intensive Treatment group was provided by UCLA undergraduate students. In order to provide intervention students had to receive an "A" or "B" in an undergraduate psychology class, *Foundations of Behavior Modification*, taught by Dr. Lovaas. Each treatment team was supervised by a graduate student in psychology or an advanced undergraduate student. Dr. Lovaas and the clinic supervisor provided clinical oversight.

Staff received a variety of training experiences. After demonstrating a thorough understanding of the principles of ABA, staff attended a series of workshops. The focus of the workshops was on how to effectively apply ABA with young children with autistic spectrum disorder. Topics included reinforcement, Discrete Trial Teaching (DTT) procedures, reductive techniques, prompting and prompt fading. Staff received further training when they worked with the children. Typically, new staff worked alongside a more experienced staff member for several weeks. Additionally, the supervisor often accompanied staff to provide additional training.

Upon completion of pre-treatment measures (i.e., observational measures, parental interviews and psychometric testing) treatment was initiated. Treatment initially focused on reducing or eliminating disruptive behaviors, such as aggression, tantrums, self-stimulation and noncompliance. Disruptive behaviors were reduced through providing extensive reinforcement contingent upon appropriate responding combined with reductive procedures such as extinction, time-out and punishment (verbal and physical). For example, if a child was aggressive to himself or others, the therapist would either completely ignore the behavior (extinction) or provide a verbal reprimand (e.g., "no, "stop it!", "don't do that", etc.). If the behavior was considered serious then physical punishment (i.e., slap on the child's thigh) combined with a verbal reprimand would be provided. When the child did not exhibit aggression or was engaging in appropriate behavior they would receive reinforcement in the form of food, physical comfort or a toy along with praise.

Concurrent with the reduction of disruptive behaviors, the children were taught more appropriate means of responding. Typically, the child was initially taught to attend visually to the therapist and then to sit on the chair properly (hands and feet still). Upon exhibiting appropriate behavior, the child received individually determined reinforcers, which included both edible and other tangible rewards along with praise and other types of social reinforcement.

Although we were targeting specific readiness skills, the initial focus of therapy was teaching the child the process of therapy, often referred to as "learning to learn". Paying attention, responding to instructions, changing behaviors based upon feedback and responding to prompts are all aspects of learning to learn. These skills were taught through systematic practice with prompting and feedback.

When the child's disruptive behavior had been reduced and mastery over sitting and attending occurred, the child's program was expanded to developing early language skills. DTT was used to teach children Non-Verbal Imitation, Matching, Receptive Commands and Verbal Imitation. Intermediate language programs involved teaching skills such as Receptive Labeling, Expressive Labeling, Pronouns and Prepositions. More advanced programming involved conversational, academic and play skills. In addition to the formal more structured curriculum the children had reinforcement breaks as well as opportunities to play.

To maintain the effects of treatment, the parents were trained in behavior management skills. Parents were trained in an "apprenticeship" fashion, largely through modeling, role playing and hands-on practice with their child, accompanied by feedback. Generalization of therapy was further achieved by conducting treatment in a variety of environments to which the child was exposed: home, school and clinic.

Initially, however, treatment was conducted exclusively at the child's home. Therapy sessions were typically three hours in length. Therapists typically worked in a team of two. This allowed therapists to alternate teaching, collect data, and provide modeling and prompting. Having two staff (i.e., "double therapy") also provided the opportunity to work on observational learning as well as school readiness skills. In addition, the overlap of staff allowed new therapists an opportunity to learn how to implement DTT by observing a more experienced therapist.

Children were enrolled in school as soon as their disruptive behaviors were at minimal levels and they were able to pay attention. This occurred at different times in treatment, depending upon the rate of the child's progress. Schools were selected based upon their willingness to have staff accompany the student in the classroom.

Each child's program was highly individualized to reflect his unique needs. The rate of progress determined not only when a child enrolled in school but when and if specific programs were introduced. Moreover, different programs were implemented, based upon the different children's needs. In other words, each child was not necessarily exposed to the same material.

The number of hours of intervention they received also differed. Although the average number of hours that children received was 40 hours weekly, there was a wide range. The range was from a low of approximately 20 hours weekly to as much as 50 hours or more weekly. People are often surprised to learn that the children who received fewer hours of treatment progressed faster. However, the dosage was determined by need and often children making rapid progress did not need the most intensive hours. When a child was progressing slowly, therapy hours were increased to help facilitate progress. There was also variability in the number of years of treatment. Whereas all children received at least two years of treatment, a few received up to 10 years of treatment. Finally, the intensity of treatment was gradually reduced as children began to approach maximum treatment benefit.

Two follow-up studies, published in 1987 and 1993, have shown that 9 of the 19 children who received the intensive behavioral treatment were able to successfully complete regular education classes and were indistinguishable from their peers on measures of IQ, adaptive skills, and emotional functioning (Lovaas, 1987; McEachin, Smith and Lovaas, 1993). The nine best outcome children were not identified by their teachers as needing any special education services and they had no extra support in the classroom. By contrast, at follow-up only one client out of the 40 children in the two control groups achieved a similar outcome. Those children receiving intensive treatment who did not attain the "best outcome" still made significant gains in language, social, self-help and play skills. All but two of them developed functional speech.

FACTORS AFFECTING GENERALITY OF RESULTS

The research that was conducted at UCLA has been very useful in guiding clinical practitioners about how to obtain the best treatment and educational outcomes for children with ASD. In drawing conclusions from the YAP it is important to keep in mind characteristics of the children included in the research, details about the intervention that was provided, and how the study's findings compare with other evidence that exists in the scientific literature regarding ABA and its application to ASD.

The application of research findings to real world clinical practice often entails making some adaptations of procedures. This can be necessary for a number of reasons, including the reduced availability of resources outside the research setting. In the Lovaas study, the use of aversives, as we will discuss below, is one aspect of the treatment that most practitioners would not currently consider as a treatment option. When adaptations are made in clinical practice this represents a departure from the research methodology which can jeopardize the generality of the research findings. However, by fully understanding what the important treatment variables are and by incorporating results from other research, one can make the necessary adjustments and still have a reasonable level of confidence in anticipated outcomes.

There are also deviations from the treatment methodology that have occurred because clinicians have misunderstood the procedures in the study and have adopted practices which they incorrectly believe are dictated by the research. Such errors can also jeopardize treatment outcomes or at the very least result in unnecessary complication of the treatment process. Therefore it is essential to correctly interpret what the study does—and does not—indicate. We would like to highlight some important treatment variables that we believe need to be more fully understood in order to come as close as possible to replicating the outcomes achieved in the YAP.

AGE CONSIDERATIONS

In the YAP there were no children older than four so the 1987 Lovaas study does not allow us to make comparisons between younger and older children. However, this should not be used to imply that children who are older than four cannot receive substantial benefit from intervention. In fact there is extensive literature demonstrating the effectiveness of ABA for older children, adolescents and adults (Lovaas, Koegel, Simmons & Long, 1973; Eikeseth, Smith & Eldevik, 2002; Fenske, et al., 1985; Matson, Benavidez, Compton, Paclawskyj & Baglio, 1996).

In our opinion it would be a mistake to deny treatment to a child who is older. Although younger children are generally found to have more impressive outcomes than older children and the probability of recovery decreases with delay in treatment onset, starting late is clearly better than never starting at all (Lovaas *et al.*, 1973; Fenske, Zalenski, Krantz, & McClannahan, 1985). The benefits for children who are older at the onset of treatment will still be substantial. Recovery is not the only outcome that deserves recognition.

ROLE OF TREATMENT INTENSITY

If one is attempting to replicate the positive outcomes obtained in the YAP, it will be essential to adhere to the level of intensity that was used in the Lovaas study. The research conducted by Lovaas and his colleagues, convincingly demonstrated that intensive intervention was a critical aspect of outcome. Not only did children who received an average of 40 hours of intervention have substantially better results, but a child who received an average of 10 hours weekly was not much better off than a child who received zero hours. Inadequate intensity of intervention will compromise treatment outcome. The National Research Council (2001) recommended a minimum of 25 hours a week. The vast majority of professionals in the field recommend between 30 and 40 hours weekly (Green, 1996).

QUALITY OF TREATMENT

In the YAP, treatment was provided under optimal conditions. The generality of findings from the UCLA research can only be assured if one is able to approximate as closely as possible the level of quality control that was in place during the YAP. The further treatments deviate from the ideal the less likely it is to produce similar outcomes. In the research setting, it is possible to control more variables and ensure that the intervention will be administered in an ideal manner. Some of the factors that enabled children to make the maximum progress included having parents become highly skilled in behavioral intervention as well as having staff with a high level of expertise. Therapists received training in the principles and application of ABA prior to working with a child. Because there was consistent and sufficient availability of trained staff, funding, and other necessary resources, the practical constraints associated with most treatment efforts were not an issue.

DIFFERENCES IN SERVICE MODELS: WORKSHOP VS. CLINIC-RUN

The UCLA Young Autism Project (YAP) utilized a clinic-run model of service delivery. YAP staff provided the direct intervention services, as well as supervision and program development. The direct-line staff were carefully selected and trained by the project's supervisory staff. Supervision occurred on a frequent and ongoing basis (i.e., a minimum of weekly and often daily). Multiple layers of supervision were provided. In addition to the direct supervisor, a clinical supervisor and psychologist provided oversight to each case.

In contrast to the YAP, the vast majority of ABA services provided throughout the world that are based upon Lovaas's research utilize a "workshop" model. This model is extremely different in many aspects from the clinic-run model. First, in the workshop model the ABA agency does not provide the direct line staff. Parents are typically responsible for recruiting and hiring staff. The training of staff is often provided by a consultant from an ABA agency. However, sometimes, out of necessity, parents or other direct line staff provide some training as well. The frequencies of consultations are also different. Whereas, frequent supervision is provided in the clinic-run model, the workshop model typically provides consultation on a much less frequent basis (e.g., quarterly). Although consulting agencies may review video tapes or communicate via phone or email, these methods cannot compare with the frequent supervision and training provided through the clinic-run model.

Although both the clinic-run and workshop model utilize ABA, there are fundamental differences that can greatly impact their effectiveness. The following chart illustrates some of the significant differences between the models:

CLINIC-RUN MODEL	TYPICAL WORKSHOP MODEL
Staff hired by agency	Staff hired by parents
Staff trained by agency	Staff trained by consultant & parents
One to two months of staff training	Three days of staff training
Weekly and sometimes daily supervision	Monthly to quarterly supervision
Weekly meetings	Monthly to quarterly meetings

The workshop model has been developed for a number of reasons. First, children often do not live in areas where comprehensive ABA services are available. Second, agencies simply cannot hire and train the number of staff that is needed to serve families. Third, agencies do not have the availability to provide more frequent supervision. Although this model may not be as effective as a clinic-run model, in our opinion it is superior to the vast majority of services that children receive!

Dr. Lovaas has been quite outspoken regarding his concerns about the workshop model of intervention (Lovaas, 2003). As he points out, intervention at UCLA utilized a clinic-run model; consequently, one cannot necessarily generalize the YAP results to a workshop model. Dr. Lovaas believes that a lower proportion of children will achieve best outcome utilizing the workshop model compared to the clinic-run model. It would seem reasonable to expect that a clinic-run model would be superior given the availability of better trained staff and more frequent ongoing supervision. Smith, Buch and Gamby (2000) conducted a study in which they compared a workshop model versus the clinic-run model. Although the workshop model produced changes in skill acquisition and parent satisfaction, the treatment outcomes were not as substantial as compared to a clinic-run model. A study conducted in the U.K. looking at the effectiveness of a workshop-based model suggests that people are not obtaining the same level of outcomes as occurred in the clinic-run YAP (Bibby, Eikeseth, Marin, Mudford & Reeves, 2001).

Given the intensity of training, level of supervision and extent of quality control, and consistency in staffing it is not surprising that the clinic-run model would produce superior outcomes. Problems with staff accountability are just one example of the difficulties encountered when staff is not in the employment of the supervisory agency.

STRONG BEHAVIORAL CONTINGENCIES

As discussed previously, Dr. Lovaas conducted extensive research in the 1960's demonstrating the effectiveness of punishment (i.e., electric shock) in reducing and eliminating severe and persistent self-injurious behaviors (e.g., Lovaas, Freitag, Gold & Kassorla, 1965; Lovaas & Simmons, 1969; Simmons & Lovaas, 1969). Research also demonstrated that punishment combined with positive reinforcement for appropriate behavior resulted in response generalization. That is, not only did punishment result in the reduction of the target behavior reduce (e.g., SIB) but other disruptive behaviors such as tantrums and self stimulation reduced without being specifically targeted. Dr. Lovaas also demonstrated that with careful application the effects generalized to other people as well as other environments. Although controversial, it was absolutely clear that the use of punishment was not only effective in reducing such behaviors but that it facilitated increases in appropriate behaviors (e.g., speech, social and play skills).

During the YAP, electric shock was not used but both verbal and physical punishments were used in order to reduce disruptive behaviors such as self-injury, aggression, self-stimulation and tantrums. Typically only one behavior was targeted at a time. Physical punishment entailed a hard slap on the child's thigh and was always accompanied with verbal punishment (e.g., a loud "no").

The use of punishment was thought to be an important component of therapy. It resulted in rapid suppression of disruptive behaviors. Often children's self-stimulation was eliminated with only a few applications of the punishment. By rapidly reducing interfering behaviors we were able to quickly teach appropriate alternative responses. Furthermore, there was increased opportunity to use reinforcement.

Staff received extensive training in the use of punishment in order to make sure that they used the correct intensity. Moreover, extensive training was provided in the use of reinforcement. It was emphasized that for every application of punishment children should receive a hundred instances of reinforcement. In other words, although punishment was a powerful treatment component, reinforcement was considered to be the more important aspect of treatment.

The use of punishment was carefully monitored. Dr. Lovaas, the Clinic Supervisor and the Senior Therapist reviewed the use of punishment to assure that it was being applied correctly. Data was continually reviewed to identify that it was resulting in significant improvement. Furthermore, during the project, two research studies were conducted demonstrating the effectiveness of punishment in the reduction of disruptive behaviors (Ackerman,1980; McEachin & Leaf, 1984).

In addition to the research conducted in the 1960's, Ackerman (1980) also demonstrated the effectiveness of physical punishment. Four children began treatment without the use of punishment. Although they received extensive reinforcement as well as other reductive procedures (e.g., response cost, differential reinforcement procedures, extinction) their disruptive behavior remained at high levels and therefore interfered with the learning process thereby impeding their progress. When punishment was finally applied, children's progress was substantially improved.

The use of punishment procedures became controversial toward the end of YAP but **NOT** because it was ineffective. Contrary to opinion, punishment was quite effective and the effects were durable. The effects also generalized across behavior, people and settings. So why did a highly effective procedure stop? First, the awareness and sensitivity to child abuse was increasing. To those outside the project, punishment may have been viewed as abusive. Second, "parenting" of the 1980's was more permissive and thus the use of punishment was viewed as abhorrent. Finally, there was a strong sentiment that ABA was a repugnant approach because it was too controlling, insensitive and disregarded personality. Punishment simply was not politically correct.

We believe there are more legitimate reasons not to use punishment:

1. It can potentially be a highly abusive procedure that requires careful control. We have witnessed instances where "professionals" have misused punishment to the extent we do consider it to be child abuse.

2. It is too easy a procedure to use. We fear that instead of using it as a last resort, it will be used too early in the process. Staff will not develop reinforcement procedures and alternative treatment procedures. Furthermore, they will not develop proactive approaches to develop appropriate alternative replacement behaviors.

3. People are likely to use it emotionally. The effective use of punishment requires that staff be incredibly positive and not use it out of anger. Furthermore, punishment was based upon careful analysis of behavior that identified target behaviors which were not readily amenable to change with positive reinforcement alone.

4. Correct use requires carefully monitoring change in behavior as well as intensive efforts at establishing appropriate replacement behaviors. People are rarely willing to put that much effort into behavior change procedures.

5. Incorrect use of punishment will further give ABA a bad reputation and thereby reduce people's willingness to use ABA. Although this may seem to be a minor point, we would not want to do anything that would reduce the utilization of intensive behavioral treatment.

Although the above constitute good reasons for not currently including punishment as part of an ABA program, we do feel it is important to understand the role that such a strong behavioral procedure potentially contributed to the superior outcomes of the YAP. Many people overlook the fact that it was a treatment component and that the generality of the YAP results may be diminished if use of strong behavioral contingencies is completely abandoned. Fortunately, there have been recent successful replications of the YAP which did not use aversive procedures (Sallows and Graupner, 2005; Cohen, Amerine-Dickens, and Smith, 2006)

PARENT EXPERTISE

One of the major features of the YAP was the extent to which parents were involved in day-to-day treatment. A parent was expected to be at home during therapy sessions, so that usually meant only one parent could work outside the home. The reason had nothing to do with liability issues. It was felt that time was needed for parents to become experts in ABA. Lovaas (1987) made it clear that parental expertise was a critical component of intervention:

"The parents worked as part of the team throughout the intervention: they were extensively trained in the treatment procedures so that treatment could take place for almost all the subjects' walking hours, 365 days a year." (Page 5)

Parents provided valuable input to the team and their presence during sessions helped ensure consistency across team members who did not have frequent opportunity for overlap. They could also provide valuable support and suggestions for the staff. Many parents became extremely talented therapists thus further enhancing progress in treatment. They were able to fill in when the student staff were on vacation. Since college students were utilized, it was not possible to provide therapists for 52 weeks of the year. During winter, spring and quarter breaks parents provided the bulk of intervention. And not surprisingly, there was not regression because parents were experts!

MAINTAINING TREATMENT BALANCE

Although parents participated in therapy on a daily basis, they were not required to participate for the entire session. We wanted them to be continuously aware of their child's progress and any changes that needed to occur in behavioral and teaching programs. However, since parents had a tremendous responsibility for treatment outside of "formal" therapy we also wanted them to have some respite during times when therapists were working with the child. Such occasions provided a much needed break for the parents. We believed their participation in "formal" therapy was vital. But even more important was their ability to consistently carry out the programs when staff went home! We felt it was necessary that the children receive treatment from the time they woke up until the time they went to bed. Even though YAP provided intensive intervention, it really only represented a small part of the child's week.

Parents quickly became the experts. Not only were they incredibly knowledgeable about all aspects of treatment but they were fabulous at implementing treatment procedures. Many of them became the best therapist on their child's team. Furthermore, parents were extremely supportive of the staff and worked collaboratively with school personnel and the professional community. Without such a high level of involvement and expertise in ABA, the effectiveness of treatment and the generality of the YAP research findings are likely to be compromised.

DOUBLE THERAPY

It was standard practice to have two therapists work every session. Although it was not done specifically as a means to provide improved therapy, there is no doubt that it positively affected the quality of treatment. We had what seemed like an unlimited number of qualified candidates who wanted to be part of YAP. And since we had limited children, double therapy was a means for us to provide students increased opportunities to enroll in an undergraduate class entitled *Fieldwork in Behavior Modification.*

By having two staff provide intervention we were able to pair a slightly more experienced therapist (i.e., approximately three months of experience) with a brand new therapist. This provided training opportunities as well as support and assistance if the newer therapist ran into problems.

Over time we have seen that double therapy can have tremendous clinical benefit. Then as now, we find using two therapists can make the sessions more productive in a number of ways:

- Simulation of play dates

- Simulation of school

- Increased opportunities to practice observational learning and group instructions

- Reduced "downtime" during set-up and record keeping

- Increase in staff's skills

Although this was potentially an important variable in the YAP research, we rarely observe ABA intervention programs including "double" therapy. This most likely is a result of the advantages of double therapy not being recognized along with the obvious higher costs associated with using two staff. However, there is a risk of reducing the generality of the YAP findings if Double Therapy is not part of the protocol.

QUALITY THERAPY

Just because one is doing ABA does not mean he or she is providing quality treatment. We have seen many times when parents and professionals are convinced they are following the UCLA protocol when in fact what they are doing is far different. They blindly follow a treatment protocol which they do not understand and which is overly prescriptive. Many seem to adhere diligently to what they believe are necessary minute procedural details and neglect the spirit of the model which is to individualize intervention to meet the needs of the child. They do not have sound rationales for the procedures they adopt and, amazingly, they attempt to cite the research as justification for following a cookie-cutter model. Because they do not have a solid understanding of the principles of ABA, they are locked into a specific protocol and automatically reject a more flexible model as being unfaithful to the ABA model. They do not understand the importance of teaching children in natural settings when possible, as well as the objective of fading 1:1 intervention sooner rather than later, all of which were essential components of the YAP.

As discussed previously, there is a great deal of misinformation regarding the project. ABA zealots often believe an extremely rigid treatment protocol was followed. We have frequently observed programs implemented by persons never associated with UCLA, but who profess to be adhering to the "UCLA" model. We did not adhere to a rigid curriculum but adapted to the needs of the children. For example we did not have a set number of trials at any one sitting (the belief is that we conducted 10 trials on every sitting), we did not work on only one curriculum at a sitting, and we did not do continuous data recording. At UCLA children were taught observational learning skills and received instruction in groups so as to facilitate their successful integration into school.

In a recent email, an "advocate" for children emphatically stated that Autism Partnership staff is "known" to have "watered down the ABA methodology to appease school systems and reduce costs". This "advocate" seems to believe that since we utilize group teaching and feel that some children need less than 30 hours of "formal" ABA per week and because we consult with school districts, we are advocating for poor ABA. This "advocate" simply does not know that a major goal of the YAP goal was for children to be in group instruction and that many of the children who achieved best outcome status received less than 30 hours per week of therapy.

This "advocate" was under the further belief that the children in the "best outcome" group had 1:1 shadows in elementary school and used this as a basis to attempt to force a school district to utilize a 1:1 staffing ratio. If he had read the research he would have realized that the children in the best outcome group not only did not have shadows, but they did not have any type of support once they started in first grade. Despite this individual's dissemination of incorrect information he has put himself in a postion of influence and can potentially do a great disservice to YAP and more importantly to children with ASD. In order for children to receive the kind of treatment that will provide maximum benefit, it is important that advocates and professionals become knowledgeable and not provide misinformation to parents. We feel it is necessary to speak out and help parents and professionals distinguish between sense and nonsense.

POST-YAP

The YAP spanned more than 15 years and there were many generations of graduate students and clinic supervisors. The first generation of graduate students included Robert Koegel and Laura Schriebman. John McEachin, Ron Leaf, Mitch Taubman, Tracee Parker and Sandy Slater were in the final generation. In between there were a number of incredibly talented professionals including Tom Willis, Buddy Newsom, Ted Carr and Dennis Russo. After the last children included in the research study had completed treatment, a number of other graduate students subsequently worked with Dr. Lovaas. Tristram Smith was essential in the analysis and write up involving the Young Autism Project. In the late 1980's, other graduate students, including Jackie Wynn, Doreen Granpeesheh, Kathy Calouri and Gregg Buch worked with Dr. Lovaas on the extension and dissemination of the YAP findings.

COMMON FOLKLORE REGARDING YAP

The children included in the Lovaas (1987) study and then followed up in McEachin, Smith, and Lovaas (1993) were investigated from 1973 until 1985. Naturally during these years there were revisions, alterations and innovations in treatment. Dr. Lovaas is a pioneer and innovator. Being such, he recognized the need for the continuous evaluation, refining and evolution of treatment. Therefore, investigating new and innovative approaches was an ongoing aspect of treatment at the UCLA Young Autism Project. In an effort to disseminate the strategies and techniques developed by the Autism Project Team, *Teaching Developmentally Disabled Children: The Me Book* (Lovaas, Ackerman, Alexander, Firestone, Perkins and Young) was published in 1980 and *Five Videotapes for Teaching Developmentally Disabled Children* (Lovaas and Leaf) were released in 1981. Although these were published in the early 1980's, one must remember that they were compiled during earlier years. While these materials were incredible resources in the treatment of individuals with autism, the book and tapes did not and could not have captured all the procedures developed on the project. We often departed from *The Me Book* and tapes as well as expanded its programs and procedures, always in the quest for individualization.

In the years following the studies, a great deal of folklore and mythology has developed. Through the years, practices and protocols attributed to the UCLA Young Autism Project have been passed on from one generation of graduate students to the next, sometimes losing accuracy in the process and resulting in widespread misperceptions that go well beyond reality. Unfortunately, some of the folklore has resulted in treatment that is not in keeping with the behavioral practices maintained on the YAP, nor with the evolution that has ensued.

In publishing the results of the YAP research, the authors were conservative and cautious in interpreting their results, as is scientifically appropriate. Unfortunately, and as is often the case, the research is interpreted by others in a manner inconsistent with what the study actually concluded. The following are the most common examples of myths and fictions that we have encountered:

MYTH 1: CHILDREN RECEIVED A MINIMUM OF 40 HOURS OF INTERVENTION WEEKLY

As discussed previously, children in the Intensive Treatment group received an **average** of forty hours. There was a range of hours, with some receiving as little as 20 hours weekly and some receiving more than 50 hours weekly.

How many hours of formal DTT should a child receive? The research is quite clear that many children with ASD generally require 30 or more hours of intervention per week (Green, 1996). However, "What counts as hours?" is a question that is often asked. Does Speech Therapy, Occupational Therapy or Physical Therapy count? If a child is in a school program does this count toward the 30 hours? There is no absolute answer. Although many of these services may be helpful, what research and our experiences have shown is that most students will require at least 30 hours of high quality and systematic ABA instruction.

In determining the range of hours necessary there are multiple considerations. For example, the degree of skill deficits would be one determinant in the number of hours. Those students with fewer deficits and who learn more rapidly may require less formal intervention. Another factor would be the child's age and stamina or tolerance of formal intervention. Intensity and rate of disruptive behaviors are another determinant of the number of hours of structured intervention necessary. Students who exhibit extreme disruptive behaviors may require more hours in order to help ameliorate acting out behaviors.

There is not an exact formula to determine the ideal number of hours. Based upon the research, however, we recommend between 30 and 40 hours per week. Then we let the child's progress guide us in determining a more exact number of hours. That is, we may decrease or increase the hours to determine what number of hours is most beneficial for the individual child.

MYTH 2: INTERVENTION WAS EXCLUSIVELY ONE-TO-ONE

A frequent myth regarding the treatment on YAP is that the intervention was exclusively one-on-one. Whereas the majority of intervention for very young children was initially provided utilizing a one-to-one teaching format, the objective in the YAP was always that children learn in small group as well as large group instructional formats as soon as possible. One-on-one was conceptualized as a more artificial teaching format that allowed for rapid acquisition of skills in the early stages of treatment. Although one-to-one was initially the primary format, we systematically exposed the children to group instruction when appropriate. It was always the goal that children become able to participate successfully in group learning and fade their dependence on one-to-one direct instruction. Toward the end of the project, there was a greater emphasis on observational learning as well as group instruction. One of the evolutions in the field of ABA has been the increased use of more natural teaching formats so that children can more easily integrate into more natural learning environments such as school.

MYTH 3: INTERVENTION OCCURRED EXCLUSIVELY AT HOME

Although the YAP is often regarded as a home-based treatment program, it actually extended well beyond the home setting in order to ensure that treatment would have an impact in all areas of a child's life. This definitely meant that school had to be part of the picture. Although often overlooked, there are several references to intervention in school contained in the Lovaas (1987) report:

"Intervention occurred at home, at school and in the community." (pg. 5)

"Treatment was also extended into the community to teach children to function within the preschool." (pg. 5)

"After preschool, placements in public education classes was determined by school personnel. All children who successfully completed normal kindergarten successfully completed first grade and subsequent normal grades." (pg. 5)

". . . successful mainstreaming of a 2-4 year old into a normal preschool group is much easier than the mainstreaming of an older autistic children into the primary grades." (pg. 8)

One of the aims of treatment was to enable children to participate meaningfully in school. Being able to receive education only at home was not considered a desirable outcome. Therefore, as rapidly as possible, children were transitioned to pre-school and other community settings as part of their ABA program. The most successful children were the ones who were able to move quickly beyond the home setting into group learning situations.

MYTH 4: INTERVENTION OCCURRED IN DISTRACTION FREE SETTINGS

There is often the belief that intervention needs to occur in environments where little or no distractions occur. It is assumed that noise, people or classroom materials will distract the child so much that they will be unable to listen and process information. Therefore, in home programs therapy is often conducted in one quiet "therapy" room. Sometimes parents have gone as far as providing extra insulation and installing a camera so that observations can be made without creating the distraction of an extra person in the room.

In classrooms, children are often placed in *isolated* cubicles or even pulled out of the classroom to minimize distractions. Sometimes, materials are even taken off the walls and windows are covered in order to provide "optimal" programming.

Although eliminating all distractions may create the seemingly "perfect" learning environment, in reality it can create tremendous problems! First, the child may become conditioned so that learning can eventually occur only under distraction free conditions, thereby severely restricting the number of environments and places where the child can learn. Teaching in other places in the house, in school or the community would be problematic at best. Moreover, the skills they have acquired may not generalize to the more natural environments.

Ostensibly, distractions can be introduced at a later time. However, all too often this does not occur. The therapist, parent and child are "reinforced" by working in a distraction free environment and unwilling to venture out! And even when there is a systematic plan, it is often not successful because the child's learning style is difficult to alter.

On the YAP, we recognized the difficulty of creating too "optimal" an environment. Therefore, we quickly moved to more natural settings. Treatment was rarely conducted in one "therapy" room. Children received intervention throughout the house, sitting on chairs, at a table, on couches and the floor. Often more distractions were created than would typically occur by turning on the radio or television, or working in front of a window or mirror. The purpose was to give the children the opportunity to learn to concentrate and stay on task in the face of typical kinds of distraction.

Today the same protocol is used at Autism Partnership. As rapidly as possible we begin working in increasingly natural settings. In home programs we work throughout the home. Similarly, in schools we do not recommend teaching children in isolation or in cubicles or behind partitions unless absolutely necessary. Naturally, if a child is having a problem learning a specific program, we would tailor the environment to enable him to be successful. But we would introduce distractions again as quickly as possible. To help a child learn with distractions, it is important to provide reinforcement for paying attention and responding under those conditions.

MYTH 5: WE WORKED ONLY ON SPEECH

Although developing language was a primary concern we also spent time working on play, social and self-help skills. Once again our mission was for children to integrate into natural environments as rapidly as possible. Therefore, if a child had limited play and social skills it would create a tremendous obstacle to our mission. Moreover, if a child did not have self-help skills, such toileting, eating or hygiene it would also hinder attending school.

A similar myth is that we worked on hundreds of programs. As we discuss in Chapter 13 *(Goals, Goals, Goals)* we utilized relatively few programs and only those programs that we felt were uniquely important to the child.

MYTH 6: CONTINUOUS DATA WAS COLLECTED

Treatment data was primarily recorded in narrative form at the conclusion of sessions. Continuous data was only collected when there was a specific question regarding a child's progress. When research was being conducted, more extensive data were also collected. It was generally easy to identify if a child had no understanding of a concept, or was in acquisition or had achieved mastery. It was not usually necessary to collect trial-by-trial data. We collected only as much data as was necessary to evaluate a child's progress.

Research has demonstrated that there are valid and practical ways to reduce the amount of data being collected. Taking representative samples of behavioral and learning data will provide an accurate picture (Haynes, 1978; Powell, Martindale & Kulp, 1975; Powell, Martindale, Kulp, Martindale & Bauman, 1977). Time sampling is a much more efficient procedure and results are similar to continuous recording. Leaf (1983) demonstrated that by utilizing time sampling data collection procedures, one can collect valid data while greatly increasing efficiency. This should not be surprising. If one is testing whether a cake has been baked long enough, you only need to test a few sections, not the whole cake! Or you can get a good idea of someone's personality after a little while, you do not usually need to know their life's story!

A recent research investigation compared the validity, efficiency and user satisfaction of three discrete trial data collection techniques: trial-by-trial, time sample and contemporaneous summaries (Papovich, Rafuse, Siembieda, Williams, Sharpe, McEachin, Leaf, & Taubman, 2002). The results demonstrated that utilizing time sampling and contemporaneous summaries as compared to continuous recordings had multiple advantages. First, and most importantly, the data proved to be every bit as reliable and valid as continuous recording. Second, more user friendly data collection procedures allowed for far more social interaction with the student. Third, by utilizing time sampling data collection procedures, more trials of learning were conducted. Therefore, because of increased learning opportunities children were able to master learning objectives more rapidly.

THE BIG QUESTION: HOW REALISTIC IS THE AIM FOR "RECOVERY"?

Many people disagree with using the term "recovery" in reference to children with ASD. This is partly due to a lack of belief that children can actually progress to a level of functioning where they become indistinguishable from peers. Lovaas is careful not to use the word "cure" because that term implies that the cause has been identified and removed. We worked directly with the children who were documented as obtaining best outcome in the Lovaas 1987 study and there is no doubt in our mind that these children started out with ASD and as a result of intensive behavioral treatment can now be regarded as normal functioning. In our recent clinical work we have seen more than 80 children who have recovered from ASD as a result of intensive behavioral treatment and many more who have made amazing progress.

A second reason why people object to discussion of recovery for children with ASD is a fear that it will cause parents to become desperate in their quest for successful treatment of their child's disorder. Parents are often overoptimistic about their child's progress in treatment and can set themselves up for incredible disappointment and heartache. If one examines the Lovaas studies, it is clear that many children are not going to recover. The children who participated in the YAP, received intervention under optimal circumstances, yet the majority of them did not achieve best outcome as defined by Lovaas. Despite the fact they began treatment before the age of four, received intensive treatment that continued as long as necessary and was carried out in all environments by well-trained staff, less than half of the children were able to successfully complete regular education on their own.

We believe expectations need to be balanced. Parents need to have hope because intensive behavioral treatment is demanding and requires hard work for a long time. But we think the goal of treatment is for each child to obtain "his own best outcome" and we know that is achievable. It is no different than it is with our non-ASD children—we can never know when they are young how they will turn out. Pilot? Doctor? Lifeguard? We have to be satisfied knowing that they have become the best person they can be, that they are happy and productive and that they will make good choices for themselves.

Of course there are things we can and should do to ensure this happy outcome. For children with ASD this means not just making sure they get the proper number of hours of intervention. From the Lovaas 1987 study we know there are a number of factors that contributed to successful outcome. These are the ones that we consider most important:

- Intensity

- Consistency of Treatment

- Early Intervention

- Utilizing Quality ABA

- Not incorporating other treatments that would dilute the impact of ABA

- Intensive supervision

- Parental Expertise

All these factors together constitute the "proper" dosage of treatment. If these elements are not included then prognosis may be lessened. It is similar to going to a physician and asking what needs to be done to get healthy again. For example, if you have cancer, the oncologist might say that to increase the likelihood of remission, you need to receive the appropriate level of chemotherapy over a certain period of time, that it needs to occur in a setting that meets certain standards from highly trained professionals, as well as follow the right diet, get enough exercise and plenty of rest. You also cannot assume that 1/2 dosage of medication will get you half of the desired results. It might have barely any effect at all. You would not want to skimp, hoping that you would get "pretty good" results. The same is true for children with ASD. When children who need 30-35 hours of intervention on a year-round basis only receive 20 hours of intervention for 45 weeks per year, or are receiving education from those who are not experts in ABA as well as receiving a regime of unproven eclectic approaches, it is highly unlikely that their child will reach their potential.

It is not our intention to cause distress to parents when we make recommendations that are difficult to follow, although we know that can happen. We believe it is our obligation to provide parents with accurate information so that they can make informed decisions. We think this is ultimately fair, kind and ethical. We also want parents to be realistic about the outcome that is attainable. In our opinion parents should not undertake intensive behavior treatment if recovery is the only acceptable result. Obviously every parent would like their child to become indistinguishable after treatment. But what we should be aiming for is to have the child fully achieve their potential whatever that turns out to be. Aim high, but know that you might not reach the target. Although a child may always have behaviors associated with ASD, ABA can still provide the best opportunity to develop life skills and thereby greatly enhance the quality of children's lives. Research clearly showed that the eight children, who attained an intermediate level of outcome, benefited substantially from intensive ABA and fared much better than they would have if they had not received treatment. Even the two children who remained nonverbal at the end of the study, most likely have a better quality of life than they would have without treatment. One could certainly say that all of the children achieved the outcome that was the best they were capable of, even though the majority did not "recover."

REFERENCES

Ackerman, A. B. (1980). The role of punishment in the treatment of preschool aged autistic children: Effects and side effects (Volumes IV). *Dissertation Abstracts International, 41*(5-B), 1899

Bibby, P., Eikeseth, S., Martin, N. T., Mudford, O. C., & Reeves, D. (2001). Progress and outcomes for children with autism receiving parent-managed intensive interventions. *Research in Developmental Disabilities, 22*(6), 425-447

Cohen, H., Amerine-Dickens, M., & Smith, T.. (2006). Early Intensive Behavioral Treatment: Replication of the UCLA Model in a Community Setting. Journal of Developmental & Behavioral Pediatrics, 27 (2), 145-155.

Department of Health and Human Services (1999). *Mental Health: A Report of the Surgeon General.* Rockville, MD: Department of Health and Human Services, Substance Abuse and Mental Health Services Administration, Center for Mental Health Services, National Institute of Mental Health.

Eikeseth, S., Smith, T., & Eldevik, S. (2002). Intensive behavioral treatment at school for 4- to 7- year old children with autism. *Behavior Modification, 26,* 49-68.

Fenske, E.C., Zalenski, S., Krantz, P.J., McClannahan, L.E. (1985). Age at intervention and treatment outcome for autistic children in a comprehensive intervention program. *Analysis and Intervention in Developmental Disabilities, 5,* 49-58.

Green, G., 1996. Early Behavioral Intervention for Autism: What Does Research Tell Us? In *Behavioral intervention for young children with autism: A manual for parents and professionals,* Maurice, C., Green, G. & Luce, S., Eds., pp15-28. Austin, TX: PROED.

Haynes, S. N. (1978). *Principles of behavioral assessment.* Oxford, England: Gardner

Leaf, R.B, 1983. A simplified measure for behavioral assessment of autistic individuals. Unpublished Doctoral Dissertation, University of California, Los Angeles.

Lovaas, O.I. (1987). Behavioral Treatment and normal educational and intellectual functioning in young autistic children. *Journal of Clinical and Consulting Psychology,* 55(1), 3-9.

Lovaas, O. I., & Leaf, R. L. (1981). *Five videotapes for teaching developmentally disabled children,* Baltimore, MD: University Park Press

Lovaas, O. I., & Simmons, J. Q. (1969) Manipulation of self-destruction in three retarded children. *Journal of Applied Behavior Analysis,* 2(3), 143-157

Lovaas, O. I., Freitag, G., Gold, V. J., & Kassorla, I. C. (1965). Experimental studies in childhood schizophrenia: Analysis of self-destructive behavior. Journal of Experimental Child Psychology, 2(1), 67-84

Lovaas, O. I., Koegel, R., Simmons, J. Q., & Long, J. S. (1973). Some generalization and follow-up measures on autistic children in behavior therapy. *Journal of Applied Behavior Analysis, 6*(1), 131-166

Lovaas, O. I., Ackerman, A. B., Alexander, D., Firestone, P., Perkins, J., & Young, D. (1981). *Teaching Developmentally Disabled Children: The Me Book.* Austin, TX: Pro-Ed.

Lovaas, O.I., 2003. UCLA Young Autism Project. Speech presented at the meeting of the Association for Behavior Analysis, 2003 Annual Convention, San Francisco, CA.

Matson, J., Benavidez, D., Compton, L., Paclawskyj, T., & Baglio, C., 1996. Behavioral Treatment of Autistic Persons: A Review of Research From 1980 to the Present. *Research in Developmental Disabilities,* 17-6, 433-465.

Maurice, Catherine (1993). *Let me hear your voice.* A family's triumph over autism. NY: Fawcett Columbine.

McEachin, J.J. & Leaf, R.B., 1984. The role of punishment in the motivation of autistic children. Paper presented at the Annual meeting of Association of Behavior Analysis, Nashville, Tennessee.

McEachin, J.J., Smith, T., & Lovaas, O.I. (1993). Long-Term outcome for children with autism who received early intensive behavioral treatment. *American Journal on Mental Retardation*, 97(4), 359-372.

National Research Council (2001): *Educating Children with Autism*, Washington, D.C., National Academy Press.

New York State Department of Health. (1999). *Clinical practice guideline: Report of the recommendations autism/pervasive developmental disorders. Assessment and intervention for young children (ages 0-3)*. Albany: Author.

Papovich, S., Rafuse, J., Siembieda, M., Williams, M., Sharpe, A., McEachin, J., Leaf, R., & Taubman, M., An Analytic Comparison of Data Collection Techniques Used with Discrete Trial Teaching in an Applied Setting for Persons with Autism. Paper presented at the meeting of the Association for Behavior Analysis, 2002 Annual Convention, Toronto, Canada, 2002.

Powell, J., Martindale, A., & Kulp, S. (1975). An evaluation of time-sample measures of behavior. *Journal of Applied Behavior Analysis, 8*, 463-469.

Powell, J., Martindale, B., Kulp, S., Martindale, A., & Bauman, R. (1977). Taking a closer look: Time sampling and measurement error. *Journal of Applied Behavior Analysis, 10*, 325-332.

Sallows, G. O. & Graupner, T. D. (2005). Intensive behavioral treatment for children with autism: Four-year outcome and predictors. *American Journal on Mental Retardation, 110*(6), 417-438

Simmons, J. Q., & Lovaas, O. I. (1969). Use of pain and punishment as treatment techniques with childhood schizophrenics. *American Journal of Psychotherapy. 23*(1) 23-36

Smith, T., Buch, G. A., & Gamby, T. E. (2000). Parent-directed, intensive early intervention for children with pervasive developmental disorder. *Research in Developmental Disabilities, 21*(4), 297-309

Chapter 3

DIVERGENCE, CONVERGENCE AND RESOLUTION?

By Ron Leaf, John McEachin, & Jennifer Styzens

THE EMERGENCE OF DIVERGENCE

It would be reasonable to think that the small, but growing, cadre of professionals who utilize ABA in the treatment of ASD would design and implement behavioral intervention programs in a similar manner. As *behaviorists,* they should all adhere to the principles of behaviorism. As discussed in **Chapter 1** (*What is ABA?*), there certainly is agreement that there are environmental determinants of behavior and therefore with effective teaching techniques we can reduce or even eliminate disruptive behaviors and increase the occurrence of desired behaviors. Furthermore, ABA practitioners would all share in common a focus on objective data and utilization of an empirical process for making treatment decisions. Therefore, it would be reasonable to think that all ABA practitioners would operate in a similar manner.

Although the scientific foundation lays out many basic principles upon which everyone agrees, there are many technical aspects of the implementation of intensive behavioral intervention that are handled in widely varying manners, such as the types of reinforcement used, the complexity of language spoken by the teacher, and where intervention is carried out. There is also lack of agreement about the type of instructional format that should be utilized (e.g., Discrete Trial Teaching, Pivotal Response Training, Natural Language Paradigm)? To greatly complicate the debate, different approaches have derived different terms often with similar meanings. Finally, there is a wide range of stylistic differences in the way practitioners approach the challenges of building skill repertoires in children with ASD. The continuum ranges from dogmatic, rigid and mechanistic at one extreme all the way to loose, inexact, unsystematic and watered down.

STYLE, TECHNIQUE AND THEORY

A widely used but not universally favored teaching technique is Discrete Trial Teaching (DTT). DTT is often viewed as an extremely rigid procedure that should only be used in highly structured settings to teach very specific skills to lower functioning young children. Our own view is that DTT has broad applicability and can be employed quite flexibly and naturally. DTT can be used to teach a wide variety of skills to individuals of all ages and functioning levels in all types of settings.

Professionals who utilize DTT are often pigeonholed as rigid and punitive. The fact is that many behaviorists employ DTT with much flexibility and are quite natural in their implementation of DTT procedures. Perhaps because of the stereotype of DTT, many professionals seem to have distanced themselves from DTT and have come up with other names and variations of teaching strategies that seem more appealing. Two notable examples are Pivotal Response Training (PRT) developed by two former students of Lovaas, Robert Koegel and Laura Schreibman (Koegel, Koegel, & Schreibman, 1991), and Incidental Teaching (IT) as described by Hart & Risley (1982) and McGee, Morrier & Daly (1999).

These approaches have attempted to distinguish themselves from DTT by emphasizing naturally occurring opportunities to teach a skill as opposed to contrived opportunities. Those who have only been exposed to a more rigid approach to DTT might view Pivotal Response Training (PRT) as being quite different from DTT and might be more inclined to favor PRT or over DTT because they perceive it as more child friendly and natural.

Prizant and Wetherby (1998) have described a Social-Pragmatic Developmental theory for treatment of ASD. They see their approach as being the antithesis of traditional DTT and theorized the following continuum of teaching strategies:

☐	☐	☐
Traditional DTT	Contemporary Behavioral	Social-Pragmatic Developmental Approaches

This continuum positions "contemporary" behavioral approaches, in which are included PRT, IT, and NLP, away from DTT. Additionally, it perpetuates a narrow view of how DTT is conceptualized and implemented. They make this distinction on the basis of purported differences in the use of more natural learning environments, more emphasis on individualization of curriculum and more natural and balanced social transactions in which learning opportunities are initiated by the child. As illustrated in the above continuum, they view the Social-Pragmatic approach as moving even further away from Traditional DTT by emphasizing the following elements:

1. *Use of Interactive-Facilitative Strategies* (i.e., taking advantage of opportunities to facilitate natural language).

2. *Degree of Acceptance of Children's Communicative Bids* (i.e., providing positive and supportive feedback of children's communication).

3. *Degree of Directiveness* (i.e., utilizing a less directive more "facilitative" style whenever possible).

4. *Adjusting Language and Social Input* (i.e., adjusting language complexity based upon the individual child).

5. *A Focus on Communicative Events* (i.e., arranging the environment to facilitate increased communication opportunities).

6. *Learning is Transactional and Affectively Based* (i.e., acknowledging and enhancing the interactive nature of communication)

In fact, there is no reason why DTT needs to be conducted in a rigid and unfriendly manner or for it to override the opportunity for the student to initiate interactions. We agree that there are advantages to incorporating these principles in teaching children with ASD. Moreover, we strongly believe that DTT can and should incorporate these principles but we would prefer to conceptualize the differences in behavioral terms.

We believe there exists a similar type of continuum which distinguishes "Rigid DTT" vs. "Flexible DTT", illustrated in the following table.

RANGE OF DISCRETE TRIAL TEACHING STRATEGIES

RIGID	STRUCTURED	FLEXIBLE
☐	☐	☐

"TRADITIONAL"	"CONTEMPORARY" PRT, IT, NLP	EVOLVED **DTT**

CONVERGENCE	TRADITIONAL	EVOLVED
SYSTEMATIC TEACHING IS CRUCIAL	One-on-one instruction	One-on-one, small and large group
REINFORCEMENT	1. Food reinforcement 2. Continuous schedules 3. Limited interaction upon delivery	1. Activities, toys & social 2. Intermittent schedules 3. Extensive interaction as appropriate
PROMPTING IS CENTRAL IN TEACHING	Wrong, wrong, prompt or Errorless prompting	Flexible prompting strategies based on student's ability to learn from a variety of prompts or learn from feedback.
ELIMINATE INTERFERING BEHAVIORS	Reactive behavioral strategies, at most	Pro-active and reactive behavioral strategies
GENERALIZATION IS ESSENTIAL	1. Initially eliminate distractions (e.g., isolation, reduce noise) 2. Identical & simple instructions	1. Start in most natural settings possible 2. Variety & complexity of instruction should reflect child's ability
DATA IS MANDATORY	Continuous data	Representative samples
MEANINGFUL CURRICULUM	Speech & academics	Communication, social, play, self-help, school learning skills, and behavior control
ULTIMATE GOAL IS CHILD'S INDEPENDENCE	1. Therapist's preferences 2. Control battles	1. Child & therapist preferences 2. Reduced control battles

CONVERGENCE: IT IS TIME TO EVOLVE

During the early days of treatment more rigid approaches were used, but there has since been an evolution in philosophy as well as treatment. We have learned to preserve the systematic and methodical approach to teaching which is the hallmark of an effective ABA program, but carry out DTT in a more natural manner. We owe a large debt to the pioneers of DTT for developing a highly effective method of teaching and do not fault them because of the imperfections.

Although it is critical to be systematic, it is also necessary to be flexible. This may seem to be a contradictory concept, but it really is not. It requires a plan, but one must be willing to adjust the plan when it is not working. To best meet the needs of the students, teachers and parents cannot become so invested in a program or methodology that they are unwilling to make necessary modifications.

Unfortunately, many people who employ ABA with children who have ASD adhere to strict rules and are unwilling to even consider changing, for example, always doing exactly ten trials within each program or following a rigid "wrong + wrong = prompt" rule. Such "rules" have applicability in some situations with some students, but not necessarily with all students. If we change "rules" to "considerations" then we can have flexibility to meet the student's individual needs which in turn may increase the effectiveness of the procedure or technique being utilized.

Although there is consensus regarding the foundations of ABA, there remain divergent directions in philosophy, conceptualization and application between various types of ABA programs. In order to converge as a behavioral community, it is important that we look at the history of DTT. Evolution occurs when we build on the strengths of a teaching approach and apply creativity to the shortcomings rather than abandoning a model that has merit, but may not be perfect. Too often people change the name of an intervention and attempt to erase the link to the evolutionary history. We believe that it fragments the field and causes confusion among lay consumers when practitioners make some changes in terminology and repackage their approach as "new and different."

RESOLUTION MEANS INDIVIDUALIZATION

As behaviorists, we should determine what intervention strategies are most effective for each child. It is critical that we not automatically revert to the formulas with which we are most comfortable, but let the data shape our behavior. An analogy would be which route to take to a specific location. Although you may utilize a map, it may be necessary to alter your route based upon the conditions (e.g., accidents, weather, road repairs, time of day, etc.). Sometimes there may be a few routes that will get you to the same location. And although the map provides a structure, the conditions require flexibility within structure.

NONSENSE
EVERYONE SPEAKS OF THE NECESSITY OF INDIVIDUALIZATION, YET MANY BEHAVIORISTS FOLLOW A RIGID APPROACH IN WHICH THERE IS LITTLE OR NO INDIVIDUALIZATION! WE SEEM TO HAVE LOST THE "I" IN IEP AS WELL AS THE "I" IN IDEA!

AUTISM PARTNERSHIP'S EVOLUTIONS

Behaviorism's roots go back to the early 1900's to the work of Ivan Pavlov and John B. Watson. The foundations and principles of Applied Behavior Analysis largely remain unchanged. However, treatment strategies and philosophy have continually evolved. It should not be surprising that the field would change, given that the hallmark of Behaviorism is modification based upon data analysis. During our days at UCLA, treatment was continually changing. Whereas in the earlier days we utilized punishment procedures, toward the end of the project we abandoned such strategies. A focus on parental expertise, intervention in schools and more advanced language programming all represented significant evolutions.

Just as ABA has evolved, Autism Partnership has also evolved since its inception in 1994. We have made changes in areas such as treatment strategies, curriculum, and philosophy. In fact the book we published detailing our beliefs was entitled *A Work in Progress*. We chose that name so as to convey the ever-changing nature of treatment of children with ASD. The following illustrate some of the evolutions we have gone through since our inception:

- There is a greater emphasis on proactive strategies to address behavior problems. Previously, there was often reliance upon reducing behavior problems through reductive strategies (e.g., extinction or response cost). Presently, there is more emphasis on teaching children replacement behaviors, for example, positive attention seeking behaviors, ways to gain control, social and play skills, as well as coping strategies such as stress management and self monitoring. And, we have increased our attention to ensuring that artificial prompts within the environment are eliminated so that the replacement behaviors are exhibited and utilized independently.

- Continued development of behavior programs to address children's deficit areas. Innovative programs designed to teach joint attention, resolve receptive learning difficulties and reduce self-stimulation have assisted parents and schools.

- Observational learning skills are addressed from very early on in intervention. At UCLA we recognized the importance of children being able to acquire information through observation. However, it was a skill that was not addressed until later stages of intervention. Now we focus on observational learning early in intervention and have greatly expanded curriculum in this area.

- Utilizing DTT in a group format has been an important addition to our ABA programming efforts. Research and experience has revealed that children can learn increased amounts of information through participation in group instruction. Procedures used in a one-to-one format have been adapted and enhanced in order to facilitate effective group learning (Taubman, Brierley, Wishner, Baker, McEachin & Leaf, 2001).

- In the beginning, the preponderance of programming had been on language development. We continue to regard communication as important, however a greater emphasis has been placed on social, play, self-help, and daily living skills. These skills provide a child greater control within his environment and treatment gains are better maintained because they provide a greater number of ways for the child to access naturally occurring reinforcement. But more importantly, the child is better able to meet his own needs in a variety of ways which greatly enhance the quality of life.

■ There has been tremendous development in programs to facilitate more natural and spontaneous language. The teaching of communication skills has been greatly improved by exposing children to more natural, "kid-like" language, setting up the environment to evoke language (e.g., sabotage), using motivational manipulations (e.g., communication temptations), developing joint attention, fluency building exercises, decreased emphasis on question answering and more emphasis on commenting.

■ Social skills programs have been developed to target increasingly complex social situations (e.g., telling/keeping a secret, knowing when and how to change a topic based on the lack of interest of others, etc.). We recognize the necessity to remain systematic and comprehensive in social skills development, therefore, are developing a social taxonomy as an attempt to capsulate the complexities of identification and teaching of social skills.

■ Because of the continued identification of needs for children with autistic disorder at various levels on the continuum, as stated, Autism Partnership has focused program development and treatment in the areas of social, play, language, self help, and school learning programs. Because of the expansive needs in the above areas, academics has been de-emphasized and often not targeted as a primary objective. Academic areas may be utilized to teach other learning skills (e.g., observational learning, joint attention, choral responding, etc.), but again academic information is not a primary learning focus. As an agency we maintain that what does need to be assessed are the processes and skills preventing the child from acquiring academic information and teaching those skills. Consequently, if a child learns the skills necessary to learn, and appropriate ways of meeting their needs, they will learn academics independent of 1:1 tutors to teach information/facts.

■ Overall programming has become more developmentally attuned. Language, academic and self-help programs, for example, will more often mirror the developmental sequences. (e.g., using age appropriate play materials and an emphasis on development of age appropriate reinforcement, utilizing a school based "typical" setting as the teaching environment, etc.) Naturally, there are times when a child does not learn in such a manner and therefore programming efforts need to be adjusted accordingly.

■ Programming has aimed to become more functional. There is a greater understanding of the skills that are important for a particular child based upon their age, instructional needs and skill level (e.g., receptive instructions such as "line up", matching skills being taught through cleaning up tasks or putting laundry away, "manding" to make a snack, materials imitation requiring the student to "build a bridge" with 3 blocks, not a non-functional structure, etc..)

■ There is an expansive use of different teaching strategies (e.g., DTT, task analysis, teaching interactions, imbedded instruction, role play, , etc).

■ Since the 1960's Dr. Lovaas recognized the importance of school placement. However, the actual intervention was often typically provided by UCLA staff. Through the years behaviorists have been increasingly committed to teaching school personnel how to effectively utilize ABA procedures so that they can independently design and implement effective teaching strategies. Autism Partnership is also committed to pursuing this mission and sees this as a vehicle for providing effective intervention for many more children.

ABA as a field must continue to evolve. We must be willing to overcome the stereotypes and dogma associated with DTT, because it is far too valuable a tool to simply discard. We must rely on data to evaluate outcomes and take steps to generalize skills. We must recognize the importance of maintaining a systematic yet flexible approach to treating children with autistic disorder as each child presents a different set of skills and deficits.

REFERENCES

Hart, B. & Risley, T. R. (1982). *How to use incidental teaching for elaborating language.* Lawrence, KS: H & H Enterprises.

Koegel, L. K., Koegel, R. L., & Schreibman, L (1991). Assessing and training parents in teaching pivotal behaviors. *Advances in Behavioral Assessment of Children and Families,* 5, 65-82.

McGee, G.G., Morrier, M.J., & Daly, T. (1999). An incidental teaching approach to early intervention for toddlers with autism. *Journal of the Association for Persons with Severe Handicaps,* 24, 133-146.

Prizant, B.M. & Wetherby, A.M. (1998). Understanding the continuum of discrete-trial traditional behavioral to social-pragmatic, developmental approaches in communication enhancement for young children with ASD. *Seminars in Speech and Language, 19,* 329-353.

Taubman, M., Brierley, S., Wishner, J., Baker, D., McEachin, J., Leaf, R.B. (2001). The Effectivness of a group discrete trial instructional approach for preschoolers with Developmental disabilities. *Research in Developmental Disabilities, 22*(3), 205-219.

Chapter 4

TO BCBA OR NOT TO B?

By Ron Leaf, Mitch Taubman, Andy Bondy & John McEachin

WHO IS QUALIFIED?

Often intensive behavioral treatment for children with autism is delivered by paraprofessional staff working under the supervision of a more qualified and experienced professional. In such a case, the effectiveness of treatment is dependent on the skill of the supervisor at providing Programmatic oversight as well as the skill of the paraprofessionals in teaching the child.

Tragically, parents of children with autism are desperate. School districts also face tremendous pressure. There are simply not enough professionals to provide the necessary intervention. Often, it would be considered fortunate just having a caring interventionist. If they happen to be conversant about ABA and autism that would be a fantastic bonus! The reality is that merely being conversant is not nearly sufficient even for the most dedicated professional.

How would a parent, or a school district for that matter, know that a professional is qualified to provide intensive behavioral intervention to children with autism? Is one qualified if they have only a Bachelors degree? Does a Masters or a Ph.D. make one even more qualified? Is practical experience more important than formal education? How many years of experience does one need in order to be considered qualified? What kind of experience should it be? What kind of training is necessary? How comprehensive should the training be and what is the necessary content? Should one consider the expertise of the supervisor who provided the training?

These questions and dilemmas have created the need for some kind of system to evaluate the skills of practitioners. A recent credential, Board Certified Behavior Analyst (BCBA) is starting to be recognized and in some cases required as a way to identify who is qualified to deliver ABA services. The Certification is overseen by a private nonprofit corporation which establishes the requirements. To become a BCBA one must have a Masters Degree which includes specified course work on theory, practice, experimental design, and ethics. In addition, one must complete a supervised internship and pass a written exam.

Since its origins in Florida in the 1990's (Starin, Hemingway, Hartsfield, 1993), there has been an increasing push for using the Board Certified Behavior Analyst (BCBA) credential to solve the dilemma of how to identify qualified professionals. However, we are concerned that the BCBA credential is not the "Gold Standard" that everyone has been longing for. In fact we think that the cure might be even worse than the illness!

BCBA SHORTCOMINGS

What is the scope of the expertise of BCBA's? Parents and school districts are hoping that by employing a BCBA, they will be assured that a professional has the expertise to provide intervention for their child with ASD and guide others in the process. There is often a false belief that BCBA's are certified as experts in autism. Many school districts require that interventionists for children with ASD have a BCBA credential without considering their level of specialized experience, knowledge and training in the design and delivery of intensive behavioral treatment of autism. Clearly there is a lack of awareness among these administrators that a BCBA may not have extensive course work or training in autism. Therefore, the BCBA credential does not fulfill the purpose of identifying those who are qualified for the job that needs to be done.

What level of training and what kind of experience is required for becoming a BCBA? Although supervisors verify that candidates have received supervision, there is no standard regarding how much training occurred or the type of training. The experience may be in areas that are quite unrelated to intensive behavioral treatment of autism and there may be little training that is specific to the design of a teaching curriculum for children with autism.

Is the examination a valid measure of therapeutic quality? Once again, there exists a false belief regarding what "expertise" a BCBA would possess. It is often believed that a BCBA has demonstrated through experience as well as the examination that they posses the skills essential for providing quality intervention. Moreover, there is not any provision for evaluating the practical skills of the candidate. The assessment method used in the certification process is a paper and pencil test. Furthermore, the examination primarily focuses on knowledge of research design and data analysis. While these are important areas, there are far more skills that are required to be a competent interventionist. In fact, it is possible to become a BCBA with very little practical experience and limited knowledge and training in the clinical aspects of working with children, parents and professionals.

Additionally, the examination simply does not reflect the breadth of ABA. There are many sub-areas within ABA, especially in the treatment of children with ASD. However, the examination primarily reflects the interests and perspective of those who have created the certification process. For example, there is strong emphasis on Applied Verbal Behavior. Although being knowledgeable about Skinner's theory of Verbal Behavior as well as practical application of the theory is worthwhile, there are many other perspectives that would be important for interventionists to know, especially given the limited research on the effectiveness of AVB in the treatment of ASD.

Moreover, many of the areas "tested" also reflect the creators of BCBA's specific perspective. Such biases are reflected in the exam's heavy concentration on research design and data (Bailey & Burch, 2002). There is an emphasis on continuous recording as opposed to time sampling. Acceleration charts are also emphasized, and the concept of clinical significance as opposed to statistical significance gets little consideration. One would expect there to be a consensus on data recording procedures and data analysis, but there are widely diverging views and therefore no clear standard to which a practitioner should be expected to adhere.

What does the examination actually measure? Ironically, the test appears to be a very non-behavioral way to certify behaviorists. Test taking behavior actually seems to be the behavior that is being measured as a supposed indicator of some larger competency. There is no demonstrated relationship between being able to answer questions about ABA and ability to help children. In fact, it appears that lately graduate programs emphasize material that is on the test, rather than training in actual service delivery skills. Although it is possible on any licensing examination, (e.g., Licensed Psychologist, Marriage Family Therapist, Licensed Social Worker) the BCBA examination is so specific that it appears much more likely that candidates are simply learning to pass the exam and aren't really demonstrating important skill areas.

The field of behavior analysis grew, in part, in reaction to relying upon secondary measures of behavior and performance. Psychology was once dominated by personality tests, paper and pencil methods of trying to determine a person's 'true self.' However, these strategies failed to help psychologists understand and predict real behaviors in meaningful situations. Behavior analysts developed strategies that directly measured behaviors and found far better predictive validity to these types of measures as well as demonstrating causal relationships between intervention and outcome. It does not make sense for the field to turn back to multiple-choice exams as an indicator of something as important as a person's clinical acumen. All model programs serving children with autism rely upon direct observations of the skills of the staff and have exacting descriptions of what constitutes "good therapy". Obtaining passing grades in courses on ABA should merely set the stage for professional growth, by getting a person in a position to begin learning good clinical skills with children, their parents, and staff who work with them. The Board of the BCBA has focused so much attention on taking **THEIR** test that they have required prominent professionals who wrote the very textbooks upon which the tests are based to sit for the test! (It would be very interesting to many of us to see the 'wrong' answers of these brilliant individuals!)

Is there really a need for certification of seasoned licensed professionals? There has existed for a long time a licensing procedure for professionals who work with developmentally disabled clients. Even now, such a license is necessary in most cases for such clinical work as assessment, inpatient care, and health plan reimbursement or one must work under the supervision of a licensed professional. A compelling case has not been made that BCBA supplants these older established credentials. It certainly has not been demonstrated in any way whatsoever that those professionals who developed the field with research in ABA or clinical application with clients prior to the existence of the BCBA should now be considered unqualified. What does make sense is that newly trained professionals can choose the BCBA route as an alternative to other professional credentials. We would also agree that BCBA's should be recognized as qualified providers of behavioral intervention within the scope of their training under medical insurance plans. We do not agree that they should be the solely qualified practitioners of behavioral intervention.

Are BCBA's more qualified than other licensed professionals to provide intervention (Harris, 2006)? In many states BCBA's with a Master's Degree receive a higher level of reimbursement than Licensed Psychologists who hold a Ph.D. In California, for example, BCBA's receive $75 per hour of service vs. $52 for Licensed Psychologists. Even though licensed psychologists have earned a Ph.D., have more years of supervised experience, have passed far more stringent examination procedures and have a much broader experience, they often receive a lower reimbursement fee from state agencies. It is not logical that someone with more education and experience, who has demonstrated competency through a more rigorous process, should receive lower compensation.

MIGHT WE BE BETTER OFF WITHOUT THE BCBA CREDENTIAL?

What are the broad goals and risks associated with certification? The BCBA process arose out of fear that many people would portray themselves as having expertise in ABA without adequate training and experience. The BCBA process can be viewed as setting a 'standard' to help parents and school personnel to recognize charlatans. However, this type of restricted interpretation of who is qualified to provide effective intervention within autism can also operate to defend a 'guild' from outside members, thus often limiting trade. Essentially, if you're not a member of my club, you cannot be good. Many professionals have spent years obtaining doctorates from programs certified by the American Psychology Association, including APA approved internships, passed state standards for licensing within psychology, taught ABA courses and published widely in the field about highly effective strategies, participated actively in ABA oriented conferences and workshops and yet resist 'club' membership. Why? Because it does not add any additional recognition to the myriad ways of having demonstrated the clinical skills needed to lead effective intervention programs to help children with autism and their families. We believe there are adequate means of demonstrating these skills without the methods adhered to by the BCBA board.

Furthermore the new certification opens the door for less qualified individuals to claim that they are the ones who should be providing service while others who truly have the breadth and depth of expertise are suddenly defined as unqualified. Finally, reliance on the BCBA credential can give a false sense of assurance to consumers. Until these concerns can be resolved we feel people will need to continue to do old fashioned due diligence and look behind the credential to gather enough information about training, experience and professionalism to satisfy themselves that a behavior interventionist knows his or her stuff. Consumers and funding agencies should not trust a piece of paper to tell them everything they need to know. A competent behaviorist's work will speak for itself.

REFERENCES

Bailey, J.B., & Burch, M.R. (2002). Research Methods in Applied Behavior Analysis. Sage Publishing Company

Harris, S.L. (2006). Ask the editor. *Journal of Autism and Developmental Disorders,* 36(2), 293.

Hopkins, B. L. & Moore, J. (1993). ABA accreditation of graduate programs of study. *Behavior Analyst,* 16, 117-121.

Moore, J., & Shook, G.L. Certification, accreditation, and quality control in behavior analysis. *Behavior Analyst,* 24(1), 45-55.

Shook, G.L. (2005). An Examination of the Integrity and Future of the Behavior Analyst Certification Board Credentials. *Behavior Modification, 29,* 562-574.

Shook, G.L., Neisworth, J.T. (2005). Ensuring appropriate qualifications for Applied Behavior Analyst Professionals: The Behavior Analyst Certification Board. *Exceptionality,* 13(1), 3-10.

Shook, G. L., Hartsfield, F. & Hemingway, M. J. (1995). Essential content for training behavior analysis practitioners. *Behavior Analyst,* 18, 83-91.

Shook, G. L. (1993). The professional credential in behavior analysis. *Behavior Analyst,* 16, 87-101.

Starin, S., Hemingway, M. & Hartsfield, F. (1993). Credentialing behavior analysts and the Florida behavior analysis certification program. *Behavior Analyst,* 16, 153-166.

Chapter 5

ECLECTICISM

By Ron Leaf, Mitch Taubman & John McEachin

THE QUEST FOR BEST PRACTICE

Attorneys and school district administrators often cite two articles to support the view that an eclectic approach to autism treatment is "best practice". Dawson and Osterling (1997) and Prizant and Rubin (1999) both reviewed various treatments and presented their conclusions. Both articles reached the same conclusions: there are common elements to all successful approaches, all research on autism treatments has flaws and limitations, and there is no evidence that any one approach is better than another. They go on to assert that; therefore, there are basic elements that are common to and necessary for effective treatment and that there are a wide variety of effective treatments. These conclusions have been widely used as evidence in support of many types of therapies and for the contention that an eclectic approach is "best practice".

HAS THE CASE REALLY BEEN MADE FOR ECLECTICISM?

On the face of it, these reviews appear to be a strong endorsement for many specific approaches to treatment, as well as for an eclectic approach. However, with a little critical thinking the power and value of these articles are greatly diminished. There are multiple problems with these two articles.

First, it is crucial to note that these two articles are not **empirical** research studies. They are simply the authors' observations and conjecture without any data to support their conclusions. There is absolutely no scientific, meta-, or statistical analysis to support their opinions. Second, even though the authors acknowledge that they have not conducted a comparative analysis, their findings are portrayed as though one has been conducted. In a comparative review or meta-analysis, various approaches are compared using standard, commonly accepted scientific and statistical methodology. This is done to systematically determine comparative effectiveness. Although the authors conclude that the treatments they reviewed were all equally effective, in reality all they did was describe the various approaches and present what each approach claimed as outcome without consideration of the legitimacy of those claims. The authors conjecture that the approaches have equivalent effectiveness without conducting any scientific comparison or providing much of a basis for their conclusions.

Third, many of the approaches included in their commentaries had limited scientific evidence as to their effectiveness, and were mixed in with studies which were highly empirical. Some of the approaches claimed effectiveness based upon case studies, without experimental evidence. Some approaches, while having some research on specific aspects of their treatment, did not present any comprehensive outcome data. And some utilized seriously flawed methodology (such as retrospective chart review); therefore, making it difficult to draw any conclusion. Papers lacking scientific evidence in support of a given treatment are given weight equal to comprehensive, long term, scientifically sound outcome studies. The authors explain that all the studies reviewed have scientific flaws and therefore conclude that all of the studies are comparable. Studies with minor flaws which did not undermine the significance of the findings are not discriminated from those with devastating, fatal deficiencies which render their conclusions meaningless.

A fourth concern is that the approaches utilized extremely different methodologies. It is next to impossible to make any valid comparisons when there are such vast differences in variables such as: subject age, diagnostic criteria, age at onset of treatment and the intensity and duration of treatment. A fair and valid comparison even with thorough statistical methodology, would be difficult at best.

Fifth, and perhaps even more problematic than differing methodologies, were the tremendous differences in "outcome" criteria between the studies reviewed. For some approaches, treatment was deemed as "successful" if the subjects were able to maintain community placement even though they may continue to exhibit disruptive behaviors or profound skill deficits. Others reported outcome success if a child was in a regular education setting with supports. In contrast, Lovaas considered it "best outcome" when the children were in regular education without any supports and indistinguishable from their typical peers. Both outcomes, however, were deemed to represent success by their authors, and are therefore treated equally by the review paper authors. Can we really say both approaches are equally effective?

Sixth, the authors pull from each of the articles components of the various approaches which they claim were important in the treatment process. They then list these components as common threads for success among all the studies and detail them as elements of "best practice". While the studies may have contained these elements, the authors offer nothing to support that these elements were important or central to the specific outcomes achieved by the various studies. For example, suppose all approaches had more female than male teachers or therapists (a strong likelihood, by the way). Would we conclude that this gender ratio was necessary to have a successful program and therefore having a preponderance of female service providers constitutes "best practice"?

Even if an element was indeed an important part of a treatment protocol, its effectiveness might be dependent on some other variable included in the original study but which did not make it to the list of consensus "best practice". No effort was made to determine all the essential elements of a given approach and generally this would not even be possible to determine given the methodologies used. Nor do they offer information to support their lack of inclusion of unique elements of a particular approach which might have been critical to the results achieved. Leaving out such variables might cripple an otherwise potent treatment approach. Intensive ABA, which was one of the approaches reviewed, has certain features that are not contained in any of the other approaches, perhaps most notably a very intensive application of direct instruction. This variable, which did not appear in the list of supposed "best practices" very likely is an important contributor to the uniquely positive outcomes obtained using the ABA approach.

Finally, these articles have taken on a life of their own. They are cited in litigation, referred to in articles and discussed as though a comparative analysis had been conducted (Nelson & Huefner, 2003). The term "best practice" is used with frequency and without caution, as if a comprehensive, valid model has been identified and compiled through careful, extensive analysis. This folklore has given credence to the eclectic approach.

THE DOWNSIDE OF ECLECTIC TREATMENT

We strongly believe that an "eclectic" approach (that is, a treatment program which contains a blend of elements from diverse intervention approaches) is a mistake. In the UCLA YAP (Lovaas, 1987; McEachin, Smith, & Lovaas, 1993), the intensive treatment group only received ABA. They did not receive occupational or speech therapy. They did not have any dietary or medical interventions. Sensory Integration was not provided. They also did not receive any interventions based upon TEACCH or traditional models of education. It was strictly ABA. If you seek the kind of results that were obtained in that study it is important to maintain the integrity of the intervention. This is borne out again in a more recent study by Howard, Sparkman, Cohen, Green, & Stanislaw (2005). In this study, ASD children receiving eclectic treatment did not fare as well as children who received only ABA. Utilizing a variety of approaches at best dilutes the effectiveness of any one approach, and potentially undermines intervention overall. Each approach is based upon some specific theoretical foundation. Consequently, the simultaneous application of multiple approaches is often couterproductive.

There are multiple reasons why using an array of procedures (i.e., an eclectic approach) is problematic:

1. "Jack of all trades and master of none." It is difficult for staff to become proficient in any one technique, let alone try to learn it all.

2. It is like a rudderless ship. Underlying philosophies help guide the application of treatment procedures. They help steer decision making and problem solving as well as evaluation of the results of such efforts. Theoretical and philosophical clarity provides direction and cohesiveness as well as facilitating uniformity and continuity. Without a unifying, underlying concept, staff have no idea what to do, why, and when.

3. Intermixing procedures can dilute the effectiveness of any one approach by reducing consistency and intensity.

4. Intermixing may even sabotage the effectiveness. Most approaches have fundamentally different foundations. Therefore each approach may actually conflict with and undo the efforts of the others, thereby undermining overall effectiveness.

5. It becomes extremely difficult, if not impossible, to analyze the effectiveness of any one procedure within the hodge-podge. Therefore, the most effective component(s) of an educational program cannot be identified.

6. Since there is not a strong commitment to a single approach, there is a strong temptation to dabble. People will try a little of this and a little of that, not being systematic in the implementation and not staying with an approach long enough to fully determine its merits.

7. Since anything can potentially be included, there is not a clear vision of what practitioners should be looking for. It is an open-ended invitation list that allows some potentially unsavory, inappropriate, and ineffectual participants through the door. The open door policy promotes constant and indiscriminate searching rather than concentrating on the interventions that are theoretically cohesive and have a proven track record.

We are not suggesting that districts be uninformed about different methodologies that have scientific evidence as to their effectiveness. But it is essential to adopt and become grounded within one orientation. Techniques and procedures from other approaches can then be incorporated within that orientation when and if necessary, but only to the extent that they are complementary and do not detract from the effectiveness of the foundational components. This reduces the amount of incongruity and interference and results in a more seamless and integrated approach. As should be clear by now, we believe that ABA is the approach that should be the core of an intervention program.

In our opinion, doing it all does not even come close to "best practice". Analogously, one would most likely be reluctant to go to a restaurant that served every kind of food (e.g., Chinese, Mexican, French, Italian, Japanese, American). One would suspect they could not do justice to all the different cuisines. This would be especially true if every dish represented a "fusion" of _every_ type of cuisine. Similarly, it would be hard to dance (and a confusing mess) using a jazz-ballet-hip-hop-ballroom-swing-country line dancing-break dancing-waltz style. There is a good reason why psychologists would not pass the licensing examination if they stated they followed an "eclectic" approach. The expectation is that psychologists should be trained in multiple areas but have expertise in a clear methodology. Their ethical obligation is to stay within their areas of expertise and call upon experts of other methodologies to assist clients when their needs fall outside one's own area of expertise.

Being eclectic has curb appeal. On the face of it, it sounds good. After all, one size cannot fit all, so it is tempting to think that a blend of philosophies and approaches has the best chance of providing what each student needs. Even though an eclectic approach is often viewed as "best practice", the research does not bear this out. If you want the best results, choose the methodology that has the best track record and do not lose your focus. Become an expert on that methodology and do not add elements that could dilute its impact. If you fall into the eclectic trap there is a serious risk of becoming a "jack of all trades and master of none" and students will end up getting mediocre and less effective services.

REFERENCES

Dawson, G. & Osterling, J. (1997). "Early intervention in autism: Effectiveness and common elements of current approaches." In Guralnick (Ed.) *The effectiveness of early intervention: Second generation research.* (pp. 307-326) Baltimore: Brookes

Dolan, B. (2004). "Legal digest: A summary of recent case law." *Journal of Forensic Psychiatry and Psychology* **15**(1): 165-172.

Eikeseth, S., Smith, T., Jahr, E., & Eldevik. S. (2002). "Intensive behavioral treatment at school for 4 to 7-year-old children with autism: A 1 year comparison controlled study." *Behavior Modification* **26**(1): 49-68.

Etscheidt, S. (2003). "An analysis of legal hearings and cases realted to indvidualized education programs for children with autism." *Research and Practice for persons with severe disabilities* **28**(2): 51-69.

Fogt, J. B., Miller, D.N., & Zirkel, P.A. (2003). "Defining Autism: Professional best practice and published case law." *Journal of School Psychology* **41**(3): 201-216.

Howard, J. S., Sparkman, C.R., Cohen, H.G., Green, G., & Stanislaw, H. (2005). "A comparison of intensive behavior analytic and eclectic treatments for young children with autism." *Research in Developmental Disabilities* **26**(4): 359-383.

Jerome, A. (1973). "Scaling the fortress walls: Some ways of working with autistic children." *Acta-Paedopsychiatrica: International Journal of Child and Adolescent Psychiatry* **29**(8-10): 263-270.

Lovaas, O.I. (1987). Behavioral Treatment and normal educational and intellectual functioning in young autistic children. *Journal of Clinical and Consulting Psychology,* **55**(1), 3-9.

Mandlawitz, M. R. (2002). "The impact of the legal system on educational programming for young children with autism spectrum disorder." *Journal of Autism and Developmental Disorders* **19**(1): 125-129.

Mandlawitz, M. R. (2005). "Educating Children with Autism: Current Legal Issues." In *Handbook of autism and pervasive developmental disorders: Assessment, intervention, and policy.* F. R. Volkmar, Paul, R., Klin, A., & Cohen, D. Hoboken, NK, John Wiley & Sons, Inc. **2**: 1161-1172.

McEachin, J.J., Smith, T., & Lovaas, O.I. (1993). Long-Term outcome for children with autism who received early intensive behavioral treatment. American Journal on Mental Retardation, 97(4), 359-372.

Nelson, C. & Huefner, D.S. (2003). "Young children with autism: Judicial responses to the Lovass and discrete trial training debates." *Journal of Early Intervention* **26**(1): 1-19.

Prizant, B. & Rubin, E. (1999). "Contemporary Issues in Interventions for Autism Spectrum Disorders: A Commentary." *Journal of the Association for Persons with Severe Handicaps.* **24**(3): 199-208.

Tutt, R., Powell, S., & Thornton, M. (2006). "Educational Approaches in Autism: What we know about what we do." *Educational Psychology in Practice* **22**(1): 69-81.

Chapter 6

ALTERNATIVE TREATMENTS FOR AUTISM SPECTRUM DISORDERS: WHAT IS THE SCIENCE?

By B.J. Freeman

Kanner (1943), in his now famous paper, "Autistic Disturbances of Affective Contact," introduced the word autism into the scientific literature. He hypothesized that autism was an inborn constitutional error where children are born lacking the motivation for social interaction (social isolation). He also described profound disturbances in communication and resistance to change. While Kanner's clinical description of autism has endured, many issues raised by his initial paper have now been refuted. For example, Kanner observed that parents were usually successful, educated people. He hypothesized that this led to problems between parent and child, particularly the mother and child. We now know that children with autism are found across all social classes and cultures. Kanner also speculated that children with autism had trouble relating to everyone in their environment. We know now that the primary deficit in autism is relating to peers. In addition, recent research has focused on genetics and other medical causes for autism. Kanner had initially speculated that children with autism could not have other medical conditions. It is now well recognized that children with other known medical conditions can also have an autism spectrum disorder, as this continues to be a behaviorally defined syndrome.

Much has been learned since Kanner's initial description of children with autism. Autism is now viewed as a spectrum of disorders, and the term Autism Spectrum Disorder (ASD) is frequently used. ASD is best viewed as social communication/learning disabilities. For example, some children have trouble learning to read, while others have trouble learning to do math. Children with ASD have trouble learning social/communication skills. ASD represents, as noted, a wide spectrum of ability and disability, and all children require intensive multidisciplinary evaluations and intensive early interventions that focus on teaching social communication skills in the natural environment.

The role of intellectual functioning in children with ASD remains a subject of debate and serves as an excellent example of why scientific inquiry is critical to its understanding. Kanner (1943) initially assumed that children with autism were not mentally retarded. As the field evolved, it was widely accepted that Kanner was incorrect and that the majority of these children were mentally retarded. (National Research Council, 2001)   Edelson (2006) in a systematic review examined 215 studies published between 1937 and 2003 investigating this claim, and reported that empirical data do not support the claim that the majority of children with ASD also have mental retardation. The majority of the studies reviewed used developmental or adaptive scales rather than measures of intelligence. It is well documented that children with ASD score significantly lower on these measures. (National Research Council, 2001) As would be expected, significantly higher rates of mental retardation were found using these measures. These findings indicate how important empirical research is in understanding ASD, its etiology and treatment and how important it is to not assume "facts not in evidence."

WHAT IS AUTISM SPECTRUM DISORDER (ASD)?

Scientific evidence indicates that ASD is a behavioral syndrome that most likely results from various brain abnormalities. These abnormalities develop as the result of genetic predispositions and early environmental (in all likelihood while in utero) insults. While recent scientific advances continue to provide important insights into the development of ASD, the etiology is complex and the specific causes remain unknown. (National Research Council, 2001)

The increase in the rate of children diagnosed with ASD has generated an increased interest in services and treatment for children (Frombonne, 2001). Since the first descriptions of the disorder, a host of different treatment modalities have been prescribed. These have generally been tied to some underlying belief system concerning the cause of ASD. The literature contains many case studies and many anecdotal reports pertaining to these treatments. However, few of these treatments have been studied in a systematic, controlled fashion. The current consensus suggests that the best approach for intervention for the core symptoms of ASD includes a program of coordinated intensive behavioral and educational interventions. The most tested of these interventions is applied behavior analysis, which has been shown to significantly improve the core symptoms in almost all children. (Simpson, 2005) Complete recovery of all symptoms is rare, but the number of children showing significant improvement has been increasing over the past few years. (National Research Council, 2001)

A broad range of autism treatments abound, and families are often persuaded to try methods that are highly unorthodox and scientifically suspect. In spite of overwhelming scientific evidence that the specific etiologies of ASD remain unknown, many treatments designed to treat a specific cause of ASD have arisen. Many of these treatments have often been publicized as "miracle cures." They are widely used in spite of the absence of supportive scientific data. Even in the presence of contradictory data and warnings from scientists, many of these treatments continue to be passionately promoted by their supporters.

Over the past few years, the lack of agreement concerning the best combination of treatment approaches and expected outcomes combined with the increase in the number of children diagnosed and the fact that many children with ASD have poor access to effective treatments have resulted in many families turning to Complementary and Alternative Medicine (CAM) strategies. In addition, many children with ASD have associated medical difficulties that standard treatments often fail to take into account. For example, sleep disorders and gastrointestinal problems are frequently reported in young ASD children and may cause significant stress to families. Many CAM treatments claim to address these ancillary symptoms. (Richdale, 1999; Horvath and Perman, 2002)

WHAT ARE CAMS?

CAMs have been identified as "a broad domain of healing resources that encompasses all health system modalities and practices and their accompanying theories and beliefs, other than those intrinsic to the politically dominant health system," and as "strategies that have not met the standards of clinical effectiveness either through randomized control, clinical trials or through the consensus of the biomedical community." (American Academy of Pediatrics, 2001) In their reviews of the safety and effectiveness of nontraditional approaches to the treatment of ASD, Hyman and Levy (2000) and Levy and Hyman (2002) divided CAMs commonly used in ASD into four categories: 1) Unproven benign biological treatments that are commonly used but have no basis in theory; 2) unproven benign biological treatments that have some basis in theory; 3) unproven potentially harmful biological treatments; and 4) nonbiological treatments. The first category includes vitamin supplements such as B6 and magnesium, gastrointestinal medications, and antifungal agents. The second category includes gluten-free or casein-free diets, vitamin C, and secretin. The third category includes immunoglobulins, large doses of vitamin A, antibiotics, antiviral agents, alkaline salts, and withholding immunizations. The fourth category includes treatments such as auditory integration training, interactive metronome, spinal manipulation, and facilitated communication.

Nickel (1996) reported that 50% of children with ASD use these and other unconventional treatment strategies. In many cases the primary physicians and therapists are unaware of the use of these treatments. Recently, Levy, Mandell, Merhar, Ittenabach, & Pinto-Martin (2003) examined the prevalence of CAM strategies and family characteristics associated with their use. The sample consisted of children recently diagnosed with autism at Children's Hospital of Philadelphia. The authors reviewed 284 charts and found that more than 30% were using some CAM strategy and that 9% were using potentially harmful CAMs. They concluded that the high prevalence of CAM use among a recently diagnosed sample points out the importance of discussing CAMs with families early in the assessment process.

More recently Hansen et al. (2007) examined the use of CAMs in ASDs and reported that of 112 families surveyed 74% were using some type of CAM treatment with their child. Most parents reported that the treatments were either not helpful or without benefit, but not harmful. The majority of parents reported trying CAMs out of fear of the safety of prescribed medications. The authors concluded, as have others, that professionals must be knowledgeable, ready, willing and able to discuss CAMs with their patients/clients. In addition, clinicians have a moral obligation to be aware of and assist parents in obtaining appropriate intervention.

WHAT IS THE SCIENTIFIC METHOD?

The majority of CAM strategies have not been subjected to rigorous scientific investigation which includes well-designed, controlled studies. While scientific studies may take many forms, ranging from double-blind, placebo-controlled studies to well-designed case reports, the gold standard for evaluation of research methodology is replicability and publication in a peer-reviewed journal. The reader is referred to Association for Science in Autism Treatment (ASAT) (asatonline.org) for a complete review.

Historically, treatment studies in the field of autism have been extremely difficult to interpret primarily because of a lack of agreement on diagnosis resulting in inadequate description of the population and small sample sizes. Currently, however, funding agencies and professional journals have set minimum standards in design and description for intervention studies. For example, all intervention studies have to provide the following information at a minimum: Adequate information concerning the sample and the families who participated, including those who chose not to participate or withdrew from participation; chronological age; Autism Diagnostic Interview-Revised (ADI-R); Autism Diagnostic Observation Schedule (ADOS); gender, race, family characteristics and socioeconomic status; relevant health or other biological impairments; and any other factors that may effect outcome (e.g., cognitive levels of functioning). Studies also need to include a description of the intervention in enough detail that an independent group could replicate the results. Detailed documentation is critical, especially because in most cases there is no treatment manual readily available. Peer review and replication is essential in the study of treatment effectiveness. The fidelity of treatment and the degree of implementation, as well as specific objective measures – such as expected outcome assessed at regular intervals – have to be independent of the intervention in terms of both the evaluators and the measures, and must include broad immediate and long-term effects on the children and families, particularly generalization and maintenance of skills. Studies should also contain appropriate control groups and detailed descriptions of the children in whom the treatment was ineffective as well as those in which the treatment was effective.

In the Complementary and Alternative Medicine field, much of the data is anecdotal. Research is often conducted by persons with a financial stake in the outcome, is based on social validity, and has not been subjected to peer review. Specifically, a treatment becomes controversial when its social validity is assessed differently by different people. Schwartz (1999) defined social validity and controversial treatments. Social validity assesses the acceptability, variability and sustainability of an intervention by asking the consumers of the intervention if it was effective. Thus, social validity does not evaluate the actual effectiveness of treatments. Rather, when parents report their child showed improvement after a specific treatment, it should be understood that this is a measure of social validity and not a scientific measure of effectiveness. A controversial treatment is one where interested parties involved have a difference of opinion regarding its effectiveness. Thus, these types of data do not contribute to the scientific literature on the overall effectiveness of the treatment. It is important to understand that the majority of studies of CAM treatments rely primarily on anectodal reports of social validity and have not been replicated or subjected to scientific peer review and criticism. With these caveats in mind, some of the more popular biological and non-biological CAMs are reviewed below. (For additional detailed reviews of both educational methodologies and CAMs, see Simpson, 2005; Schreibman, 2005; and Jacobson, Foxx & Mulick, 2005.)

BIOLOGICAL CAM TREATMENTS[1]

Several factors have come together to increase the popularity of biologically oriented treatments for ASD. These include increasing consensus that ASDs are neurological conditions; the increased use of psychotropic medication in psychiatry; and the increased use of homeopathic, herbal, vitamin and other alternative medical approaches. In general, some of these treatments have been promoted as producing extraordinary benefits and miraculous cures even in the absence of supportive data and in some instances in the face of disconfirmatory data. These treatments are based on both plausible and implausible theories of the etiologies of ASD. This distinction is often blurred in CAM reports.

Furthermore, proponents may attempt to legitimize their treatment by the use of "medical tests." The use of these tests and thus the treatments are generally based on unproven theories regarding the underlying cause of ASD. Barrett (2004) on the website quackwatch.com reviewed the use of what he labeled "dubious medical tests" or those that have little or no diagnostic value. These can include: blood tests (e.g., circulating IgE and IgG, food immune complexes, EIISA/ACT, mercury testing for "amalgam toxicity" to name a few); saliva tests (e.g., candida, yeast, mercury test); urine tests (e.g., amino acid analysis used for prescribing supplements, mercury testing); dubious devices (e.g., Electronic-Allegro Sensations Test); imaging procedures; physical examination procedure (e.g., muscle testing for allergies and nutrient deficiencies, auto-immune disregulate testing, phrenology); skin tests (e.g., patch test for mercury amalgam hypersensitivity); questionnaires (nutrient deficiency); internet testing; and various miscellaneous analyses (e.g. hair analysis, brain mapping, etc). Many of the tests listed are recommended to families of children with ASD.

One example of how "medical" tests can be misused can be found in hair analysis

---

[1] The author has attempted to include all studies published at the time of writing this chapter. Any omissions and/or errors are completely unintentional.

(Barrett 1985; 2004), a test frequently used in ASD to test for the presence of heavy metals. Hair analysis involves sending a sample of a person's hair taken from the back of the neck to a laboratory for analysis. Proponents of hair analysis claim that it is useful in evaluating a person's general state of nutrition and health, as well as detecting the presence of certain metals, e.g., mercury. Hair analysis supposedly enables determination as to whether mineral deficiency, mineral imbalance or heavy metal pollutants in the body are the cause of a child's ASD. These claims are simply false. Scientific research has shown that although hair analysis may have limited value as a screening for heavy metal exposure, it is not reliable in evaluating a person's nutritional status. Furthermore, most commercial hair analysis laboratories have not validated their techniques against standard reference materials. In addition, hair mineral content can be affected by exposure to substances such as shampoos, bleach and hair dyes. The level of certain minerals can be affected by color, diameter, rate of growth, season, geographic location, age, and gender, and normal ranges have not been established. In order for hair analysis to be a meaningful index of nutritional states, a correlation with other known indicators of nutritional status would be necessary. Since this has not been done, along with the fact that hair grows slowly, analysis of it does not represent the current nutritional status of the body and should be viewed skeptically. (Barrett, 1985; 2004)

Table 1 lists some of the many alternative medical therapies that have been proposed as treatments for children with ASD. While proponents of these therapies are usually well-intentioned, the recommended use of some of the tests described above before beginning therapy may make it appear more "scientific/medical" and this is misleading to parents and persons with ASD.

TABLE 1. COMPLEMENTARY & ALTERNATIVE BIOLOGICALLY-BASED TREATMENTS

Treatment	What It's Supposed to Do	Research/Data to Support
A. Nutritional		
1. Vitamins	Unspecified improvement in behavior	15 studies/Anecdotal reports
2. Magnesium	(Given with B-6)	Only anecdotal data
3. Dimethylglycine/DMG	Increases eye contact, decreases frustration	Double-blind placebo controlled study/Found no effect
4. Gluten-free/Casein-free diet	Reduce GI symptoms	Case studies
5. Pancreatic enzymes	May solve problem of loose stools	None
6. Colloidal Silver	Taken in water, helps diarrhea	None
7. Super Nu Thera	Improve taste of B-6/Magnesium	None/Anecdotal/May increase irritability
8. Omega-3 Fatty Acids	Improves digestion and heals leaky gut	Double-blind studies/Not helpful in ADHD
9. Calcium	Used for twitching in sleep	None
10. Aloe Vera	Helps digestion; leaky gut	None
11. Flower of sulphur	Improves digestion	None
12. Efalex oil/DHA oil	Heal leaky gut; improve vision, fine motor skills	None
13. Food allergies/Feingold diet	Removing additives results in general improvement	Yes/Feingold diet disproven
B. Secretin	Overall improvement in behavior	Yes/Phase III trials found no effect
C. Hyperbaric Oxygen/Ozone	(Based on theory that autism is a viral brain infection)	None

Treatment	What It's Supposed to Do	Research/Data to Support
D. Fibroblast Growth Factor 2	Improve behavior; used for seizures	None
E. Live cell/Stem cell therapy	Reportedly keeps body organs healthy	None
F. Anti-fungal treatment/ (Diflucan, Nizoral, Nystatin)	Treats over growth of bacteria/ decreases aggression, hyperactivity	Anecdotal
G. Antibiotic therapy (Vancomycin)	Activates immune system; "bursts of words"	Anecdotal
H. Naltrexone (NTX) Therapy	Blocks opiods; some functional improvements	Open-label trial
I. Immunoglobulin Therapy	Views autism as autoimmune disease; improves behavior	Double-blind study/Needs further research
J. EEG Bio-feedback	Normalizes brain waves	None
K. Detoxification of heavy metals	Removes heavy metals from CNS; improvement in behavior	Yes/Chelation therapy proved ineffective for lead poisoning. No research in autism.
L. Somatic Therapies	(Disorders of nervous system caused by dislocations of spine)	None
M. Cranio-Sacral Therapy	Alters rhythmic movements of the brain	None

N. Traditional Chinese Medicine
  1. Acupuncture
  2. Herbal medicine
  3. Nutrition
  4. Massage
  5. Aromatherapy
  6. Spinal mani
  7. Lifestyle counseling
	Heart, spleen and kidneys responsible for autism; chooses individual therapies to bring into balance.	None

O. Magnet Therapy	Redirects flow of energy	None
P. Melatonin	Improves sleep	Yes/Panksepp 2004
Q. Psychotropic medication	Used to treat specific behavioral symptoms	Very few studies specific to autism

NUTRITIONAL THERAPIES

Perhaps the most widely used class of alternative treatments in ASD involves nutritional therapies. The assumption many consumers make is that because you can buy these supplements over the counter, they are harmless. As Levy and Hyman (2002) have pointed out, this is far from correct and many of these commonly used supplements may result in serious harm to the child.

Vitamin B-6 and Magnesium are perhaps the most widely studied of this type of therapy. Smith (1996) reviewed 15 studies that reported that B-6 with magnesium may produce some beneficial effect for children with ASD. However, reports are mixed with studies showing no effects with high doses or no difference when compared to placebo control groups. (Findling et al., 1997) All of the studies that have reported positive effects have serious methodological flaws such as relying only on parent and staff reports instead of assessments from independent evaluators. Since large/mega doses of these substances are often recommended, safety concerns have been raised regarding the use of these substances. For example, high doses of B-6 can cause nerve damage and high doses of magnesium can cause reduced heart rate and weakened reflexes. (Deutsch and Morrill, 1993)

Dimethylglycine (DMG) is also marketed as a treatment for autism. Some professionals claim that DMG increases eye contact and speech, and decreases frustration levels among individuals with ASD. (Rimland, 1996) In response to the large number of anecdotal reports on the effectiveness of DMG, Kern et al. (2001) conducted a double-blind placebo crossover study (the scientific gold standard for drug studies) and found no significant difference between DMG and placebo. In spite of the absence of scientific evidence supporting claims of effectiveness, proponents continue to advocate for the use of B-6, magnesium and DMG.

The second most commonly used nutritional treatment is dietary. Despite the absence of scientific evidence, some dieticians and parents have long believed that symptoms of ASD may be reduced by eliminating gluten and dairy products. This treatment is closely tied to the observation that children with ASD have increased frequency of gastrointestinal (GI) symptoms (e.g., diarrhea and food selectivity including excess carbohydrate ingestion) and may have celiac disease. Levy, Souders, Coplan, Wray and Mulberg (2001) reported results of a study to determine the frequency of GI symptoms in a well-defined population of children with ASD and their relationship to dietary intake. While children with ASD had a high frequency of GI symptoms, particularly involving loose stools, none had medical evidence of celiac disease. Preliminary results suggest symptoms were related to carbohydrate intake and food selectivity rather than underlying disease process.

As a result of the reports of increased GI symptoms, dietary interventions have become common. The most frequently proposed is the gluten-and casein-free diet. Gluten is a mixture of protein found in grain products such as wheat bread. Casein is a protein found in milk. There have been increasing numbers of anecdotal reports that some persons with ASD demonstrate increased negative behavior following the consumption of milk, wheat bread or similar products. There is some evidence that eliminating these proteins from the diet can lead to improvements in behavior. (Kvinsberg, Reichelt, Nodland and Hoien, 1996; and Whiteley, Rodgers, Savery and Shattock, 1999) However, due to methodological problems (anecdotal reports and case studies), it is not possible to rule out alternative explanations for any observed improvements following gluten- and casein-free diets. (Adams and Cowen, 1997) Much more rigorous research is needed before recommending this diet as part of a comprehensive treatment program. However, if a child has gastrointestinal issues, the child should be examined and treated by a physician.

There are few, if any, studies of the remaining nutritional therapies described in Table 1 regarding their effectiveness for ASD. Support is provided by anecdotal case reports. Clearly, much more research is needed regarding the use of all the nutritional therapies before they should be incorporated as part of a comprehensive program for a child with ASD.

SECRETIN

Secretin is a hormone that stimulates digestive fluids from the pancreas, the production of pepsin from the stomach, and bile from the liver. The use of secretin in the treatment of ASD gained widespread attention following a 1998 report of a child who appeared to show significant improvement following a single dose. (Horvath, Stefanatos et al., 1998) Parents by the thousands began requesting the drug. However, research has not been able to confirm these results.

Sandler, Sutton et al. (1999) in a study published in the New England Journal of Medicine reported no effect on the behavior of 56 autistic children after a single dose administration of secretin. Other studies have also found no effect. (Dunn-Geier, 2000; Owley et al. 1999) Chez and Buchanan et al. (2000) in summarizing the scientific evidence regarding secretin concluded they "cannot rationalize the use of secretin as a treatment modality." (p. 85) More recently, a well controlled third-phase drug trial funded by Repligen (the manufacturer of secretin) failed to find differences between placebo and secretin groups after multiple injections.

Esch and Carr (2004) reviewed 17 studies comparing the effects of secretin forms, dosage levels and dosing intervals on outcome measures with approximately 600 children with ASD. Twelve of 13 placebo-controlled studies failed to demonstrate the differential efficacy of secretin. Kern, Miller, Evans Trivedi (2002) did report some improvement in children with chronic diarrhea. However, the study is difficult to interpret due to its many methodological flaws.

Lightdale et al. (2001) observed that interest in secretin should diminish as scientific studies continued to demonstrate its lack of efficacy. In spite of the fact that Esch and Carr (2004) concluded that their findings are conclusive, some advocates continue to recommend the use of secretin and are still encouraging parents to seek physicians who will administer the drug to their children. (ARI, 2004)

ADDITIONAL BIOLOGICAL CAMS

The logic of using Hyperbaric Oxygen Treatment (HBOT) for developmental disorders, including ASD, relates to autoimmune and/or viral theories of the disorder. Hyperbaric oxygen has been studied for autoimmune disorders. In this treatment, oxygen is delivered in a pressurizing chamber. Theoretically, this increases absorption of oxygen by the body. Encephalitis, or inflammation of the brain, is hypothesized to play a role in the etiology of autism. The encephalitis can be initiated by viral infection, exposure to vaccines, and/or by other autoimmune procedures. While Hyperbaric Oxygen Therapy has been used to treat a number of medical conditions (e.g., Wallace, Silverman, et al.), there has not been a single study examining its effect in ASD. However, the therapy continues to have its proponents. Liptak (2005) in a systematic review concludes that HBOT is an untested treatment for ASD. In addition, he points out that the equipment may be a fire risk and may have damaging effects on middle/inner ears, and raise blood pressure.

Variations of this therapy include ozone therapy, aroma therapy and steam/sauna therapies. While ozone therapy has been recommended as a treatment for a variety of different conditions, effectiveness and safety have not been demonstrated scientifically. (InteliHealth, 2007)

Fibroblast Growth Factor 2 has been reported to both improve behavior as well as cause children to regress and become more hyperactive. It is primarily used in autistic children with seizures. Its proponents believe that seizures among children with ASD are caused by a build-up of peptides and the chemical imbalance caused by partially digested protein, gluten, dairy, or other foods, which this treatment supposedly eliminates. As with so many of the other treatments described, there are no controlled studies to support its use. (McKinnon, 2004)

Live Cell and Stem Cell Therapy was developed in Switzerland and is aimed at keeping the organs of the body healthy. As yet, this treatment has not been studied systematically in ASD (Johns Hopkins, 1997).

Anti-fungal treatments grew out of a study of the bowel problems frequently exhibited by children with ASD. This theory hypothesizes that poor bowel ecology often promotes the overgrowth of fungi and other microbes. These microbes are proposed to be involved in the etiology of ASD as they are sometimes found in the urine of autistic children. Rimland (1988) reported that many children score high for yeast and anaerobic bacteria, and recommended treatment with anti-fungals.

One type of a single-cell fungus is Candida-Albicans, which belongs to the yeast family. It is treated with Nystatin, a medication used to treat yeast infections in women. Of particular interest has been the observation by some clinicians that autistic symptoms are made worse by the overgrowth of candida. Overgrowth is made possible by a dysfunctional immune system. The "leaky gut" theory of autism implies that correcting gut allergies and treating yeast overgrowth should help return the gut to normal and thus improve autistic symptoms. It has also been reported that children with ASD may have frequent ear infections when young and may have taken large amounts of antibiotics. These are thought to exaggerate the yeast problem. This theory has resulted in treatment of autism by potent anti-fungal agents such as Diflucan, Nizoral or Nystatin. The assumption is that after one to two months of treatment the yeast will die off and the symptoms of ASD will improve. In spite of a lack of scientific evidence to support the theory or the treatments, these medications are still prescribed and may cause liver damage.

Anecdotal studies have reported that the frequency of inappropriate noises, teeth grinding, biting, hitting, hyperactivity and aggressive behavior all decrease. Rimland (1988) hypothesized that five to ten percent of children with ASD showed improvement with treatment for candida infections. Furthermore, proponents often recommend Nystatin be given to children whose mother had candidiasis during pregnancy, whether or not the child showed signs of infection. This is in spite of the fact that there is no evidence that mothers of ASD children have a higher incidence of candidiasis than mothers in the general population. The research to date is based on case studies and anecdotal reports. Without reliable and valid evidence to the contrary, case reports cannot rule out a host of confounding variables including natural remission, change in symptoms due to developmental maturation or merely the passage of time. In addition, there is absolutely no evidence that even severe candidiasis in humans can produce the brain damage that leads to the deficits exhibited by autistic children. (Herbert and Sharp, 2001)

In direct contradiction to the theory of Candida-Albicans and autism is treatment with antibiotics. This treatment supposedly addresses the possibility that bacterial pathogens that cause autism are in the gut and bloodstream. There are only one or two anecdotal reports of the use of antibiotics in autism. As noted above, chronic use of antibiotics can cause yeast infections. (Bolte, 2000)

Naltrexone is a medication that blocks the action of endogenous opiods. One theory states that individuals with ASD have too much beta endorphins in their central nervous system. This theory is based on research which demonstrates that the opiod antagonists (e.g., Naltrexone and Naloxone) increased prosocial behavior in monkeys. (Panksepp, 1979) The theory goes on to posit that some of the improvements attributed to autistic individuals who have taken Naltrexone include: increased socialization, eye contact and general happiness; normalized pain sensitivity; and a reduction in self-injury and stereotypic (self-stimulatory) behaviors. There are no known side effects of Naltrexone, although possible long-term effects are difficult to assess given the relatively short amount of time since Naltrexone has been used for autistic individuals. However, there are reports that some vision loss may occur when Naltrexone is given with Haldol. (Caccullo, Musetti et al., 1999; Panksepp, Lensing et al., 1991) Schreibman (2005) concludes that recent well-controlled studies have not supported the use of Naltrexone and the opiod theory of autism remains speculative.

Intravenous Immunoglobulin Therapy (IVIG) is based on the theory that autism is an autoimmune disease that may be triggered by a virus or bacteria. Treatment involves administration of IVIG to correct immune abnormalities. Singh (1997) reported improvement in the behavior of some autistic children after administration of IVIG. However, much more research is needed to identify when and for which children this may be a useful treatment.

EEG Biofeedback: The EEG is a measure of the arousal level of the central nervous system. The purpose of this treatment is to help the brain remain in a given state of arousal. Autism is thought to represent over-arousal of the brain. Proponents claim the ability to "take autistic children to the point where they shed their diagnosis of autism." (Othmer, 2004) Unbelievably, these claims are made in the absence of scientific data.

A variation of this therapy is the use of SPECT (single photon emission tomography) scans, which measure cerebral blood flow. These scans are used in an attempt to identify parts of the brain that are not functioning properly, and to use this information as part of an assessment and to prescribe treatment. (Amen and Carmichael, 1997) They further state to date that we do not fully understand how the brains of children with ASD function differently from those of typical children. Thus, use of this technique to help direct treatment is premature. (Flaherty, 2005) The American Psychiatric Association (APA) Council on Children, Adolescents and their Families has raised serious doubts about both the usefulness and safety of SPECT scans.

Detoxification of Heavy Metals: There recently have been public concerns about the use of vaccinations as playing a major role in the increase in prevalence of ASDs. Rimland (2000) described it as "medical over-exuberance" in producing a tradeoff in which vaccinations protect children against acute diseases, while simultaneously increasing their susceptibility to many chronic diseases including ASD. More recently, a number of scientific studies have reviewed the prevalence of autism and the relationship with the increase in the number of vaccinations that children receive. No causal relationship between vaccines and ASD has been found. The American Medical Association, Institute of Medicine (USA), World Health Organization, American Academy of Pediatrics, Population and Public Health Branch of Health Canada, Ireland Department of Health and Children, and Centers for Disease Control all have come out in support of the use of vaccines.

In spite of these findings, questions persist and many children continue to undergo detoxification therapy. The concept behind detoxification (or chelation therapy) is that heavy metals have accumulated in the child and that removal of these heavy metals (and other toxins) will improve symptoms. (Barrett, 2004) One source of heavy metals is thought to have been the thimerosal (mercury) in vaccinations. The first step often is testing for heavy metals in the urine or hair (see discussion above). Typical treatments include administration of DMSA (dimercaptosuccinic acid) as well as adding other medications (e.g., adding lipoic acid is thought to help remove mercury from the central nervous system). These drugs are not approved for this purpose nor are they approved for use in children. (Ricks, 2007). Detoxification is a long process and may take months. In spite of the fact that liver toxicity to DMSA can develop and the absence of scientific data, many children are continuing to undergo this procedure. (Nelson & Bauman, 2003) The Association for Science in Autism Treatment (www.asatonline.org/resources/treatments/chelation.htm) summarized the medical issues associated with chelation therapy. They point out that not only is it based on a non-plausible theory, it is unacceptably risky. Furthermore, there have been reports of deaths involved with some forms of chelation therapy. (Kane, 2006)

The role of the MMR (Measles, Mumps and Rubella) and other vaccinations and detoxification of heavy metals in the treatment of autism hold several important lessons for the student of ASD. First, parents and professionals alike can easily misinterpret events that could occur temporally as being causally related. Second, the MMR-autism link reveals the self-correcting nature of science. Like many hypotheses in science, the MMR-autism hypothesis, although reasonable when initially proposed, turned out to be incorrect or at best incomplete. Third, the issue illustrates the persistence of incorrect ideas concerning the etiology and treatment of autism, even in the face of convincing evidence to the contrary. Recent research indicates that the MMR as well as other vaccines cannot be responsible for the sharp increases in diagnosed cases of ASD. The real harm is the public health concern raised by encouraging parents to avoid vaccinating their children from serious diseases that can easily cause ongoing problems and physical as well as emotional issues. It has been reported that MMR vaccination fell from 92% to 80% when Wakefield's initial study was published. (Katelaris, 2007) More research is needed to determine if giving vaccinations at a young age may result in adverse effects in some children. (Simpson, 2005)

Somatic therapies include such procedures as cranio-sacral therapy and some forms of Chinese medicine. <u>Cranio-Sacral Therapy</u> has become a popular alternative treatment for ASD. It is one of many terms used to describe various methods which are said to alter the central nervous system pathology associated with ASD. Cranio-Sacral therapy involves a gentle noninvasive manipulation technique that purportedly improves central nervous system function and can also be used to boost the immune system. This has been used for a multitude of infantile disorders including ASD. Barrett (2004) reviewed the various cranio-sacral therapies and concluded that not only are the effects unproven, but the therapy is based on an untenable theory.

Traditional Chinese Medicine first began to be used as a treatment for autism around 1993. Chinese Medicine (CM) is a comprehensive health care system with its own system of diagnostics. It includes not only acupuncture but also herbal medicine, nutritional therapies, massage techniques, aromatherapy, spinal manipulation and lifestyle counseling. The practitioner utilizes different combinations of techniques based on the constitution and specific needs of the individual child. CM is recognized as a treatment for many disorders and its reported effectiveness in treating physiological and neurological disorders serves as the basis for its treatment of autism. (Majebe, 2002) There is no scientific evidence to support this theory or treatment. However, it is important to note that advocates of Chinese medicine also point out the importance of educational therapies in the overall treatment.

Magnet therapy takes several forms (e.g., placing magnets on the body, sleeping under a blanket with magnets, and sleeping on a bed of magnets) and purports to redirect the flow of energy in the body. According to ASAT (www.asatonline.org/resources/treatments/magnets.htm), no scientific studies of this therapy have been conducted on children with ASD and thus it should be presented to parents as an untested treatment.

One of the most common disturbing symptoms for parents is their autistic child's difficulty sleeping through the night. This has led to the widespread use of Melatonin, a natural sleeping aid. Unfortunately, there are presently not enough data to determine if it is actually effective. However, it appears to be safe and may help some autistic children settle to sleep. (Giannotti et al., 2006)

Psychopharmacology: There are several excellent reviews of the effects of medication in ASDs. (AACAP, 1999; Aman and Langworthy, 2000; King, 2000) As with other alternative treatments, placebo-controlled, double-blind crossover design studies (the gold standard for evaluating medications) are few. The most recent study by McDougle, Holmes et al. (2004) utilizing this design did show improvement in some symptoms with risperidone, which was recently approved for use in ASDs by the Food and Drug Administration for treating irritability in ASD. All medication should be used cautiously. It is important to remember psychotropic medication may be utilized to ameliorate specific symptoms, which then will allow the child to benefit from behavioral and educational programs. However, all medications have side effects and should be monitored closely. Since persons with ASD often show idiosyncratic responses to medications, it is important that the physician monitoring the treatment have knowledge of both ASD and medication.

NON-BIOLOGICAL CAM TREATMENTS

Just as the biological CAM treatments, nonbiological therapies have also come into common use. Many of these therapies are now accepted as standard treatments for ASD, in spite of the fact that scientific support is at best minimal. Table 2 lists some of the nonbiological-based interventions frequently proposed for treating ASD. At times, there is overlap with the biological treatments. In addition, some information could only be found on web sites and not in scientific journals.

TABLE 2. NON-BIOLOGICAL BASED INTERVENTIONS

Treatment	What It's Supposed to Do	Research/Data to Support
A. SENSORY TREATMENTS		
1. Sensory Integration Therapy	Increase ability to process sensory information	One control study found little support; other studies had no comparison group; more research needed.
2. Music Therapy	Requires no verbal interaction; seeks to effect changes in cognitive, physical, social and emotional skills.	Studies to date involve small samples and anecdotal data.
3. Auditory Integration Training 　a) Berard Method 　b) Tomatis Method 　c) Samonas Method 　d) Rhythmic Entainment	Normalize hearing to allow brain to process auditory information more efficiently.	No controlled studies reporting positive effects; 23 studies reporting positive results rely on parent report; 3 studies report no effect; 2 studies had mixed results. American Academies of Pediatrics and Audiology warn there are no well-controlled studies.
4. Irlen Lenses/Irlen Method	Improve reading skills and depth perception to improve learning skills	Testimonials/Little scientific evidence to support
5. Ambient Lenses	Improve awareness of body in space	No controlled studies
6. Vision Therapy	Correct eye coordination, perception and processing, focusing, tracking and other vision difficulties	None

Treatment	What It's Supposed to Do	Research/Data to Support
A. SENSORY TREATMENTS (cont.)		
7. Aromatherapy	Improve relaxation	None
8. Squeeze Machine	Involves deep pressure stimulation; reduces tactile defensiveness	None
9. Massage Therapy	Reduce anxiety	No controlled studies
B. RELATIONSHIP-BASED THERAPIES		
1. Psychoanalysis	Focuses on maternal rejection as cause of autism	None/Considered harmful.
2. Son Rise Options	Cures autism; based on unconditional love and acceptance	None/Anecdotal testimonials
3. Floor Time - child centered play therapy	Emphasizes relationship & engagement; child developing sense of self	No controlled studies.
4. Relationship Development Intervention (RDI)	Improve communication and social skills	One study showing improvement; no control group
5. Holding Therapy	Increase parent-child bonding	None
6. Gentle Teaching	Decrease inappropriate behaviors and teach new skills	None
C. MOTOR THERAPIES		
1. Doman/Delacato Patterning	High levels of motor and sensory exercises can train nervous system and overcome the handicap	Research shows may be harmful for families
2. Facilitated Communication	(Persons with autism suffer from motor apraxia)	Yes/shown to be ineffective
3. Rapid Prompting	Increase attention and decrease self-stimulatory behaviors	None
4. Physical Exercise and Dance Movement Therapy	Decrease stress and self-stimulatory behaviors/Reduces anxiety	None

Treatment	What It's Supposed to Do	Research/Data to Support
D. ANIMAL ASSISTED THERAPIES		
1. Pet Visitation	Fosters rapport/improves communication	None
2. Animal-Assisted Therapy/ Social Dog	Improves social interaction	None
3. Therapeutic Horseback Riding/Hippotherapy	Calming effect and improves balance, posture, and mobility	None
4. Dolphin-Assisted Therapy	Improves speech and motor skills	None
E. COMPUTER THERAPIES		
1. Discrete Trial Trainer	Based on principles of ABA; repetitive presenting of material	Needs more research regarding its effectiveness
2. Fast ForWord	Improves auditory processing by slowing down sounds	Only research from manufacturer
3. Earobics	Teaches auditory, phonological skills	None
4. Train Time	Developed by speech therapist to improve attention	None
5. Interactive Metronome	Strengthens motor planning, sequence and timing	None
6. Virtual Environments	Increases emotional recognition	One exploratory study
7. ADAM Autistic Internet Interface	Goal is to restore people who are labeled autistic; educational program for telepathic communication	None
F. MISCELLANEOUS		
1. Miller Method	Uses boards elevated above ground/teaches children to follow directions	None
2. Lindamood-Bell	Multi-sensory approach to improve cognitive functioning	Only research from manufacturer

Treatment	What It's Supposed to Do	Research/Data to Support
F. MISCELLANEOUS (cont.)		
3. Video Modeling	Uses videos to motivate ASD children	Needs more research
4. HANDLE Institute	Holistic approach for neurodevelopment and learning efficiency	None
5. Epsom Salt Baths	Improves sleep, decreases irritability, increases language	Anecdotal
6. Art Therapy	Increases creativity	Case studies

SENSORY TREATMENTS

The most commonly used non-biological treatments focus on the fact that children with ASD show unusual sensory responses and may have difficulty modulating sensory perception. Ayres (1979) developed Sensory Integration (SI) therapy. She hypothesized that autistic children possess deficits in registering and modulating sensory input and a deficit in the brain that initiates purposeful behavior. Treatment attempts to facilitate reintegration, engaging the child in full-body movement designed to provide vestibular, proprioceptive and tactile stimulation. These activities are designed to correct the underlying neurological imbalances (Hoehn and Baumeister, 1994). Controlled studies have found little support for the efficacy of SI for treating children with various disabilities (e.g., Mason and Iwata, 1990; Iwasaki and Holm, 1989). Dawson and Watling (2000) reviewed studies that utilized objective behavioral measures investigating the efficacy of sensory integration in ASD. Only one of the four studies had more than five participants and no study had a comparison group. In the study with the largest sample size (Reilly, Nelson, and Bundy, 1984), a randomized ABAB counter-balanced design was used to compare SI and tabletop activities. They reported that structured teaching resulted in a larger increase in verbal behavior than SI activities.

There have been single case studies reporting beneficial effects when SI is compared with no treatment baseline in ASD (Case-Smith and Bryan, 1999; Linderman and Stewart, 1999). These designs cannot demonstrate that the benefits were attributable to the SI alone. As Green (1996) has pointed out, while children may find SI activities enjoyable, this does not provide evidence of any significant long-lasting benefits in the child's behavior or underlying neurological deficits, which cannot be measured. While SI has become an integral part of many children's programs, much more research is needed to establish SI as an effective treatment. Simpson (2005) after an exhaustive review of research on sensory integration therapy suggests the theory is appealing because it explains some of the unusual ASD behaviors. He goes on to conclude that much more research is needed to demonstrate a positive effect.

Music Therapy has been organized as a scientific profession only in the last century. Music therapy, which does not require verbal interaction, is used in ASD to improve cognitive, physical, social and emotional skills. Brownell (2002) compared intervention with and without music and found that the latter intervention was more effective. While many ASD children are musically talented and enjoy music, much more research is needed to establish this as a proven intervention technique.

Auditory Integration Training (AIT) was developed by Berard in the 1960s in France. The theory is that autistic children often have hearing that is disorganized, hypersensitive, different between the two ears or otherwise abnormal. The purpose of AIT is to reduce sound sensitivities and improve auditory processing. There are four different types of AIT therapies: Berard, Tomatis, Sammos and Rhythmic Entrainment Intervention.

Edelson and Rimland (2004) reviewed 28 studies of AIT. They concluded that 23 studies showed some benefit, three showed no benefit and two produced contradictory results. However, the 23 studies showing positive benefit were fraught with methodological problems (e.g., no control group, single subject design, anecdotal reports, etc.). The three studies showing no benefit all had control groups. As even Edelson and Rimland (2004) point out, all of the studies had serious methodological problems. Mudford, Cullen et al. (2000) reviewed studies of AIT from a methodical point of view and found no support for its use in ASD or other developmental disabilities. The American Academy of Pediatrics and the American Academy of Audiology have warned that no well-designed scientific studies demonstrate that AIT is useful (Barrett, 2004). Furthermore, AIT devices do not have FDA approval for treating ASD or any other medical condition. The American Speech and Hearing Association recently issued a statement regarding the ineffectiveness of AIT.

In the Irlen Method (Irlen, 1983) the participant receives an individual evaluation to determine if they have difficulties with certain light frequencies. The participant is then given colored overlays or eyeglasses with tinted lenses designed to filter out those light frequencies, which reportedly improves the brain's ability to process visual information. Simpson (2005) in review of the scientific literature concluded that there is little evidence to support this method.

Only anecdotal reports exist to support other sensory treatments based on vision (ambient lenses, vision therapy), smell (aroma therapy), and tactile (Squeeze Machine, massage therapy) senses.

RELATIONSHIP BASED THERAPIES

All of these therapies hypothesize that the primary social deficit in ASD arises from a disturbed relationship between the child and the primary caregiver.

Psychoanalysis in treatments of ASD arose from Kanner's original assumption (1943) that the etiology of autism centered on a disturbed mother-child relationship. Despite overwhelming evidence that these theories are inaccurate, psychoanalytic treatment of ASD continues. (Beratis, 1994; Bromfield, 2000) These treatments can be harmful. The focus on parental, particularly maternal, rejection can lead to misplaced blame and guilt. Furthermore, the unstructured nature of psychoanalytic treatments including allowing autistic individuals wide latitude to pursue preferred activities in treatment, and lack of focus on contingencies between behavior and their consequences, can lead to a worsening of autistic symptoms (Smith, 1996).

Options Therapy grew out of the book "Son-Rise" (Kaufman, 1976). The book was written by parents who reported that they spent many hours every day mirroring the actions of their autistic child without placing demands on him. They theorized that they entered their son's world and drew him out so that he was no longer autistic. To date, while the Options Institute continues to advocate its use, there are no scientific studies of effectiveness.

Floor Time is a form of child-centered play therapy developed by Greenspan (1992). It emphasizes interaction and engagement while following the child's lead. The goal of the therapy is to motivate the child to communicate by helping the child develop a sense of self and a sense that communication with others is pleasurable. While Greenspan has published several books and articles regarding this theory of autism (which he calls multi-system developmental disorder), no controlled studies exist demonstrating the effectiveness of the therapy/theory. (Greenspan, 1992; Greenspan & Weider, 1998)

Relationship Development Intervention (RDI) is a parent-based, clinical treatment where parents teach their autistic children motivation and dynamic intelligence. Dynamic intelligence is made up of emotional references, social coordination, declarative language, flexible thinking, relational information processing, foresight and hindsight. Deficits in these areas characterize children with ASD. Guttstein (2004) compared a group of 17 autistic children receiving RDI to 14 autistic children receiving other interventions. Results indicated that 70 percent of children in the RDI group improved over time. However, methodological issues regarding effects of developmental trajectory and specifically what other types of treatment the children were receiving make this study difficult to interpret. In spite of the fact that RDI addresses perhaps the major deficit in ASD, as Simpson (2005) points out, much more scientific research is needed to establish its superiority to other social interventions.

Holding therapy was first developed in the 1970s (Welch, 1988). It involves having the child sit or lie face-to-face with the parent. The parent tries to establish eye contact and to share feelings verbally to increase bonding. Over the years some variations have been developed including using holding as a negative reinforcer. This therapy has no support in the scientific literature and is particularly counter indicated as a treatment for ASD because of its emphasis on a disturbed parent-child relationship.

Gentle Teaching was originally utilized as a nonaversive approach for teaching children with ASD. The philosophy is one of behavior management and centers on the relationship between the therapist/teacher and the child. The technique has also been used to both decrease inappropriate behaviors and teach new skills. (McGee, 1990) As Simpson (2005) points out, the individual child's needs should dictate the method used and all methods should have a built-in, objective monitoring system. Gentle Teaching does neither. Not only have there been no scientific studies, but allowing children to engage in serious behavior (e.g. aggression and self-injury) when other methodologies may reduce the frequency of the behaviors more quickly, is not appropriate.

MOTOR THERAPIES

Motor therapies focus on improving symptoms of ASD by emphasizing movement and the remediation of supposed motor deficits.

Doman-Delacato Method, also called patterning, was developed during the mid-1950s and is offered by the Institute for Human Potential in Philadelphia, Pennsylvania. Its proponents claim that the great majority of cases of mental retardation, learning problems, behavioral disorder and autism are caused by brain damage or poor neurological organization. The treatment is based on the idea that high levels of motor and sensory stimuli can train the nervous system and lessen or overcome handicaps caused by brain damage. Parents following the program may be advised to exercise the child's limbs repeatedly and use other measures said to increase blood flow to the brain and decrease brain irritability (Doman and Doman, 1974). In 1999, the American Academy of Pediatrics issued position statements concluding that "patterning" has no special merit and its proponents' claims were unproven, and that the demands on families was so great that it may actually be harmful in its use (AAP, 1999). Novella (2001) reviewed the scientific literature and concluded that patterning was pseudoscience and of no use in treating children with developmental disabilities.

The theory behind Facilitated Communication holds that the major problem in autism is one of initiating motor movements. Thus, a "facilitator" supports the hand or arm of the person with ASD who spells out a message using a typewriter, computer keyboard or other device containing a list of letters, numbers or words. It is alleged to help individuals strike the keys they desire without influencing the choice of keys. Proponents claim that it enabled such individuals to communicate. However, many scientific studies have demonstrated that the procedure is not valid, because the outcome is actually determined by the facilitator. (Jacobson, Mulick & Schwartz, 1993; Wheeler et al.,1993) In one study, for example, autistic persons and facilitators were shown pictures of familiar objects and asked to identify them under three conditions: a) assisted typing with facilitator unaware of the content of the stimulus picture; b) unassisted typing; and c) a condition in which the participants and the facilitators were each shown pictures at the same time. In this last condition, the paired pictures were either the same or different, and the participant typing was facilitated to label or describe the picture. No autistic person gave the correct response when the facilitator had not been shown the picture. The researchers concluded that facilitators were not aware that they were influencing the autistic person's choice. (Jacobson, Mulick and Schwartz, 1995) The American Psychological Association has denounced facilitated communication and warned that using it to elicit accusations of abuse by family members or other caregivers threatens the civil rights of both the impaired individual and those accused. (APA 1994)

Rapid Prompting Method (Soma, 2004) is a method for teaching by eliminating responses through intensive verbal, auditory, visual and or tactile prompts. RPM was developed by a mother, Soma Mukhopadhyay, to aid her son, Tito, in communicating. The teacher matches the student's speed of self-stimulatory behavior while continuously speaking and requesting student's responses in order to keep the student on task and focused. Soma has copyrighted the method through the non-profit organization HALO, and she teaches mostly nonverbal autistic children. As yet no research is available on the effectiveness of RPM.

Physical exercise and dance therapy have also been proposed as treatments for ASD. While no one would deny the benefits of physical exercise in general, whether or not it is a therapeutic intervention would depend on how it is utilized. It is reported to decrease stress as well as self-stimulatory behaviors in ASD. However, its use has not been studied systematically or scientifically.

ANIMAL-ASSISTED THERAPIES

As intervention, animal-assisted therapies have been utilized on various levels and in various settings from pediatrics to geriatrics. (Levinson, 1969) These interventions are based on the idea that the human-animal bond, particularly with horses, dolphins and dogs, can be utilized in an approach to aid in recovery from illness. With respect to ASD, it is assumed that animals provide unconditional acceptance of the individual and thus facilitate social interaction and communication.

The simplest form of therapy is called Pet Visitation, which involves bringing pets into the therapeutic environment. It is said to improve rapport between the child and the therapist and to improve communication. Pet visitation led to "Animal-Assisted Therapy" where an animal, usually a dog, is an integral part of the treatment team. One popular form of this treatment for ASD is the Social Dog. The person with ASD always has the dog with them. It is said to facilitate social interaction and improve communication. There are no data to support this position. In addition, since most children do not take their dog to school, this would make the ASD child stand out even more.

Hippotherapy and therapeutic horseback riding have also been proposed as treatments for ASD. Reportedly, these therapies have physical, psychological and social benefits. The rationale for using horseback riding as a therapeutic intervention has focused on the concept that it provides the person with disabilities a normal sensorimotor experience. This experience involves vestibular input and stimulates the rider's balance mechanism. (Mackinnon, Noh, LaLiBerte, Lariviere and Allen, 1995) In addition, relating to and successfully maneuvering a large animal, such as a horse, results in a sense of accomplishment in the individual. Again, there are no data to support this.

Dolphin Assisted Therapy is a therapeutic approach used to increase speech and motor skills in children and adults with varying diagnosis, including ASD. The theory behind this controversial therapeutic approach is that when the child with special needs interacts with a dolphin, it improves his attention, which results in an improvement in behavior and communication. (Nathanson and deFaria, 1993) While no one can deny the benefits of owning a pet, there is no scientific evidence that supports the use of pets as a meaningful, rational, therapeutic intervention for ASD. (Marino and Lilienfeld, 1998)

COMPUTER-ASSISTED TECHNOLOGIES

As the use of computers has become common place, there has been a concomitant increase in the number of computer-based therapies for ASD children. In addition, many children with ASD show a particular affinity for computers. This has led to the proliferation of therapies which attempt to use this affinity to improve communication. Computer-assisted therapies show a great deal of potential for use in ASD. Many, such as the Discrete Trial Trainer, are based on the principles of applied behavior analysis (ABA) and hold great promise while awaiting scientific validation. (Butler and Mulick, 2001) Only the more frequently utilized therapies will be reviewed here.

Fast ForWord was originally developed to improve reading skills in learning disabled students. This program targets auditory processing by slowing down the rate of presentation of sounds and then speeding them up as the brain is trained to better process them. The manufacturers of Fast ForWord (Scientific Learning Corporation) reported that children with ASDs (ages 5 to 13 years) showed improvement in both expressive and receptive language after completing the Fast ForWord program. Richard (2000) reviewed the use of Fast ForWord in autism and raised concerns about the generalization of the drilled skills found in the program. He goes on to suggest that additional carry over activities would be necessary to ensure generalization of skills. Simpson (2005) reviews results of Fast ForWord research and concludes the claims made by the manufacturer (e.g., that children gain 1-2 years in language in 4-6 weeks) have not been subjected to rigorous scientific scrutiny. He points out that there are few if any studies of Fast ForWord in ASD and classifies the program as having "limited supporting information for practice." (p.113)

Earobics is a well researched reading program that teaches auditory and phonological skills, including auditory attention, phonemic identification and rhyming. As yet there is no research on its use with children with ASD.

Train Time was developed by a speech pathologist for autistic children who may have a specific interest in trains, a common interest among children with ASD. The program consists of various games at different levels and is reported to increase visual and auditory attention. No research data is available and references were found only on a list of therapies provided by a non-profit parent group. (Foothill Autism Alliance, Power Pak Guide, 2001)

Interactive Metronome was originally developed for children with attention deficit hyperactivity disorder (ADHD). It involves using a computer-based interactive version of a traditional music metronome. The idea behind the interactive metronome is to strengthen motor planning, sequencing, timing and rhythmicity to improve attention and language. To date, no scientific controlled studies in ASD exist. (Stemmer, 1996)

Virtual Environments is a computer-generated three-dimensional simulation of a real or imaginary environment. Moore, et al. (2005) conducted an exploratory study of collaborative virtual environment in 36 autistic children. They reported that 90% of the subjects correctly identified emotions displayed by the representatives in the virtual environment. They concluded the technique holds promise, but much more research is needed.

ADAM Autistic Internet Interface is perhaps the most unconventional method examined. The goal of this treatment is to utilize technology to allow autistic persons to unlock themselves by reaching deep inside themselves and developing knowledge that, with the ADAM technology, will return them to normalcy. (www.dimensionallife.com) The proponents do not clarify how this works and there are no control studies. This therapy represents one of several that utilize the paranormal. (See Jacobson and Mulick (2005) for a complete review.)

MISCELLANEOUS

Some treatments did not seem to fit into any of the above categories, and none have supporting data from scientific studies.

The <u>Miller Method</u> is a teaching methodology developed for children with ASD (Miller, 1989). It seeks to help children who may be withdrawn or disordered learn how to cope with their world. A specialized assessment is used to determine how each child experiences reality and a treatment plan is developed. One unique aspect of the method is the use of elevated boards two or four feet above the ground on which the children can better follow directions. To date, no controlled studies are available.

<u>Linda Mood-Bell</u> is a multi-sensory approach using intensive instruction that reports to improve cognitive and language development. (Bell, 1991) This method uses visualization and verbalization to improve language skills. Although there are a number of studies of its effectiveness in children with reading difficulties, no studies were found regarding its use with children with ASD.

Video modeling, including <u>Video Self-Modeling</u> (VSM), is another treatment that shows promise in teaching new behaviors and eliminating undesired behaviors in persons with a variety of disabilities. However, there are few studies in children with ASD. Buggey (2005) studied the effects of VSM across a variety of behaviors (e.g., language, social initiation, tantrums and aggression) in five ASD children. The results suggested that VSM may be effective in some children. Buggey points out the need for more research to validate the use of this method.

The <u>HANDLE</u> (Holistic Approach to Neurodevelopment and Learning Efficacy) <u>Institute</u> is a developmental drug-free approach that includes principles and perspectives drawn from medicine, rehabilitation, psychology, education and nutrition. Programs are individualized and seek to treat neurodevelopmental differences at their roots. This procedure appropriates many of the procedures already discussed and as with many others has no scientific basis.

<u>Art Therapy</u> uses art as a teaching tool. It reportedly assists persons with ASD in expressing themselves nonverbally. While some individuals with ASD may be talented artists, the treatment of ASD involves much more than developing this talent. (Steinberg, 1987) To date, there are no scientific studies to support this therapy.

Epsom Salt Baths is therapy based on the theory that autistic children have a shortage of pseudo neurotransmitters. Soaking in magnesium sulfate (Epsom salt) is reported to correct this shortage. As would be expected, there are no data on its use with children with ASD.

EVALUATING TREATMENTS

It is important to remember that there is a very fine line between controversial practices that merit consideration, review and study, and controversial practices that are hopelessly flawed. Choosing who decides and what decision making process is used may mean the difference between a stagnating and a vibrant field, the difference between current outcomes and better outcomes for children and families. The question is: What process can parents use to avoid "dumping out the baby with the bath water"? At this point, the suggestion is to use the results of the National Research Council (2001) position which attempts to synthesize and integrate information on both controversial and not so controversial treatments.

In addition, according to the National Research Council, over the past several years there has been increased interest in helping parents evaluate these "pseudo scientific studies." Jacobson, Foxx and Mulick (2005) published a comprehensive review, "Controversial Therapies for Developmental Disabilities," which included ASD. Schriebman (2005) also reviewed the "Science and Fiction of Autism." Both reviews stress the importance of consumer awareness of what constitutes scientific research and how to evaluate results and treatment. There is no position paper, however, that can substitute for empirical study.

In a systematic review of the scientific literature on treatment of ASD, Simpson (2005) identified more than 30 commonly used interventions and evaluated whether they were supported by research. He organized these into five categories: 1) interpersonal/ relationship based; 2) skill based; 3) cognitive; 4) physiological/biological/neurological; and 5) other. In addition to a description of the interventions, reported outcomes, qualifications of persons implementing the intervention, how, where and when the intervention is best carried out, potential risks, costs and methods of evaluating effectiveness were examined. Interventions and treatments were then graded as falling into one of four groups: scientifically-based; promising practice; practice having limited supporting information; and not recommended.

Scientifically-based practices were all skill-based and involved direct teaching utilizing the principles of applied behavior analysis, e.g., ABA in general and discrete trial training in particular. One intervention, Learning Experiences: An Alternative Program for Preschoolers and Parents, was identified as a scientifically-based cognitive treatment.

Promising practices were those with some scientific support, but more research is needed to recommend them as an intervention. Interpersonal/relationship-based interventions in this category included play-oriented strategies. Skill-based interventions that hold promise were the Picture Exchange Communication System; incidental teaching; structured teaching (e.g. TEACCH); augmentative alternative communication; assistive technology; and joint action routines. Cognitive interventions placed in this category included cognitive behavioral modification; cognitive learning strategies; Social Stories; and social decision-making strategies. Sensory Integration was listed as a promising physiological/biological/neurological intervention.

Practices with limited supporting information include the majority of the interpersonal/relationship-based interventions, (i.e., Gentle Teaching, the Options Method, FloorTime, pet/animal therapy, and relationship development intervention). Skill-based interventions included Van Dijk's curricular approach and the FastForword reading program. Cognitive strategies found to have limited supporting information included cognitive scripts, cartooning and Power Cards. Therapies categorized here as physiological/biological/neurological interventions included: Scotopic Sensitivity Syndrome/Irlen Lenses; Auditory Integration Training; megavitamin therapy; the Feingold Diet; and the use of herb, mineral and other supplements.

Of all the interventions reviewed, two were not recommended. These included holding therapy as an interpersonal/relationship-based intervention, and Facilitated Communication as a skill-based intervention. These interventions, as discussed, may result in harm to the child.

Freeman (1997) developed guidelines for parents in evaluating alternative treatments. These include the following: Parents should approach any alternative treatment with hopeful skepticism. Remember, the goal of any treatment should be to improve the quality of life for a person with an autism spectrum disorder, and help that person become a fully functioning member of society. Parents should be wary of any treatment – with the exception of a structured, individualized program based on the principles of applied behavior analysis – that is said to be effective or desirable for every person with ASD. Parents should also be wary of any alternative treatment that thwarts individualization, which can result in inappropriate programming decisions. In addition, all treatments should always depend on an individual multidisciplinary assessment that identifies the individual child's strengths and weaknesses. We should also consider that no alternative treatment be implemented until its proponents can specify these individualized assessment procedures as well as the risks, possible side effects and potential benefits for each individual.

We should all be aware that the debate over the use of various alternative treatments is often reduced to superficial arguments over who is right, moral and ethical, as opposed to who is the true advocate for the child. The true advocate for the child with ASD is the one who wants the child to become a fully functioning member of society. Finally, it is important that everyone be aware that the great majority of complementary and alternative treatments discussed in this chapter have not been validated scientifically and often represent "political" positions. Currently, the only treatment whose efficacy has been demonstrated in well-designed, scientific studies is an individualized program based on the principles of applied behavior analysis.

Below is a list of questions that people should ask regarding any alternative treatment. For example, what is the treatment's purpose and rationale? Is it logical? Is it based in theory that makes some sense? Is there written information available for the family? Most people respond much better when written information is given to us, so that we can review it, as opposed to having to make a decision on the spot. It is also important to know what is involved for the child and the family, i.e., the length of treatment, frequency of sessions, time and cost to the family. Families should also know whether this is a treatment that focuses on one skill or is it a comprehensive program for the child? Will the treatment result in harm to the child? Harm to children can occur in more than one way. Not only may there be direct harm to the child, as with detoxification with mercury, but also indirect harm to the child that occurs when unproven treatments are used in lieu of treatments that we know work, such as a comprehensive educational program based largely upon the principles of applied behavior analysis.

QUESTIONS TO ASK REGARDING SPECIFIC TREATMENT

1. What is the treatment program's rationale and purpose?
2. Is there written information?
3. What is involved for child and family?
4. What is length of treatment, frequency of sessions, time and costs to the family?

5. Does the treatment focus on one skill or is it a comprehensive program?

6. Will the treatment result in harm to the child?

7. Is the treatment developmentally appropriate?

8. What is the background and training experience of the staff?

9. Does the treatment staff allow input from the family?

10. Are assessment procedures specified and is the program individualized for each child?

11. How will progress be measured?

12. How often will effectiveness of the intervention be evaluated?

13. Who will conduct the evaluation?

14. What criteria will be used to determine if treatment should be continued or abandoned?

15. What scientific evidence supports the effectiveness of the program?

16. How will failure of treatment affect child and family?

17. How will treatment be integrated into the child's current program?

One final recommendation is to not become so infatuated with a given treatment that functional curriculum, vocational, life and social skills are ignored.

We also need to ask ourselves if the treatment is developmentally appropriate, as well as verifying the background and training experience of staff. ASD is a complex disorder and requires ongoing training. It is important to know that staff need experience and ongoing training to be able to effectively administer treatment for children with ASD. It is not enough to have a two-day workshop for training. Training needs to be ongoing and it is necessary to constantly update one's skills. It is also important to know if the treatment staff allow input from the family. No one should enroll their child in a treatment program that does not allow some input from the family. As noted, one should ask - is the assessment procedure specified and how is the program to be individualized for each child? If a provider says this is a treatment that is appropriate for every child with ASD, one should become extremely skeptical.

In addition, before anyone enters treatment, how progress will be measured, how often will the effectiveness of the treatment be evaluated, and who will conduct the evaluation should be specified. It is critical that people who are evaluating the effectiveness of the treatment do not have a vested interest, whether emotional or financial, in the outcome of the treatment. Parents should also be aware of what criteria will be used to determine if the treatment should be continued or abandoned, and what scientific evidence supports the effectiveness of the treatment.

Finally, parents and advocates should ask themselves how failure of the treatment would affect the child and the family. If parents put all of their hopes in a specific treatment and it does not work, how will this affect them as a family and how will it affect the child? How will treatment be integrated into the child's current program? It is critical not to become so absorbed with a specific complementary alternative treatment that functional curriculum, vocational life, behavior and social skills are ignored.

CONCLUSIONS

As noted throughout this chapter, several factors have rendered ASD vulnerable to etiological ideas and intervention approaches that make bold claims yet are inconsistent with established scientific theories and unsupported by research. Despite their absence of grounding in science, these theories and techniques are often passionately promoted by their advocates. Several reasons exist for this. The diagnosis of ASD is typically made during the preschool years and is often devastating news for parents and families. In addition, unlike most other physical or mental disabilities that affect a limited sphere of functioning while leaving other areas intact, the effects of ASDs are pervasive, generally affecting all domains of functioning, particularly social. Parents are typically highly motivated to attempt any promising treatment, rendering them vulnerable to promising "cures." The normal appearance of autistic children may lead parents, caregivers and teachers to become convinced that there must be a completely "normal or intact child lurking inside the normal exterior."

Furthermore, autism comprises a heterogeneous spectrum of disorders and can vary considerably among individuals. This fact makes it difficult to identify potential effective treatments for two reasons. First, there is a great deal of variability in response to treatments. Giving psychotropic medication, for example, may improve certain symptoms in one individual while actually making them worse in others. Secondly, as with all other developmental problems, persons with ASD sometimes show developmental gains or symptom improvement in a particular area for unidentified reasons. If any intervention has recently been implemented, such improvement may be erroneously attributed to the treatment, even when the treatment is actually ineffective. Thus, ASD is a fertile ground for Complementary and Alternative Medicine treatments. The purpose of this chapter has been to review these CAMs and their use in autism, and to help parents develop guidelines for how to evaluate them. Most of the treatments evaluated have been a part of what is often called "pseudo scientific treatments" with exaggerated claims of effectiveness that are well outside the range of established scientific procedures. They are often based on implausible theories that cannot be proven false. They tend to rely on anecdotal evidence and testimonials rather than controlled studies for support. When quantitative data are available, they are considered selectively. That is, confirmatory results are highlighted whereas unsupported results are either dismissed or ignored. Finally, many of these treatments are often associated with individuals or organizations with a direct and substantial financial stake in the treatments. The more of these problems that characterize a given theory or technique, the more scientifically suspect it becomes.

The intervention approaches discussed in this paper are extremely heterogeneous in theory and approach. However, many share the characteristic of possessing little or no scientific evidence of effectiveness. What is even more distressing is that some of these treatments continue to be promoted even after controlled studies have clearly demonstrated that they are ineffective or even dangerous. The interventions reviewed in this chapter may appear to give us little reason for hope in the treatment of autism. Fortunately, the situation is not bleak. Developmental educational programs based on principles of applied behavior analysis result in remarkable improvement for children with ASD. What is important for parents and professionals alike is to be aware of how to evaluate the current treatments that are out there and how to determine what an appropriate program is for the child challenged by Autism Spectrum Disorder. With an understanding of what is appropriate for children with autism, they can become functioning members of society and we can focus on their abilities rather than their disabilities.

REFERENCES

ADAM, www.dimensionallife.com; www.dolphinitp.org; www.quackwatch.com

Adams, L., and Cowen, S. (1997): Nutrition and its Relationship to Autism. Focus On Autism and Other Developmental Disabilities, 12:53-58.

Aman, M. and Langworthy, K. (2000): Psychopharmacotherapy for hyperactivity in children with autism and other pervasive developmental disorders. Journal of Autism and Developmental Disorders, 30:451-459.

Amen, D.G. and Carmichael, B. D. (1997): High resolution SPECT imaging in ADHD. Annals of Clinical Psychiatry, 9:81-86

American Academy of Child and Adolescent Psychiatry (AACAP) (1999): Practice parameters for the assessment and treatment of children, adolescents, and adults with autism and other pervasive developmental disorders. Journal of the American Academy of Child and Adolescent Psychiatry, 38:32-54.

American Academy of Pediatrics (2001): Counseling parents who choose complementary and alternative medicine for their child with chronic illness or disability. Committee on children with disabilities. Pediatrics, 107:591-601.

American Academy of Pediatrics (1999): Policy statement: The treatment of neurologically impaired children using patterning. Pediatrics, 104:1149-1151.

American Academy of Pediatrics Committee on Children with Disabilities (1998): Auditory integration training and facilitative communications for autism. Pediatrics, 102:431-433.

American Academy of Pediatrics (1998).

American Psychological Association (1994): Resolution on facilitated communication, August 1994.

Autism Research Institute (2004). Secretin activates amygdale, affects glutamate and GABA levels in Hippocampus. Autism Research Review International, 18(2)2-7.

Ayers, A.J. (1979): Sensory Integration in the Child. Western Psychological Services, Los Angeles CA.

Barrett, S. (1985): Commercial Hair Analysis: Science or Scam? Journal of the American Medical Association, 254:1041-1045.

Barrett (2004): Commercial Hair Analysis: A Cardinal Sign of Quackery. www.quackwatch.com

Barrett, S. (2004): Mental Health: Procedures to Avoid. www.quackwatch.com

Barrett, S. (2004): Craniosacral Therapy. www.quackwatch.com

Barrett, S. (2004): Chelation Therapy: Unproven Planes and Unsound Theories. quackwatch.com

Bell, LindaMood: www.lindamoodbell.com

Bell, N. (1991): Gestalt imagery: A critical factor in language comprehension. Annals of Dyslexia, 41:246-260.

Berand, G. (1993): Hearing Equals Behavior. New Canaan, CT: Keats.

Beratis, S. (1994): A Psychodynamic Model for Understanding Pervasive Developmental Disorders. European Journal of Psychiatry, 8:209-214.

Bolte, E. (2000): Short-Term Benefit of Oral Vancomycin Treatment of Aggressive-Onset Autism. Journal of Child Neurology, 15:430.

Bromfield, R. (2000): It's the Tortoise's Race: Long-term psychodynamic psychotherapy with a high-functioning autistic adolescent. Psychoanalytic Enquiry, 20:732-745.

Brownell, M.D. (2002): Music adapted social stories to modify behavior in students with autism: Four case studies. Journal of Music Therapy, 39:117-124.

Buggey, T. (2005): Video self-modeling application with students with autism spectrum disorder in a small private school setting. Focus on Autism and Other Developmental Disabilities, 20(1):52-63

Butler, E.A. and Mulick, J.A. (2001): ABA and the computer: A review of the Discrete Trial Trainer. Behavioral Interventions, 16(4):287-291.

Caccullo, A.G., Musetti, M.C., Musetti, L., Bajo, S., Sacerdote, P., Panerai, A. (1999): Beta endorphin levels in peripheral blood; Mononuclear cells and long-term naltrexone treatment in autistic children. European Neuropsychopharmacologia, 9:361-366.

Case-Smith, J. and Bryan, T. (1999): The effects of occupational therapy with sensory integration emphasis on preschool children with autism. American Journal of Occupational Therapy, 53:489-497.

Chamberlain, R. and Herman, B. (1990): A novel biochemical model linking dysfunction in the brain melatonin, proopiomelanocortin peptides, and serotonin in autism. Biological Psychiatry, 28:773-793.

Chez, M., Buchanan, C., Began, B., Hammer, M., McCarthy, K., Ovrutskaya, I., Nowinsky, C., Cohen, Z. (2000): Secretin and Autism: a Two-Part Clinical Investigation. Journal of Autism and Developmental Disorders, 30:87-94.

Dawson, G. and Watling, R. (2000): Interventions to facilitate auditory, visual, and motor integration in autism: a review of the evidence. Journal of Autism and Developmental Disorders, 30:415-421.

Deutsch, R. and Morrill, J. (1993): Realities of Nutrition, Palo Alto CA. Bull Publishing.

Doman, G.J. and Doman, G. (1974): What to do about your brain damaged, mentally retarded autistic child. Parason Press, Homesdale PA.

Dunn-Geier, J. (2000): Effect of secretin on children with autism: A randomized control trial. Developmental Medicine and Child Neurology, 42:796-802.

Edelson, M.G. (2006): Are the majority of children with autism mentally retarded?: A systematic evaluation of data. Focus on Autism and Other Developmental Disabilities, 21(2):66-83.

Edelson, S. and Rimland, B. (2004): The Efficacy of Auditory Integration Training: Summary and critique of 28 reports. (www.autism.com/ari)

Esch, B.E. and Carr, J.E. (2004): Secretin as a treatment for autism: A Review of the evidence. Journal of Autism and Developmental Disorders, 34:543-556.

Physician's Statement: Auditory Integration Training (1993): Executive Committee, American Academy of Audiology. Audiology Today, 5:21.

Findling, R., Maxwell, K., Scotese/Wojtila, L. and Huang, J. (1997): High-dose Paroxetine and an Absence of Salutary Effects in Double-Blind Placebo-Controlled Study. Journal of Autism and Developmental Disorders, 27:467-478.

Flaherty, R. (2005): Brain imaging and child and adolescent psychiatry with special emphasis on SPECT. Position paper of the American Psychiatric Association. (psych.org/psych_pract/clin_issues/populations/children/SPECT.pdf.)

Foothill Autism Alliance Power Pak (2001): Foothill Autism Alliance, Glendale CA.

Freeman, B.J. (1997): Evaluation of Treatment Programs: Questions Parents Should Ask. Journal of Autism and Developmental Disabilities, 27:641-651.

Frombonne, E. (2001): The Epidemic of Autism. Pediatrics, 107:411-413.

Giannotti, F., Cortesi, F., Cerquiglinia, A., and Bernabei, P. (2006): An open label study of controlled release Melatonin in treatment of sleep disorders in children with autism. Journal of Autism and Developmental Disorders; 2006, 36:741-752.

Green, G. (1996): Evaluating Claims about Treatment for Autism. In C. Maurice (Ed), G. Green and S. Luce (Co-Eds), Behavioral Intervention for Young Children with Autism. A Manual for Parents and Professionals. (15-28) Austin TX, PRO-ED, Inc.

Greenspan, S. (1992): Reconsidering the diagnosis and treatment of very young children with autistic spectrum or pervasive developmental disorders. Zero to Three, 13(2):1-9.

Greenspan, S. and Weider, S. (1998): The Child with Special Needs, Washington D.C.; Perseus Publishing.

Guttstein, S. (2004). www.rdiconnect.com

Hansen, E., Kalish, L., Bunce, E., Curtis, C., McDaniel, S., Ware, J. and Petry, J. (2007): Use of Complementary and Alernative Medicines among children diagnosed with autism spectrum disorder. Journal of Autism and Developmental Disorders, 37:628-636.

Harvard Medical School, Consumer Health Information: InteliHealth 2007. (www.intelihealth.com)

Heflin, L. and Simpson, R. (1998): Interventions for Children and Youth with Autism. Focus on Autism and Other Developmental Disabilities, 13:194-211.

Herbert, J. and Sharp, I. (2001): Pseudoscientific Treatments for Autism. Priorities for Health, 13:23-26.

Hoehn, G. and Baumeister, A. (1994): A Critique of the application of Sensory Integration Therapy to children with learning disabilities. Journal of Learning Disabilities, 27:338-351.

Horvath, K., Stefanatos, G., Sokoloski, K., Wachtel, R., Nabors, L., Tildon, J. (1998): Improved social and language skills after secretin administration in patients with autistic spectrum disorders. Journal of the Association for Academic Minority Physicians, 9:9-15.

Horvath, K. and Perman, J. (2002): Autistic Disorders and Gastrointestinal Disease. Current Opinions in Pediatrics, 14:583-587.

Hyman, S. and Levy, F. (2000): Autistic Spectrum Disorders: When traditional medicine is not enough. Contemporary Pediatrics, 17:101-116.

Intellihealth (2007). Complementary & Alternative Medicine. www.intellihealth.com

Irlen, H. (1983): Successful treatment of learning disabilities. Paper presented at the American Psychological Association, Anaheim CA.

Iwasaki, K. and Holm, V. (1989): Sensory treatment for the reduction of stereotypic behaviors in persons with severe multiple disabilities. Occupational Therapy Journal, 9:170-183.

Jacobson, J.W., Foxx, R.M. and Mulick, J.A. (2005): Controversial therapies for developmental disabilities: Fact, fashion and science in professional practice. (Eds) Manual. Manwah NJ, Lawrence Erlbaum Associates.

Jacobson, J.W. and Mulick, J.A. (2005): Developmental disabilities and the paranormal. In Jacobson, J.W., Foxx, R.M., and Mulick, J.A. (Eds). Controversial Therapies for Developmental Disabilities. Manwah NJ, Lawrence Erlbaum Associates.

Jacobson, J.W., Mulick, J.A., and Schwartz, A. (1995): A History of Facilitated Communication: Science, Pseudoscience, and Antiscience. Science Working Group on Facilitated Communication. <u>American Psychologist</u>, 50:750-765.

Johns Hopkins (1997): Spec sheet on stem cell selection. Baltimore: Johns Hopkins Press.

Johnson-Glenberg, M.C. (2000): Training reading comprehension in adequate decoders/poor comprehension: Verbal versus visual strategies. <u>Journal of Educational Psychology</u>, 92(4):772-782.

Kane, K. (2006): Death of a 5-year-old boy linked to controversial chelation therapy. Pittsburgh Post Gazette, January 6, 2006.

Kanner, L. (1943): Autistic disturbances of affective contact. <u>Nervous child</u>, 2:217-250.

Katelaris, A. (2007): Wakefield Saga: A study in integrity. <u>Australian Doctor</u>, August 2007.

Kaufman, B. N. (1976): <u>Son Rise</u>. New York, Harper Row.

Kennedy, K. and Backman, J. (1993): Effectiveness of the Linda-Mood Bell auditory discrimination in depth program with students with learning disabilities. <u>Learning Disabilities Research and Practice</u>, 8(4):253-259.

Kern, J.K., Miller, B.S., Cauller, P.L., Kendall, P.R., Mehta, P.J., Dodd, M. (2001): Effectiveness of N, n-dimethylglycine in autism and Pervasive Developmental Disorder. <u>Journal of Child Neurology</u>, 16(3):169-173.

Kern, J.K., Miller, V.S., Evans, P.A., Trivedi, M.H. (2002): Efficacy of porcine secretin administration in patients with autism spectrum disorders. <u>Journal of Autism and Developmental Disorders</u>, 32:153-160.

King, B. (2000): Pharmacological treatment of mood disturbances, aggression and self-injury in persons with pervasive developmental disorders. <u>Journal of Autism and Developmental Disorders</u>, 30:439-445.

Kvinsberg, A., Reichelt, K., Nodland, M., Hoien, T. (1996): Autistic syndromes in diet: A follow-up study. <u>Scandinavian Journal of Educational Research</u>, 39:223-236.

Levinson, B.M. (1969): Pet-oriented child psychotherapy. Springfield IL, Charles C. Thomas.

Levy, S. and Hyman, S. (2002): Alternative/complementary approaches to treatment of children with autism spectrum disorders. <u>Infants and Young Children</u>, 14:33-42.

Levy, S., Souders, M., Coplan, J., Wray, J., Mulberg, A. (2001): Gastrointestinal abnormalities in children with autistic spectrum disorders. <u>Journal of Developmental and Behavioral Pediatrics</u>, October 2001.

Levy, Mandell, Merhar, Ittenabach & Pinto-Martin (2003): Use of complementary and alternative medicine among children recently diagnosed with autistic spectrum disorders. <u>Journal of Developmental and Behavioral Pediatrics</u>, 24:418-423.

Lightdale, J.R., Hayer, C., Duer, A., Lind-White, C., Jenkins, S., Siegel, B., et al. (2001, November): Effects of intravenous secretin on language and behavior of children with autism and gastrointestinal symptoms: A single-blinded, open-label pilot study. <u>Pediatrics</u>, 108:Article e90. Retrieved June 11, 2002 from www.pediatrics.org.

Linderman, T. and Stewart, K. (1999): Sensory integrated based occupational therapy and functional outcomes in young children with pervasive developmental disorders: A single subject study. <u>American Journal of Occupational Therapy</u>, 53:207-213.

Liptak, G. S. (2005): Complementary and alternative therapies for cerebral palsy. <u>Mental Retardation and Developmental Disabilities Research Review</u>, 11:156-163

MacKinnon, J., Noh, S., Laliberte, D., Lariviere, J., Allen, D. (1995): Therapeutic horseback riding: A review of the literature. <u>Physical and Occupational Therapy in Pediatrics</u>, 15:1-15.

Majebe, M. (2002): Chinese medicine for autism. <u>New Life Journal</u>.

Marino, L. and Lilienfeld, S. O. (1998): Dolphin assisted therapy: Flawed data, flawed conclusion. Anthrozoos, 11(4):194-200.

Mason, S. A. & Iwata, B. A. (1990). Artifactual effects of sensory-integrative therapy on self-injurious behavior. *Journal of Applied Behavior Analysis, 23*(3), 361–370

McDougle, C., Holmes, J., Carlson, D., Pelton, G., Cohen, D., Price, L. (2004): A double-blind placebo-controlled study of risperidone in adults with autistic disorder and other pervasive developmental disorders. Archives of General Psychiatry, 55:633-641.

McGee, J.J. (1990): Gentle Teaching: The basic tenet. Mental Handicap Nursing, 86(32):68-72

McKinnon, R. (2004): Deflection of growth factors in the central nervous system during CNS development and the role of growth factors in repair after injury or disease. www.autismtreatments.com

Miller, A. (1989): From Ritual to Repertoire: A cognitive-developmental systems approach with behavior disoriented children. New York NY, John Wiley.

Moore, D.J., Cheng, Y., McGrath, P., Powell, N.J. (2005): Collaborative virtual Environment technology for people with autism. Focus on Autism and Other Developmental Disabilities, 20(4):231-243.

Mudford, O.C., Cross, B.A., Breen, S., Cullen, C., Reeves, D., Gould, J., et al. (2000): Auditory integration therapy for children with autism: No behavioral benefits detected. American Journal of Mental Retardation, 105:118-129.

Nathanson, D.E. and deFaria, S. (1993): Cognitive improvement of children in water with and without dolphins. Anthrozoos, 6(1):17-29.

National Research Council (2001): Educating Children with Autism, Washington, D.C., National Academy Press.

Nelson, K.B. and Bauman, M.L. (2003): Thimerosal and Autism: Is There a Connection? Pediatrics, March 2003; 111(3):674-679.

Nickel, R. (1996): Controversial therapies for young children with developmental disabilities. Infants and Young Children, 8:29-40.

Novella, S. (2001): Psychomotor patterning. www.quackwatch.com

O'Sullivan, J. (2004): Seeing the World through Rose-Colored Glasses: Skeptical Inquiry.

Othmer, S. (2004): The Emerging Frontier of Neurofeedback. Latitude, 6:2-5.

Owley, T., Steele, E., Coresello, C., Risi, S., McKaig, K., Lord, C., Leventhal, B., Cook, E. (1999): A double-blind placebo controlled trial of secretin for the treatment of Autistic Disorder. Abstract, October 1999. Medscape General Medicine.

Panksepp, J. (1979): A neurochemical theory of autism. Trends in Neuroscience, 2:174-177.

Panksepp, J., Lensing, P., Leboyer, M., Bouvard, M. (1991): Naltrexone and other potential new pharmacological treatments of autism. Brain Dysfunction, 4:281-300.

Reilly, C., Nelson, D., and Bundy, A. (1984): Sensorimotor versus fine motor activities in eliciting vocalizations in autistic children. Occupational Therapy Journal of Research, 3:199-212.

Richard, G. J. (2000): The Source of Treatment Methodologies in Autism. East Molino, IL; LiguiSystems.

Richdale, A. (1999): Sleep problems in autism: Prevalence, course and intervention. Developmental Medicine and Child Neurology, 41:60-66.

Ricks, D. (2007) Autism "cures" may be deadly. Newsday, Aug. 21, 2007.

Rimland, B. (1988): Candida-caused Autism. Autism Research Review International Newsletter, 1988; 2(2):3.

Rimland, B. (1990): Dimethylglycine (DMG), A Nontoxic Metabolite, and Autism. Autism Research Review International Newsletter 1990; 4(2):3.

Rimland, B. (2000): Do Children's Shots Invite Autism. Los Angeles Times.

Robinson, G. (2003). Australasian Association of Irlen Consultants, Inc. www.membersozemail.com

Sandler, A., Sutton, A., DeWeese, J., Cirardi, A., Sheppard, V., Bodfish, J. (1999): Lack of benefit of a single dose of synthetic human secretin in the treatment of Autism and Pervasive Developmental Disorder. New England Journal of Medicine, 341:1801-1806.

Schreibman, L. (2005): The Science and Fiction of Autism. Cambridge MA, Harvard University Press.

Schwartz, I. (1999): Controversy of lack of consensus: Rethinking interventions in early childhood special education. Topics in Early Childhood Special Education

Scientific Learning Corporation (2004). www.fastforward.com

Simpson, R.L. (2005): Evidence-based practices and children with autism spectrum disorders. Focus on Autism and Other Developmental Disabilities, 20(3):140-149.

Simpson, R. L. (2005): Autism Spectrum Disorders: Interventions and Treatments for Children and Youth. Thousand Oaks CA, Corwin Press.

Singh, V. (1997): Immunotherapy for Brain Diseases and Mental Illness. Progress in Drug Research, 48:129-146

Smith, T. (1996): Are Other Treatments Effective? In C. Maurice, G. Green and S.C. Luce (Eds). Behavioral Interventions for Young Children with Autism. Manual for Parents and Professionals (45-59). Austin, TX. PRO-ED, Inc.

SOMA (2004): Rapid Promotions Method. www.halo-soma.org

Stemmer, P.M. (1996): Improving motor integration by use of interactive metronome. Paper presented at America Educational Association meeting. Chicago IL.

Steinberg, E. (1987): Long-term art therapy with an autistic adolescent. The American Journal of Art Therapy, 26:40-47.

Wallace, D., Silverman, S., Goldstein, J., and Hughes, D. (1995): Use of hyperbaric oxygen in rheumatic diseases: Case reporting critical analysis. Lupus, 4:172-175.

Welch, M., (1988): Holding Time: How to Eliminate Conflict, Temper Tantrums and Sibling Rivalry and Raise Happy Loving Successful Children. New York NY, Simon and Schuster.

Wheeler, D., Jacobson, J., Paglieri, R., and Schwartz, A. (1993): An experimental assessment of facilitating communication. Mental Retardation, 31:49-59.

Whiteley, P., Rodgers J., Savery, D., and Shattock, P. (1999): A gluten-free diet as an intervention for autism and associated spectrum disorders: Preliminary findings. Autism, 3:45-65.

---

[1] *The author has attempted to include all studies published at the time of writing this chapter. Any omissions and/or errors are completely unintentional.*

Chapter 7

CRITICAL THINKING

By Ron Leaf, Mitch Taubman & John McEachin

IT'S TIME TO SPEAK OUT

When we look around and see what people are doing in an effort to help children with autism we see things that make sense and things that do not make sense. Some of the interventions that we have observed are disturbing because they capitalize on people's desire for an easy remedy, create a nice warm feeling, and shy away from objective measurement of treatment benefits. We all can be fooled into thinking we are seeing something that is not really there or that something is substantial when it is actually trivial. We gravitate to the conclusions that are most appealing and then selectively attend to evidence that justifies our conclusions.

The amount of contradictory information on autism is simply enormous. Whether it pertains to diagnosis, prognosis, prevalence, cause or treatment there are hundreds of theories and beliefs. So how does one avoid being fooled? We believe the answer lies in learning to think critically and being scientific in our approach to distinguishing between fact and fiction.

In this chapter and throughout this book we have tackled difficult and controversial issues. We are not thrilled to be in the role of troublemakers, but someone must speak out when the emperor has no clothes. We feel that it would be wrong to stand by silently when something can be done that truly will make a difference in the lives of children with autism.

THINKING CRITICALLY ABOUT AUTISM

Autism is an extremely mystifying disorder. Trying to understand where it may come from and what to do about it can be overwhelming to a parent. A child may have remarkable strengths and crushing weaknesses. Some days things may seem to be going relatively well and others very poorly. If autism is anything it is unpredictable and variable. Anything that could fill this void of uncertainty and provide some assurance would be highly welcomed. It is therefore absolutely understandable that parents, in their confusion and desperation, would be willing to try anything that presents even a hint of success. It would not be any different from someone whose loved one is facing a life-threatening illness. Analogously, it is a fight for quality of life and hope for remission! Autism is no less devastating to those who are closest to the child with the disorder. It must feel to a parent as though they have lost their child and that there is no future. Naturally they would be willing to try anything to get it all back. Who would not? And who would not try anything that sounded plausible?

In trying to better understand Autism Spectrum Disorder (ASD), one must be prepared to sift through a vast amount of information, some of which is of dubious value and may even constitute outright misinformation. If you surf the Internet, you will find hundreds of treatment options. Most sound plausible and each proponent makes a strong and often passionate argument regarding its effectiveness. Parents and professionals will continually hear differing opinions regarding diagnosis, etiology, treatments and outcome. ASD is a disorder that is already difficult, but having to separate fact from pseudo-fact only makes everyone's mission more complicated.

Every year there is a new treatment which is declared to be highly effective in treating individuals with ASD. Some of these treatments have even been purported to be "cures." Unfortunately, none of these treatments have turned out to produce the hoped for miracle. ABA is the one exception that has proven to be consistently effective (Lovaas, 1987; McEachin, Smith, & Lovaas, 1993), but it too is no miracle. Unfortunately, proponents of ABA have, at times described it with the same fervor as other "cures of the year." Not only is this misleading, but it creates a negative impression regarding ABA.

This problem is not limited to the promotion of purported "cures". Every few years there is a new theory about the cause of ASD. Dr. Lovaas has commented in various public addresses that some investigators have found the cause two or three times! Not that there should not be research attempting to determine the etiology. These efforts are critical to understanding, prevention, and treatment. However, autism is a complicated disorder, most likely a set of disorders, and easy answers as to the cause are not likely to be found. As any responsible medical researcher states, long-term, painstaking, rigorous, and sophisticated scientific investigation is necessary to gain reliable understanding of the causes of complex phenomena. Professional responsibility and ethics demand that care be taken not to over-speculate about the causes of autism, misrepresent information about them, nor present mere hypotheses as fact.

Catherine Maurice (1999) commented:

> *"Every treatment fad in autism, from the scandal of facilitated communication to the excesses of biological experimentation on children, is the result of desperate parental need, combined with irresponsible professional encouragement-or silence."* (page 3)

Unfortunately, proponents of these movements typically show disdain for scientific verification. Every month, for example, you will read in a newsletter about purchasing some product that will produce outstanding results. But of course, they have absolutely no data whatsoever to show any effectiveness. They rely often on their impressions and do not even consider any other explanations for the alleged or "apparent" effectiveness. In many cases, long papers are written, creating extended cases of pseudo-logic in support of the purported treatment (Green, 1999).

Bernie Rimland, a psychologist who founded Autism Research Institute and the father of a child with ASD, pointed out that crusades such as these are typically based upon "*...good wishes and fantasies rather than on factual information and rational thought*"(Rimland, 1993) However, just as with medical procedures, it is critical that autism treatment procedures be carefully examined. Following are some major red flags that have been associated with disappointing "panaceas of the week":

1. Exaggerated Claims of Effectiveness

2. Reported Effective for Most or All

3. Limited Empirical or Field Testing Demonstrating Effectiveness

4. Claims Based upon Individual Case Studies & Testimonial

5. Followers Often Do Not Understand the Treatment, Rationales, and Underpinnings, but Focus Primarily on the Supposed Results

6. Treatment Does Not Require Extensive Training

7. Approach Becomes Big Overnight

8. Heavy on The "Curb Appeal" and Promises of Results, Weak on the Techniques or the Theory Behind Them

9. Treatment is Not as Strong as the Charm and Charisma of the "Professional" Promoting It

So how does one decide which treatment to select? Start by looking for treatments that have been scientifically investigated and for which the results have been reported in well-respected, peer-reviewed journals. These can be found on the shelves of university libraries and in scholarly texts such as those adopted for college level psychology courses. Professionals making recommendations for treatments should be able to provide references to controlled studies published in scientific journals. Only through extensive field testing and careful scientific analysis such as found in these publications, is it possible to distinguish treatments that can be expected to produce significant changes. It is important to separate those procedures that merely sound good, make sense, or feel right from those that actually produce positive change. This really is no different from what we would expect or want when it comes to medical treatment. If one had a life-threatening medical illness, one would not take a drug merely based on the claims of the manufacturer. The patient would look for medications that have gone through scientifically rigorous examination and have proven to be effective. That way the patient would also know the risks associated with taking them. The same should be true for any psychological treatment, including treatment for ASD.

We have heard professionals say, "So what is the harm in trying this treatment? Autism is a serious disorder. As long as the side effects are not serious, everything should be tried". There are several problems with this attitude. Firstly, in most cases, possible side-effects have not adequately been investigated. Secondly, a waste of time, energy, and often times, substantial amounts of money are frequently a built-in downside of the pursuit of ineffective treatments. And this is most often at the expense of mainstream, helpful approaches. It is impossible (as well as inadvisable) to try everything and the irony is that those things that would make the greatest difference get left behind. Finally, the most consistent and perhaps most overlooked side effect of the fruitless pursuit of panaceas is the over-building and then the crushing destruction of hope. This takes its toll on all who care about and care for the person with autism, adding more dips and precipitous plunges to the roller coaster that is ASD, and depleting precious emotional reserves.

While the vast majority of those who support the panaceas are well intended, in our opinion a small minority have been less noble in their intent. Beware of unscrupulous individuals who promote treatments much like the snake oil salesmen of the old west. Those who desire to profit financially, personally, or both, will make baseless grandiose claims that prey on the vulnerabilities, uncertainties, and hopes and dreams of those looking for answers. They are recognizable by their self-promotion and pomposity, their bombastic, too-good-to-be-true claims, and the offense they take at any suggestion that evidence of effectiveness is necessary for any treatment or that careful examination of their approach should be undertaken. These approaches and their proponents should be treated with extreme caution.

Again, it is understandable that parents would not want to leave any stone unturned and would feel desperate for any possible cure. However, what is deplorable are professionals that encourage parents to seek such unfounded treatments. We would hope that professionals would understand the importance of careful scrutiny and scientific investigation to validate effective treatments.

BE CAUTIOUS!

As efforts to further understand autism continue, and as the pursuit of enhanced treatment is furthered, it is incumbent upon parents, professionals and all interested parties to maintain a responsible sense of what is current in relevant fields. The following may serve as a helpful guide as one is attempting to successfully navigate through the abundance of information that is continually generated, as attempts are made to fill the often bewildering void that can be autism:

■ Be cautious of approaches and therapies that have not been researched, replicated, and field tested. Case studies can often be misleading, since no two cases are identical, and the varying nature of the disorder may mean that change occurred coincidentally with the experience of a particular treatment. With pharmacological and similar treatments, blind clinical trials are essential for the reliable demonstration of effects and side effects.

■ Be careful of promises which are too lofty, approaches which are all the rage, and treatments which represent style over substance or personality over content. If a therapy seems to have sprung from nowhere, not as an outgrowth of earlier efforts, theory, or research, then caution is advised.

■ Be reasonable and remember that every day you experience the complexity that is autism and that overly simplistic conceptualizations and treatments may, at best, produce simple results.

■ Be a critical consumer. Do not believe everything you read or hear. Consider the derivation of information and seek additional material as well as confirmation from other, independent sources. Peer reviewed medical, psychological and educational journals often represent reliable sources. Unreviewed, unedited sources should be approached with reserve and wariness. This is particularly true in the Internet Age. Although the World Wide Web is a resource of tremendous information, support, and networking, often there is no critical screening of what is disseminated. Even published books may merely represent the non- or pseudo-scientific opinions of their authors.

■ Be sensible as you pursue treatments and resources, apportioning your time based on your sense of your child or client, what seems to fit, and what has been demonstrated to best address his or her needs

■ Consider alternative explanations for the positive results being reported. These include things like placebo effects and misinterpreted direction of causality. Alternative explanations will be discussed in greater detail later in this chapter.

■ When you encounter professionals who seem to be touting an unproven treatment do not allow them to make you feel unqualified to evaluate or question claims. If they react with disdain to your skepticism, you should seek a second opinion by consulting another professional.

RESEARCH DESIGN

Most careful research in autism uses scientific methodology. No social science research is scientifically flawless, nor able to prove beyond a shadow of a doubt that a treatment is effective or what is the cause of a psychological disorder. However, the use of scientific methodology helps reduce the level of inference and increase the believability and convincingness of research findings. In autism treatment research, the scientific method includes the manner in which subjects are selected and assigned to treatments, the objectivity and consistency of the measures used, and the research design which is utilized to show the effectiveness of treatments, as well as utilizing control procedures to determine what is responsible for producing the effects. Using an experimental design is essential in order to identify if it is the actual treatment or other factors that account for the study participants' improvement. There are many factors that may be responsible for gains besides the treatment itself (Campbell, D.T., Stanley, J.C., Gage, N.L., 1963). The following are common extraneous factors which could lead us to make false conclusions:

1. **Placebo Effect** is when people perceive or even experience improvement even when no treatment has actually occurred (Campbell, et.al., 1963). A common example is the improvement experienced by some members in the "sugar pill" group in double-blind medication research. This often occurs because of expectations. We hope and believe that the intervention will result in change. Under any condition it is difficult to be an objective observer. But when we know that our child is beginning a new intervention, we become biased observers and selectively attend to evidence that is consistent with our expectation. We want to see improvement because we have invested time, money, effort and emotions into the treatment. Thus, we may really believe that the treatment has produced change, even if it actually has not.

   There are many research strategies to eliminate placebo effects. Sometimes it means that some clients receive the treatment and some do not. However, those judging change are not aware who is actually receiving the treatment (i.e., they are "blind"). Another way to reduce placebo effect is to utilize objective measurement so as to validate that actual change has occurred. Using scientific investigation and research design, placebo effect can be eliminated.

2. **Confounding Variables.** Often when a new treatment begins other things are changing as well. If a child starts on a diet (e.g., gluten free-casein free), this may coincide with a significant increase in structure of daily life and there may be subtle changes in the kind of interactions that occur between parent and child (Campbell, et.al., 1963). Heightened expectations often produce a new era of conscientious effort. At such times parents tend to become more aware of behavioral issues and provide different consequences than before. There may also be changes in routines. Therefore, the improvement in a child may not be directly from the diet, but actually because of all these other changes, these non-specific events. Additionally, parents

have had to invest so much energy and expense in preparing food that they may be extra vigilant for signs of positive change and tend to overlook negative indications.

3. **Maturation** is sometimes a factor that may be responsible for change (Campbell, et.al., 1963). As time passes there may be positive growth that occurs simply as the natural course of development, and this would happen with or without intervention. If treatment occurs over an extended period of time, we need to take into account what improvement might have occurred if we simply did nothing. Good experimental design can control for this variable.

4. Most children receive **Multiple Treatments** (Campbell, et.al., 1963). For example, in addition to ABA, they might also be participating in Speech Therapy, O.T., Vitamins, and/or special diets. So what is the treatment or the combination of treatments that are actually responsible for change? It is likely that one will attribute the change in behavior to the treatment one most believes in. If one strongly believes in ABA, then one is likely to believe that the improvements are because of ABA.

5. A well-known phenomenon is called "**Regression to the Mean.**" This term describes the tendency of phenomena that are occurring at extreme levels to soon move back to the more typical range (Campbell, et.al., 1963). Children with ASD may be exhibiting extreme behaviors when they begin treatment. In fact these extremes may be the reason that parents have sought treatment. If they have been exhibiting a high rate of disruptive behaviors like aggression, tantrums, and noncompliance it is likely that they will soon be moving back toward a more moderate level. In a sense, they have only one way to go—down. Therefore, it may not be the treatment at all that is responsible, but simply an averaging out of the behaviors.

The *Sports Illustrated* "jinx" is a well-known example of "regression to the mean." The jinx is that once an athlete's picture appears on the cover of *Sports Illustrated* their performance deteriorates soon afterward. However, a more scientific explanation is that such high level of performance (whatever great feat put them on the cover) cannot continue to be sustained. It is not because they appeared on the cover! Their performance would have naturally returned to a more typical level even if they did not appear on the cover.

6. **Biased observations** can occur when we are selectively attending to available information (Campbell, et.al., 1963). If we have adopted a pet theory, we become more

convinced of its merit whenever we observe something that is consistent with our belief and we tend not to notice events which could tend to disprove our theory because we are not looking for them. Reputation, whether it be of a person or a product can long outlive its validity because it influences people's perceptions. The advertising industry thrives on our tendency to be unscientific in the way we collect and interpret information.

Use of experimental designs control for these possible alternative explanations for observed changes and help us rule them out while confidently identifying treatments and interventions that really do make a difference.

MULTIPLE INTERPRETATIONS

We are continually attempting to identify what is effective for our children. When the relationship between antecedent events and outcomes seems unclear and complicated we proceed cautiously. However, when the connection seems rather obvious we may be satisfied that we have identified a plausible explanation and not consider other possible interpretations. Critical thinking requires openness to a variety of possibilities as well as a healthy dose of skepticism regarding what may seem to be the obvious causative factor. There may be other factors operating alongside the one that first captured our attention.

We are constantly observing events and looking for causal relationships. We are not always objective in drawing conclusions and may be swayed by our belief systems and what we have read and heard from professionals. For example, a parent may have observed that when their child is distressed and then receives deep pressure, the child quickly stops crying. Perhaps this is advice that came from a professional. Observing the desired change in the child's behavior, the parent is likely to continue to use this strategy and gain confidence in the belief that children with ASD have difficulty integrating or accommodating sensory input and that Sensory Integration Therapy (SI) can help them cope with the world. However, what other possible explanations could there be for why the child stopped crying? Might there be other causative factors besides the one that seems most obvious?

The following are events that may take place in the life of a student with ASD. The first interpretation listed is the one that most of us would think of first and may seem to be obvious or the one that has the most "support." As you will see, however, there are other possibilities that may be every bit as valid as the mainstream interpretation.

EVENT

1. Child is crying.
2. A Sensory Integration procedure (e.g., deep pressure, joint compression, brushing) is administered.
3. Child stops crying.

POSSIBLE INTERPRETATIONS

1. **The SI procedure assists student in integrating overwhelming stimuli.**
2. SI engages the student's attention and it is the attention that produces behavior change.
3. During the time SI is provided, student is able to avoid disliked activity.
4. SI distracts student from what was upsetting.
5. SI is being employed as a reactive stress management procedure.
6. SI procedures are pleasant and crying is a learned means to access the pleasant experience. Good data would reveal whether SI should be used proactively or reactively.

EVENT

1. Child is calm.
2. Child eats sweets (e.g., candy, soda, cake).
3. Child appears to become "hyperactive."

POSSIBLE INTERPRETATIONS

1. **Sugar causes hyperactivity.**
2. Adults assume children become hyperactive when they ingest sugar and thus observations are prejudiced.
3. Sugar is provided during fun and unstructured events (e.g., cake and ice cream at a birthday party.) The high level of stimulation and lack of structure might be the real culprits.
4. Child rarely receives sugar and therefore is excited.
5. Parent reacts differently because they expect the child is going to "bounce of the walls" so they do not place the same limits that they would normally.

EVENT

1. Child exhibits behaviors characteristic of ASD.
2. Child begins Treatment X.
3. Child appears to improve.

POSSIBLE INTERPRETATIONS

1. **The treatment is responsible for improvement.**
2. Another treatment that coincided with Treatment X may be causing improvement.
3. Child is receiving other treatments and it may be the combination of the two treatments that is producing positive results.
4. Child is receiving increased attention.
5. Treatment has resulted in an increase of structure.
6. Child is more occupied.
7. Observations of improvements are actually biased due to hopeful expectations.
8. Natural (and typical) variation in performance occurred coincidentally.
9. Maturation.

EVENT

1. Child is calm.
2. Teacher has child wear a long sleeve shirt.
3. Child starts crying.

POSSIBLE INTERPRETATIONS

1. **Child is tactile defensive (i.e., finds clothes painful perhaps because of some organic disturbance in the sensory system).**
2. Child has rituals regarding clothes and one of the child's "rules" has been broken.
3. It was not the shirt but simply a matter of the child wanting attention.
4. Child "enjoys" control battle.
5. When child starts crying, teacher removes clothes and dresses child in preferred clothing.

EVENT

1. Student is agitated.
2. Student swings on "vestibular" swing.
3. Student becomes calm.

POSSIBLE INTERPRETATIONS

1. **The swing helped student "integrate and assimilate" sensory input.**
2. Student enjoyed the swing and thus became calm.
3. Student was able to avoid non-preferred tasks while on the vestibular swing.
4. Student is receiving attention and thus is happier.
5. Student has become preoccupied with self-stimulatory activity and forgets about what was distressing.

EVENT

1. A loud noise occurs (e.g., plane, siren, school bell).
2. Student covers ears.

POSSIBLE INTERPRETATIONS

1. **Student has "auditory hypersensitivity" (i.e., the noise is painful and there is an "organic" or underlying systemic cause)**
2. Student does not like the noise but there is not any "organic" or underlying cause.
3. Noisy situations are typically avoided and thus student has not had the opportunity to learn to adapt to everyday noises.
4. Student covers his ears not only to block out the noise but to avoid hearing any demands.
5. Noise interferes with student's self stimulation and is therefore aggravating to him.

EVENT

1. Children with ASD have higher rates of constipation as compared to their siblings and peers.

POSSIBLE INTERPRETATIONS

1. **Children with ASD have gastrointestinal disorders which indicate metabolic problems which cause ASD.**
2. If constipation rates were compared to peers who do not have ASD it might turn out that there is not a significant difference.
3. Children with ASD have unusual eating patterns which results in constipation.
4. Children with ASD have poor toileting skills (e.g., bowel retention) which results in constipation.

EVENT

1. Child performs better with visual tasks as opposed to auditory tasks.

POSSIBLE INTERPRETATIONS

1. **Children with ASD are visual learners and therefore visual strategies should be used.**
2. Auditory tasks require increased attention.
3. Visual strategies are easier to learn.
4. Visual strategies are easier to teach.
5. We assume this to be true and thus use visual strategies and therefore children have less practice with auditory strategies.
6. We should expose children to tasks requiring auditory processing so that child becomes better at this skill.

EVENT

1. Student's performance on an intelligence test does not accurately reflect student's ability.

POSSIBLE INTERPRETATIONS

1. **Testing is inaccurate or tester is unskilled.**
2. Student is anxious when tested.
3. Student may have partially learned the concepts but has not learned the words or format that is used on the I.Q. test.
4. Skills may not have been learned independently, and student is dependent on prompts.
5. Although student can perform skills in certain situations, the skills are not sufficiently generalized. Because of the lack of fluency in skills being tested, the low I.Q. score correctly predicts student will have difficulty learning in traditional classroom settings.

EVENT

1. Peers in full inclusion are friendly toward the student with ASD.

POSSIBLE INTERPRETATIONS

1. **Inclusion facilitates development of friendships.**
2. Peers are demonstrating sensitivity but do not consider student as a true friend.
3. Peers consider the child someone to whom they should pay special attention.
4. Peers receive extra attention for playing with child.
5. Certain peers enjoy caring for others.

EVENT

1. Student is passing all subjects in school.

POSSIBLE INTERPRETATIONS

1. **Classroom placement is appropriate and student is able to learn in a regular education class.**
2. Evaluations are not as stringent as for other students.
3. Student has previously been taught the required skills.
4. Curriculum at early grade levels is based upon concrete skills rather than abstract ones.
5. Student is receiving performance-oriented assistance.

EVENT

1. Consultant is observing in a classroom.
2. Student is exhibiting disruptive behaviors.
3. Teacher reports student is having an "unusual" day.

POSSIBLE INTERPRETATIONS

1. **Student is indeed having an unusual day**.
2. Presence of additional person is distressing to student.
3. Presence of additional person is distressing to teacher and causes teacher to be distracted and less effective than usual.
4. Student is disrupted because teacher has altered some of the routines due to the observation.
5. It is actually a typical day, but the teacher is more aware of the behavior problems because of the observation. On other days, teacher is not as tuned in to behavior problems and does not notice them as much.
6. It is a typical day but teacher is embarrassed and making excuses.

EVENT

1. Student is yawning and not participating.

2. Teacher or parents comment that student is tired.

POSSIBLE INTERPRETATIONS

1. **Student did not get enough sleep.**

2. Student is bored or unmotivated.

3. Student is avoiding the task.

4. Student is engaged in self-stimulation.

EVENT

1. Four year old child with ASD reads.

POSSIBLE INTERPRETATIONS

1. **Child has "hyperlexia"**

2. Child reads at same level as other four year olds but appears to be hyperlexic because staff do not expect child with ASD to have such an advanced skill.

3. Child can decode well but does not have understanding of what child is reading

4. Child self-stimulates on letters and words and therefore is highly motivated to develop this skill.

CORRELATION DOES NOT EQUAL CAUSATION

When attempting to determine the effectiveness of treatments for autism, as well as the potential causes for the disorder, two types of investigation might typically be used. The first, intended to establish a causal relationship between variables, involves the systematic presentation of the suspected causative factor and the examination of what happens subsequently. It also involves a control or comparison situation in which the suspected factor is not presented but results are still examined (Campbell, et.al., 1963). Except for the presence of the causative variable, the two conditions are to be as similar as possible. That way, any differences in results can be attributed to (i.e., confirmed as being caused by) the suspected factor. Such experimental control is necessary to establish cause and is often used to demonstrate that a particular treatment has "caused" intended benefits (Campbell, et.al., 1963).

As noted earlier in this chapter, with the exception of ABA, little or none of this type of research has been done to examine the effectiveness of autism treatments. Most frequently, if research is done at all, it is of an associative or correlational sort. That is, a treatment has occurred and a purported change is also observed leading to the conclusion that there is a connection between the two. The problem with this is that correlation does not demonstrate causation (Campbell, et.al., 1963). When two factors occur together, even with some consistency, it is often unclear which one causes the other. Furthermore, it is a possibility that some third variable actually caused both factors. Take for example, an individual who is exercising more and sleeping better. We could infer that he is sleeping better because he is exercising more. However, it is entirely possible that the opposite is true, i.e., he is exercising more because he is sleeping better and has more energy. A third possibility is that he has stopped eating pepperoni pizza as a late night snack. Because of the change in his eating behavior he now is sleeping better and feels less sluggish and bloated and exercising requires less effort. In that case the third variable is responsible for producing the change in both of the first two factors. Although the first two factors are correlated neither one causes the other–another example of how correlation does not equal causation.

In regards to investigation into the cause or causes of autism, this issue becomes even more complicated. Obviously, one cannot manipulate suspected causative factors in an attempt to produce autism. Experimental control is not desired here. What little research does exist, attempts to use what is in essence a correlational approach in an attempt to determine causation. While we cannot rely on correlation to prove causation, this is a good example of where we must learn what we can from the less reliable technique. Fortunately, there are factors that can strengthen our confidence in such relationships, and assist us in evaluating research which is about the cause of ASD.

When a correlational relationship is strong, that is, when one variable is consistently found in conjunction with the other, then an association between the two can be more comfortably inferred. For example, with twins who are identical, if one of them has ASD then there is a very high probability that the other will also have ASD (a high correlation). In contrast, with fraternal twins, if one of them has ASD, the likelihood of the second having ASD is considerably lower (a low correlation). This strongly indicates that genetics is a factor in the cause of autism. However the nature of that relationship is complex and not yet very well understood.

When correlated variables occur in the right temporal order (the supposed cause precedes the supposed effect), and there exists a strong and consistent relationship, then the potential for causality is more likely. In the example of genetics and autism, it is likely that the genetic anomaly precedes the autism, rather then the autism causing mutation in the individual's genetic makeup.

Finally, the comfort we have with the possibility of causality between two variables is strengthened by its predictive value. That is, when that "causal" variable is identified as present there is a consistently high likelihood that the "effect" is also present. Conversely if the causal variable is not present this should predict that the effect is also not present. So far, there is no known variable, including specific genetic structure, that consistently precedes the development of autism and that when it is absent we can be confident that autism will not develop.

CRITICAL EYE AND THE ANALYTIC PROCESS

As mentioned previously, correlational information has been generated in research designed to examine treatment effectiveness in addition to investigations into the causes of autism. In such cases, much care should likewise be taken in arriving at conclusions about whether a treatment caused a particular result or outcome. However, many supposed studies concerned with treatment are not of the correlational type. Instead, they purport to be of a scientific nature, designed to demonstrate cause (particular treatment) and effect (improvement in an area or areas of functioning).

It is recommended that one examine, at every level of a study, the assumptions, procedural elements, and supposed relationships. While no study is perfect, in the end the question becomes: "Did the study do a convincing job of demonstrating that the treatment was responsible for the change, and that it was not other factors (alternative hypotheses) that were responsible for the effect?" It is not enough to show a positive outcome. Any report of individuals making progress is deserving of notice; however, for there to be benefits to the field of autism treatment, it is necessary for a study of convincing evidence as to what was and was not responsible for those effects. That is the only way we can learn how to obtain those same positive effects for other individuals.

To be able to have confidence in a researcher's claim requires rigor in the methods of how the research was conducted. To determine the level of rigor, one can examine the following elements and considerations: participant characteristics and how they are selected; targets that are considered and how meaningful and valid they are; measures used and what in fact they measure; how data is collected and how objective or subjective it is; the soundness of experimental designs that are utilized in an attempt to show what is responsible for effects and to control for alternative variables; which results are reported (or excluded) and how honestly they are presented and depicted; and whether discussions seem to accurately reflect data obtained, avoid rampant speculation, and openly address the study's flaws and limitations. Each of these elements reduces the chances that other factors are responsible for the effects and help us rule out alternative hypotheses.

Confidence can also be increased by examining both how the researcher handled his main hypothesis and how seriously alternative hypotheses were considered. There are also signs to watch for that would indicate a researcher is going beyond what his data actually show. These signs include:

- Positions with strong agendas, and which arise from political "movements"

- Positions that substitute correlation for causation

- Positions that are too single factor oriented and which outright dismiss the possibility that multiple factors could be operating

- Analyses which do not show adequate examination of alternative hypotheses or provide no explanation why a particular factor was singled out

- High drama/National Enquirer type hypothesis and/or substitution of emphasis on hypothesis for demonstration of a strong and consistent relationship

- A "house of cards" built upon assumption after assumption, often individually weak and highly tentative

- The "oft repeated lie" which has never been substantiated and derives its credibility merely from having been repeated often

- Substitution of attack on alternative hypotheses for established strength of relationship

- Attack on the character of proponents of a competing hypothesis, rather than evaluation of the hypothesis itself.

As we said before, no study is perfect. But the stronger and sounder the above elements are, the more confidence we can have in a study's findings. Replication of a study and its effects only adds to our confidence (Sidman, 1960). While publication in a peer review journal may add to our comfort, it offers no guarantee of soundness. Some journals are more rigorous than others, while some that show experimental rigor may lack clinical relevancy. One should bring a critical eye, thorough analysis, and good consumerism to every study one encounters, no matter how promising or intuitively resonant the findings. There is just too much riding on our treatment decisions not to do so.

REFERENCES

Allgood, N. (2005). Parents' perceptions of family-based group music therapy for children with autism spectrum disorder. *Music Therapy Perspectives* 23(2): 92-99.

Bernard-Optiz, V., Ing, S., & Kong, T. Y. (2004). Comparisons of behavioural and natural play interventions for young children with autism. *Autism* 8(3): 319-333.

Bondy, A., & Frost, L. (2001). The picture exchange communication system. *Behavior Modification* 25(5): 725-744.

Bondy, A., & Frost, L. (2002). *A picture's worth: PECS and other visual communication strategies in autism.* Bethesda, MD, Woodbine House.

Bondy, A., Tincani, M., & Frost, L. (2004). Multiply controlled verbal operants: An analysis and extension to the Picture Exchange Communication System. *Behavior Analyst* 27(2): 247-261.

Bondy, A. S., & Frost, L. A. (1993). Mands across the water: A report on the application of the Picture Exchange-Communication System in Peru. *Behavior Analyst* 16(1): 123-128.

Bondy, A. S., & Frost, L. A. (1994). The picture exchange communication system. *Focus on Autistic Behavior* 9(3): 1-19.

Cafiero, J. (1998). Communication power for individuals with Autism. *Focus on Autism and Other Developmental Disabilities* 13(2): 113-121.

Campbell, D.T., Stanley, J.C., & Gage, N.L. (1963). *Experimental and quasi-experimental designs for research.* Boston, MA, Houghton, Milfflin and Company.

Carr, E. G., Kologinsky, E., & Leff-Simon, S. (1987). Acquisition of sign language by autistic children: III. Generalized descriptive phrases. *Journal of Autism and Developmental Disorders* 17(2): 217-229.

Cermak, S. A., & Mitchell, T. W. (2006). Sensory Integration. In *Treatment of language disorders in children.* R. J. McCauley, & Fey, M. E. Baltimore, MD, Paul H Brookes: 435-469.

Charlop-Christy, M. H., Carpenter, M., Le, L., LeBlanc, L. A., & Kellet, K. (2002). Using the picture exchange communication system (PECS) with children with autism: Assessment of PECS Acquisition, speech, social-communicative behavior, and problem behavior. *Journal of Applied Behavior Analysis* 35(3): 213-231.

Charlop-Christy, M. H., Carpenter, M. H. (2000). Modified Incidental Teaching sessions; A procedure for parents to increase spontaneous speech in their children with autism. *Journal of Positive Behavioral Interventions* 2(2): 98-112.

Crozier, S., Tincani, M. J. (2005). Using a modified social story to decrease disruptive behavior of a child with autism. *Focus on Autism and Other Developmental Disabilities* 20(3): 150-157.

Delano, M., & Snell, M. E. (2006). The effects of social stories on the social engagement of children with autism. *Journal of Positive Behavioral Interventions* 8(1): 29-42.

Duker, P. C., Wells, K., Seys, D., Rensen, H. (1991). Brief report: Effects of fenfluramine on communicative, stereotypic, and inappropriate behavior of autistic type mentally handicapped individuals. *Journal of Autism and Developmental Disorders* 21(3): 355-363.

DuVerglas, G., Banks, S. R., Guyer, K. E. (1989). Clinical effects of fenfluramine on children with autism: A review of the research. *Annual Progress in child psychiatry and child development:* 471-482.

Gharani, N., Benayed, R., Mancuso, V., Brzustowicz, L. M., & Milloning, J. H. (2004). Association of the homeobox transcription factor, ENGRAILED 2, 3, with autism spectrum disorder. *Molecular Psychiatry* 9(5): 474-484.

Greenspan, S. I., & Wieder, S. (2000). A developmental approach to difficulties in relating and communicating in autism spectrum disorders and related syndromes. *Autism Spectrum Disorders: a Transactional Developmental Perspective.* A. M. Wetherby, & Prizant, B. M. Baltimore, MD, Paul H Brookes Publishing: 279-306.

Greenspan, S. I., & Wieder, S., & Simmons, R. (1998). *The child with special needs: Encouraging intellectual and emotional growth.* Reading, MA, Addison-Wesley/Addison Wesley Longman.

Gutstein, S. E., & Sheely, R. K. (2002). *Relationship Developmental Intervention with Young Children: Social and Emotional Development Activities for Asperger Syndrome, Autism, Pdd, and nlD.* Philadelphia, PA, Jessica Kingsley Publishers.

Handen, B. L., Hofkosh, D. (2005). Secretin in children with autistic disorder: A double blind, placebo-controlled trial. *Journal of Developmental and Physical Disabilities* 17(2): 95-106.

Haring, T. G., Neetz, J. A., Lovinger, L., Peck, C., et-al. (1987). Effects of four modified incidental teaching procedures to create opportunities for communication. *Journal of the Association for Persons with Severe Handicaps* 12(3): 218-226.

Hart, D. (2005). Writing and developing Social Stories. *Education Psychology in Practice* 21(1): 79-80.

Hedges, D., & Burchfield, C. (2005). The placebo effect and its implications. *Journal of Mind and Behavior* 26(3): 161-180.

Jacobson, J. W., Foxx, R. M., & Mulick, J. A. *Controversial Therapies for Developmental Disabilities: Fad, Fashion, and Science in Professional Practice.* J. W. Jacobson, Foxx, R. M., & Mulick, J. A. Mahwah, M. J. Lawrence Erlbaum Associates: 363-383.

Jayachandra, S. (2005). Is Secretin effective in treatment for autism spectrum disorder (ASD)? *International Journal of Psychiatry in Medicine* 35(1): 99-101.

Josefi, O., & Ryan, V. (2004). Non-directive play therapy for young children with autism: A case study. *Clinical Child Psychology and Psychiatry* 9(4): 533-551.

Kane, A., Luiselli, J. K., Dearborn, S., & Young, N. (2004-2005). Wearing a weighted vest as intervention for children with autism/pervasive developmental disorder: Behavioral assessment of stereotypy and attention to task. *Scientific Review of Mental Health Practice* 3(2): 19-24.

Kaplan, R. S., & Steele, A. L. (2005). An analysis of Music Therapy program goals and outcomes for clients with diagnoses on the Autism Spectrum. *Journal of Music Therapy* 42(1): 2-19.

Koegel, R. L., O'Dell, M. C., & Koegel, L. K. (1987). A Natural Language teaching paradigm for nonverbal autistic children. *Journal of Autism and Developmental Disorders* 17(2): 187-200.

Kozloff, M. A. (2005). Fads in general education: Fad, fraud, and folly. *Controversial Therapies for Developmental Disabilities: Fad, fashion, and science in professional practice.* J. W. Jacobson, Foxx, R. M., & Mulick, J. A. Mahwah, NJ, Lawrence Erlbaum Associates: 159-173.

Kroeger, K. A., & Nelson, W. M. III. (2006). A language programme to increase the verbal production of a child dually diagnosed with Down Syndrome and autism. *Journal of Intellectual Disability Research* 50(2): 101-108.

Landreth, G. L., Sweeny, D. S., Ray, D. C., Homeyer, L. E., & Glover, G. J. (2005). *Play therapy interventions with children problems: Case studies with DSM-IV-TR.* Lanham, MD, Jason Aroson.

Laski, K. E., Charlop-Marjorie, H., & Schreibman, L. (1988). Training parents to use the natural language paradigm to increase their autistic children's speech. *Journal of Applied Behavior Analysis* 21(4): 391-400.

LeBlanc, L. A., Esch, J., Sidener, T. M., Firth, A. M. (2006). Behavioral language interventions for children with Autism: Comparing Applied Verbal Behavior and Naturalistic Approaches. *Analysis of Verbal Behavior* 22: 49-60.

Leibowitz, G. (1991). Organic and Biophysical theories of behavior. *Journal of Developmental and Physical Disabilities* 3(3): 201-243.

Leventhal, B. L., Cook, E. H., Morford, M. R., et-al. (1993). Clinical and neurochemical effects of fenfluramine in children with autism. *Journal of Neuropsychiatry and Clinical Neurosciences* 5(3): 307-315.

Levy, S. E., & Hyman, S. L. (2005). Novel treatments for Autistic Spectrum Disorders. *Mental Retardation and Development Disabilities Research Reviews* 11(2): 131-142.

MacDuff, G. S. Krantz, P. J., MacDuff, M. A., & McClannahan, L. E. (1988). Providing Incidental teaching for autistic children: A rapid training procedure for therapists. *Education and Treatment of Children* 11(3): 205-217.

Martineau, J., Barthelemy, C., Rouz, S., Garreau, B., & LeLord, G. (1989). Electrophysiological effects of fenfluramine or combined vitamin B-Sub 6 and magnesium on children with autistic behavior. *Developmental Medicine and Child Neurology* 31(6): 721-727.

Maurice, Catherine (1999). "ABA and us: One parent's reflections on partnership and persuasion." Address to Cambridge Center for Behavioral Studies Annual Board Meeting, Palm Beach, Florida, November, 1999.

McGee, G. G., Krantz, P. J., & McClannahan, L. E. (1985). The facilitative effects of incidental teaching on preposition use by autistic children. *Journal of Applied Behavior Analysis* 18(1): 17-31.

McGee, G. G., Krantz, P. J., & McClannahan, L. E. (1986). An extension of incidental teaching procedures to reading instruction for autistic children. *Journal of Applied Behavior Analysis* 19(2): 147-157.

McGee, G. G., Krantz, P. J., Mason, D., & McClannahan, L. E. (1983). A modified incidental teaching procedure for autistic youth: Acquisition and generalization of receptive object labels. *Journal of Applied Behavior Analysis* 16(3): 329-338.

McGee, G. G., Morrier-Michael, J., & Daly, T. (1999). An incidental teaching approach to early intervention with autism. *Journal of the Association for Persons with Severe Handicaps* 24(3): 133-146.

Mesibov, G. B. (1995). Facilitated Communication: A warning for pediatric psychologist. *Journal of Pediatric Psychology* 20(1): 127-130.

Mesibov, G. B. (1997). Formal and informal measures on the effectiveness of the TEACCH programme. *Autism* 1(1): 25-35.

Mesibov, G. B., Shea, V., & Schopler, E. (2005). *The TEACCH Approach to Autism Spectrum Disorder*. New York, NY, Springer Science & Business Media.

Miranda-Linne, F., & Melin, L. (1992). Acquisition, generalization, and spontaneous use of color adjectives: A comparison of incidental teaching and traditional discrete trial procedures for children with autism. *Research in Developmental Disabilities* 13(3): 192-210.

Miranda, P. (2003). Toward a functional augmentative and alternative communication for students with autism: Manual signs, graphic symbols, and voice output communication aids. *Language, Speech, and Hearing Services in Schools* 34(3): 203-216.

Murphy, C., Barnes-Holmes, D., Barnes-Holmes, Y. (2005). Derived manding in children with autism: Synthesizing Skinner's verbal behavior with relational frame theory. *Journal of Applied Behavior Analysis* 38(4): 445-462.

Nichols, S. L., Hupp, S. D., Jewell, J. D., Zeigler, C. S. (2005). Review of Social Story interventions for children diagnosed with autism spectrum disorders. *Journal of Evidence Based Practices for Schools* 6(1): 90-120.

Normand, M. P., & Knoll, M. L. (2006). The effects of a stimulus-stimulus paring procedure on the unprompted vocalizations of a young child diagnosed with autism. *Analysis of Verbal Behavior* 22: 81-85.

Paczynski, M. (1997). A novel therapy for autism? *Journal of Autism and Developmental Disorders* 27(5): 628-630.

Pierce, K., & Schriebman, L. (1997). Multiple peer use of pivotal response training social behavior of classmates with autism: Results from trained and untrained peers. *Journal of Applied Behavior Analysis* 30(1): 157-160.

Rogers, S. J. (2005). Play Interventions for young children with Autism Spectrum Disorders. In *Empirically Based Play Interventions for Children.* L. A. Reddy, Files-Hall, T. M., & Schaefer, C. E. Washington DC, American Psychological Association: 215-239.

Rose, M., & Torgerson, N. G. (1994). A behavioral approach to vision and autism. *Journal of Optometric Vision Development* 25(4): 269-275.

Rimland, B. (1993). "Beware The Advozealots: Mindless Good Intentions Injure the Handicapped." *Autism Research and Review International* 7(4): pg. 3

Rust, J., & Smith, A. (2006). How should the effectiveness of social stories to modify the behaviour of children on the autistic spectrum be tested? Lessons from the literature. *Autism* 10(2): 125-138.

Scahill, L., & Martin, A. (2005). Psychopharmacology. In *Handbook of autism and pervasive developmental disorders: Assessment, interventions, and policy.* F. R. Schopler, E., Mesibov, G. B., & Hearsey, K. (1995). Structured teaching in the TEACCH system. In *Learning and cognition in Autism.* E. Schopler, & Mesibov, G. New York, NY, Plenum Press: 243-268.

Schreibman, L., & Koegel, R. L. (1996). Fostering self-management: Parent-delivered pivotal response training for children with autistic disorder. In *Psychological Treatments for Child and Adolescent Disorders: Empirically Based Strategies for Clinical Practice.* E. D. Hibbs, & Jensen, P. S. Washington DC, American Psychological Association: 525-552.

Schreibman, L., Stahmer, A. C., Pierce, K. L. (1996). Alternative applications of pivotal response training: Teaching symbolic play and social interaction skills. In *Positive Behavioral Support: Including People with Difficult Behavior in the Community.* L. K. Koegel, Koegel, R. L., & Dunlap, G. Baltimore, MD, Paul H Brookes Publishing: 353-371.

Sidman, M. (1960). *Tactics of scientific research.* Oxford, England, Basic Books.

Stahmer (1999). Using Pivotal response training to facilitate appropriate play in children with autistic spectrum disorders. *Child Language Teaching and Therapy* 15(1): 29-40.

Stahmer, A. C. (1995). Teaching symbolic play skills to children with autism using pivotal response training. *Journal of Autism and Developmental Disorders* 25(2): 123-141.

Strong, G., & Winter, E. C. (2006). Teaching Children with autism and related spectrum disorders: An art and a science. *Child Care in Practice* 12(2): 185-187.

Sundberg, M., & Michael, J. (2001). The benefits of Skinners analysis of verbal behavior to teach mands for information. *Behavior Modification* 25(5): 698-724.

Sundberg, M., Loeb, M., Hale, L., & Eigenheer, P. (2001-2002). Contriving establishing operations to teach mands for information. *Analysis of Verbal Behavior* 18(15-29).

Tincani, M. (2004). Comparing the Picture Communication System and Sign Language Training for Children with Autism. *Focus on Autism and Other Developmental Disabilities* 19(3): 152-163.

Tincani, M., Grozier, S., & Alazetta, L. (2006). The Picture Exchange Communication System: Effects on Manding and Speech Development for School-Aged Children with Autism. *Education and Training in Developmental Disabilities* 41 (2): 177-184.

Varley, C. K. & Holm, V. A. (1990). A two-year follow-up of autistic children treated with fenfluramine. *Journal of the American Academy of Child and Adolescent Psychiatry* 29(1): 137-140.

Volkmar, F., Paul, R., Klin, A., & Cohen, D. Hoboken, NJ, John Wiley & Sons, Inc. 2: 1102-1117.

Whipple, J. (2004). Music Intervention for children and adolescents with Autism: A meta-analysis. *Journal of Music Therapy* 41(2): 90-106.

Wieder, S., & Greenspan, S. I. (2003). Climbing the symbolic ladder in the DIR model through floor time/interactive play. *Autism* 7(4): 425-435.

Yodel, P., & Stone, W. L. (2006). Randomized comparison of two communication interventions for preschoolers with Autism Spectrum Disorders. *Journal of Consulting and Clinical Psychology* 74(3): 426-435.

Chapter 8

COMPARING TREATMENT APPROACHES

By Ron Leaf, Mitch Taubman & John McEachin

If one were to search the internet for information about ASD, one would find literally hundreds of treatments touted as highly effective. Some even guarantee cures. While some "treatments" may appear laughable, the situation in fact is tragic, as those who are desperate may waste their valuable resources and emotion as well as their child's time in the hopes that something will work. Many other so-called treatments seem plausible. Especially, with convincing and passionate appeals and just a hint of pseudo-research.

It is essential to scrutinize the various treatments and inquire whether there is scientific evidence supporting their claims of effectiveness. One must be a careful consumer. In *Chapter 6: Alternative Treatments For Autism Spectrum Disorders: What is Science?*, we presented a list of treatment approaches that have been used with ASD. It is a long list and certainly not complete, but there are a few that have been widely adopted that require closer examination to determine whether indeed they deserve the presumption of benefit that has been accorded them. We feel that the adoption of a treatment approach must be based on a truly informed decision. In this chapter we will examine again briefly ABA, as well as Floor Time, Sensory Integration, TEACCH, and Relationship Development Intervention (RDI).

LIMITED COMPARATIVE ANALYSIS

Research that actually compares different approaches, in a head-to-head manner, is extremely limited. Sound, long term comparative outcome studies of separate treatment programs for individuals with ASD are extremely difficult to conduct. Such studies would require (along with other design elements) random assignment of ultimately comparable participants to complete treatment programs, conducted by true proponents of the separate approaches. Ethically and practically such efforts would be next to impossible to carry out.

More common are studies which settle for comparative examination of the differing procedures (typically targeting specific problem areas) of two or more approaches. Such studies have been conducted, for instance, to examine differing prompt strategies and teaching approaches (Gast, Ault, Wolery, Doyle, & Belanger, 1988; Leaf, McFadden, Tyrell, Sheldon, & Sherman, 2007; Soluaga, Leaf, Taubman, & McEachin, (2008); Tekin & Kircaali-Iftar, 2002). However, the studies are often conducted (and both procedures are performed) by supporters of only one of the procedures. It is no surprise that findings are favorable toward the author's preferred intervention.

It is important to note, however, that it is not always necessary to carry out such a comparative analysis in order to conclude that one approach is superior to another. For example, if an approach demonstrates long term effectiveness utilizing sound scientific methodology and another approach cannot provide such evidence then it would be valid to render a conclusion. In this chapter we will examine some approaches in widespread use within school systems to assist in choosing a treatment that can be expected to provide meaningful educational benefit.

ABA

Two studies from the 1960's gave an early hint about how ABA would compare with other approaches and show that the concept of procedural comparative analysis is not new. Lovaas, Freitag, Gold and Kassorla (1965) and Lovaas and Simmons (1969) conducted comparisons between ABA and psychoanalysis in the treatment of self-injurious behavior (SIB). The data revealed that children's self-injury increased when providing children "positive regard". The psychological treatment was ineffective but by contrast ABA procedures resulted in the elimination of SIB.

The 1987 outcome study conducted by Lovaas (discussed in detail in Chapter 2) could be considered close to long term, comparative program analyses. In that study, Lovaas uti-

GROUP 1	GROUP 2	GROUP 3
Intensive ABA only	Traditional Special Education, Speech Therapy, Occupational Therapy and limited ABA	Traditional eclectic range of services provided through School Districts

lized a comparison of three groups:

The data showed that the Group 1 (ABA only) outcome was significantly better than the other two groups which received a broad range of services.

Another programmatic comparison type of study was conducted by Eikeseth, Smith, Jahr and Eldevick (2002). They compared an intensive ABA approach versus an "eclectic" approach. They defined eclectic as incorporating Project TEACCH (Schopler, Lansing & Waters, 1983), sensory-motor therapies (Ayers, 1972) and ABA. The results suggested that children made larger gains utilizing a purely ABA approach. However, these articles must be interpreted with much caution. Although in some ways they represent the closest to comparative analyses that exist in the current literature, their limitations, and the potential for bias, reduce what conclusions we can draw and assume about head to head, comparative effectiveness.

There have been some other notable efforts to make legitimate comparisons: New York State Department of Health Early Intervention Clinical Practice Guideline Report of Recommendations, 1999; A Report of The American Surgeon General, (Department of Health and Human Services, 1999); Committee on Educational Interventions For Children With Autism: National Research Council, 2001. All three have indicated that ABA is "best practice". The American Surgeon General reported:

1. ABA was effective in reducing disruptive behaviors & increasing learning, communication and appropriate social behavior

2. Follow-up of comprehensive ABA intervention found that nearly half of the experimental group, but almost none of the children in the matched control group were able to participate in regular schooling

Additionally, the New York State Department of Health Report showed no evidence to support the efficacy of a number of commonly used methodologies including Floor Time, Secretin, Diets, and Sensory Integration.

Smith (1999) conducted a review of 12 published, peer-reviewed autism outcome studies in which early intervention was provided to children with ASD. The following demonstrates the IQ gains of participants in the articles reviewed:

	IQ GAINS
Lovaas (intensive treatment group)	22 - 31
Other ABA Investigations	7 - 28
Denver Model (Play School Model)	4 - 9
TEACCH	3 - 7

It was impossible for Smith to conduct a comparative analysis since there was tremendous variation in age of clients, age at onset of treatment, diagnostic criteria, length of treatment as well as evaluation measures. Nevertheless, it is relatively clear that Behavior Intervention (ABA) resulted in the best outcomes. It is also worth noting that the intervention described by Lovaas occurred substantially longer than the other behavioral treatments. As discussed previously, there are also other factors (e.g., punishment, double therapy, parent expertise, exposure to appropriate peer models, young age of children) which may also account for the differing outcomes.

Finally, the two most commonly cited reports purporting to be comparative reviews—Dawson & Osterling (1997) and Prizant & Rubin (1999)—are seriously flawed in their conclusion favoring an eclectic approach to treatment of ASD (see Chapter 5 Eclecticism). A few points which deserve to be mentioned here are:

- Although they struggle to convince us that all the approaches they examined have some degree of credibility, they actually concede that the most scientifically sound research methodology was that utilized by Lovaas and his colleagues

- Eight of the 10 approaches employed ABA strategies, which was a central feature of the Lovaas intervention program. (The authors gloss over the fact that Lovaas used ABA far more intensively than any of the other approaches.)

- The Lovaas research had the most extensive follow-up

- The Lovaas research also has the best documented effectiveness

FLOOR TIME

Floor Time has its philosophical foundation in psychoanalytic theory. According to the theory, the root of autism is the parents' inability to connect meaningfully with their children. This is a throwback to Bettleheim (1967), during a period when ASD was not well understood. Current research clearly indicates that ASD has an organic basis rather than psychological (Mesibov, Adams & Schopler, 2000). It is interesting to note that Floor Time was originally developed with a totally different population and was extended to autism without any empirical validation.

Because of its psychoanalytic foundation, it is recommended that the bulk of intervention be provided by the child's primary caregivers, so as to develop the necessary and missing bond (Greespan & Wieder, 2000). Additional intervention may be provided by individuals available to provide consistent instruction and relationship building. The approach itself does not provide a curriculum or systematic teaching goals by which to develop the students' potential. Again, this is a product of its basic philosophy that once the student can interact and communicate in a meaningful, connected way they will be able to learn from the environment. Further, again coming from the psychoanalytic perspective, Floor Time sees therapy as art as much as science. Therefore the intervention can be difficult to replicate and depends greatly upon unspecified clinical process.

There is no scientific evidence to support the efficacy of Floor Time. The one study that Greenspan and Wieder (1997) conducted has fatal methodological flaws. Although Greenspan reported almost identical results to Lovaas, the criteria used were never specified. Therefore, one has absolutely no idea what was considered as "best outcome." By comparison in the Lovaas study, this category was operationally defined in terms of IQ, class placement and clinical symptoms.

The second fatal methodological flaw of the investigation was that the individual who categorized the children was Greenspan's colleague. In other words, there was no effort to ensure unbiased measurement.

The third problem with the study was that evaluations were based upon retrospective chart review. This involves looking back at case records after treatment has been completed. In other words, an actual evaluation was never conducted. Among the problems with chart reviews is that what is measured (e.g. IQ, social skills, behavioral performance) is not set ahead of time (before treatment starts). In legitimate outcome studies such decisions are always made in advance and treatment then succeeds or fails based on those pre-determined criteria of success. In chart reviews, what is measured is determined at the time. It is very easy for bias to creep in. That is, what looks good in the files is reported and what does not look so good is left out. Who is included and what is included in the review is often based purely on what makes the approach look favorable.

Fourth, it was not a scientifically controlled study because there was not any degree of random assignment to the treatment condition. There is no way of knowing if the children in the comparison group had the same characteristics as those who received Floor Time. They may be comparing apples and oranges.

Fifth, the study was not peer reviewed. Moreover, the study appeared in Dr. Greenspan's self-made journal. This "study" is a prime example of poor methodology and design and pseudo-research.

If one were to accept Greenspan's study on face value one would conclude that it is quite an effective approach. However, when critically analyzed it becomes extremely difficult to draw any conclusions. The American Surgeon General (2000) did not recognize Floor Time as effective and the New York State Department of Health Early Intervention Clinical Practice Guideline Report of Recommendations (1999) likewise reported that there was not any evidence to document its effectiveness. One has to wonder how Dawson and Osterling (1997) concluded Floor Time was equally effective as ABA.

We certainly concur with Greenspan's position that it is critical to work on social and conversational skills in the most natural context possible. Good ABA programs have adhered to this philosophy well before Greenspan started working with children with ASD. However, it may also be necessary for these skills to be developed in a more artificial context. There are children for whom it is necessary to work in a more structured environment in order to receive the concentrated practice that helps build fluency. As fluency progresses, the structure can be systematically faded and the child can successfully transition to the demands of a natural learning context. Intervention must be individualized to best meet the unique needs of the student.

Besides the philosophical foundation differences, there exist some other significant differences between ABA and Floor Time. These differences would result in very different treatment strategies. Whereas someone utilizing Floor Time would accept self-stimulation and perhaps even reinforce it, ABA interventionists would not sanction the behavior. And whereas a Floor Time therapist would loathe "intruding" upon the child, a behaviorist would do everything possible to disrupt self-stimulatory behaviors because of their detrimental effects. It would be virtually impossible to utilize both procedures as they were intended to be implemented and in a manner that maintains their respective theoretical roots. They are in direct conflict and their combined implementation would not only be confusing to the child but would operate at cross purposes and potentially render each other ineffective.

SENSORY INTEGRATION

Sensory Integration (SI) is an approach which the majority of children with ASD in the U.S. receive. Many people are surprised to learn there is virtually no empirical data to support the theory or the effectiveness of SI treatment. The theory, as well as procedures, are based on speculation at best and run contrary to ABA.

For example, what is a common recommendation made by a SI therapist when a child has tantrums? The typical strategy is to apply deep pressure, whether through joint compression, brushing or a weighted vest (Kane, Luiselli, Dearborn, & Young, 2004). Indeed, the child typically does stop crying. This, of course, reinforces the belief that the "deep pressure" helped the child integrate sensory input. However, as discussed in the chapter on Critical Thinking, there could be a number of different reasons why the child may have stopped crying (e.g., received attention, task avoidance, distraction, etc.) Moreover, since children often enjoy being massaged, like a great many adults and "typically developing" children, the deep pressure may have only served to reinforce the tantrum.

The following are other areas where the theoretical roots and procedure collide:

SENSORY INTEGRATION	ABA
Sensory Diets are Essential	Sensory Diets can be Harmful
Child "needs" to Self Stimulate	Child "likes" to Self Stimulate
Often used when student is agitated	Use stress Management prior to Agitation

The "sensory" issues and responses to sensory input displayed by children with ASD are not very different from those without ASD. It is not surprising that children with ASD like deep pressure. So do all the people who are willing to spend a great deal of money on massages. And who would not enjoy settling down under a nice heavy comforter?

These common sensory preferences can be explained by "learning theory". From an early age, through associations (i.e., Pavlovian Conditioning), "deep pressure" is associated with other pleasant events, such as eating and being nurtured by parents and being safe. Similarly, it is not surprising that children enjoy lights, spinning, trampolines and swings. Once again so do most children and adults. Such products are readily available at most stores and not because they are being carried to cater to children with ASD. Obviously, the extent to which such sensory oriented behaviors may be pursued by children with ASD, and the degree to which they interfere with learning and appropriate responding can be highly problematic. However, there is to date no evidence that underlying sensory malfunctions are somehow central causes of autistic functioning.

In general, much of what Sensory Integrationists report as validating their theory can be accounted for by a behavioral interpretation. The difference, however, is that procedures based upon ABA have extensive research demonstrating the effectiveness. Whereas, there are virtually no scientific investigations reported in peer-reviewed journals that demonstrate the effectiveness of SI. While some studies exist, they once again contain fatal methodological flaws which greatly inhibit any supportive interpretation. Furthermore, research on the underling theory of SI, arousal theory, has long been shown not to be accurate *(Cummins, 1991; Gresham, Beebe-Frankenburger & MacMillan, 1999; Hoehn & Baumeister, 1994; Shaw, Powers, Albelkop & Mullis, 2002).*

In a stinging review of SI, Steven Shaw (2002) wrote:

"There is no evidence that SI therapy is or has ever been an effective treatment for children with learning disabilities, autism, or any other developmental disability. This is not one of those common cases where there is not enough information upon which to effectively evaluate the treatment. In fact, there are plenty of quality outcome studies (41 as of this writing). There is no study that uses a quality research design (e.g., random assignment of subjects, match control groups, consideration of the effects of maturation, evaluators blind to treatment conditions) that finds SI therapy to be effective in reducing any problem behaviors or increasing any desired behaviors. There is plenty of evidence from which a verdict can be drawn. And the verdict is that, despite the intuitive appeal and glowing testimonials, SI therapy is not an effective treatment." (Page 2)

But certainly most children enjoy SI. SI does have appeal for many children. Who would not want to play with great toys? And most SI interventionists know how to interact in fun and engaging ways. But fun does not in any way assure therapeutic benefit.

NONSENSE
FUNDING AGENCIES SUPPORT SENSORY INTEGRATION, YET THEY WILL NOT FUND ABA BECAUSE IT IS "INEFFECTIVE" AND "EXPERIMENTAL"

TEACCH: TREATMENT AND EDUCATION OF AUTISTIC AND RELATED COMMUNICATION-HANDICAPPED CHILDREN

TEACCH, developed by Dr. Eric Schopler, is a cradle-to-grave support system based on the assumption that the major deficits in autism are lifelong disabilities (Mesibov, Shea, & Schopler, 2005; Schopler, 2001). A central aspect of TEACCH is making environmental accommodations (Mesibov, et.al., 2005). Classrooms are organized to limit distractions and provide students with clear visual cues about routines. There is an emphasis on schedules, work systems, and using visual materials.

Although ABA and TEACCH are both behaviorally based, they are founded upon a fundamentally different premise. TEACCH is based upon the hypothesis that one must make accommodations for a child with ASD (Mesibov, et.al., 2005; Schopler 2001). Whereas, ABA is based upon the premise that through intervention the child needs to learn how to accommodate the environment. Although accommodations may need to be made, it is not automatic and only considered as a last resort.

The differing premises are largely based upon different views of the disorder. TEACCH is thought of as a "cradle to grave" approach. Although TEACCH personnel certainly believe children with ASD can make progress, it appears they also believe the vast majority of students with ASD will remain significantly impaired. Therefore it follows that, according to TEACCH philosophy, accommodations should be made and maintained throughout the students' lifetimes. ABA has a different view of the disorder. ABA believes that ASD does not necessarily need to be a life long disorder. Naturally, this is based upon a number of factors, including the age of the child at the onset of intervention, the quality and intensity of intervention, and the child's cognitive ability. Regardless of these factors, it is our view that students are extremely capable with most being able to function well and in a quality manner without gross accommodations needing to be made.

Since TEACCH is based upon the premise that a person most likely will always be quite impaired, their objectives are much more modest. Staying busy and perhaps becoming prepared to live in a group home and working in a sheltered workshop might be the objectives. Therefore, TEACCH is often implemented in arrangements by which students are independently kept busy while working on seemingly meaningless tasks. We have too ofter observed students learning to complete a task as quickly as possible in order to proceed to the next meaningless task. This does not provide an opportunity to learn appropriate concepts or meaningful skills in depth.

Further, ABA and TEACCH tend to define independence differently. Independence from a TEACCH perspective means completing tasks free from human contact (Schopler, 2001). The task completion may involve many structural assists (e.g., schedules and materials that guide performance), but no human assists. Within an ABA framework, independence means performance of skills without any undue assists—material, structural, or whatever—and may involve much appropriate social contact with others in the performance of those behaviors.

TEACCH certainly has a great deal to offer. The utilization of visual procedures and tasks to keep students occupied can be an important adjunct to ABA programming. ABA, however, utilizes visual strategies when it best meets the needs of a student. Often, there is a myth that ABA only uses auditory strategies. Certainly, it is our goal that a student can process information auditorily. But when a child is unable to do so, then naturally visual strategies would be employed. However, an objective would be to use visual strategies to help a student become an auditory processor. It should also be noted, that although children with ASD may prefer visual strategies, there is a significant number of children in which auditory is the preferred input. Moreover, it is critical that students can eventually process information utilizing both input modalities. We believe with effective intervention most children can learn to process information auditorily.

There are also similarities between TEACCH and ABA. They are both behavioral and therefore utilize contingencies to reinforce appropriate behaviors as well as correct disruptive responses. Both approaches utilize systematic teaching strategies. And both believe in collecting data.

However, because of the difference in philosophical underpinnings and goals, like ABA and SI, there can again be a colliding of approaches between ABA and TEACCH.

RELATIONSHIP DEVELOPMENT INTERVENTION (RDI)

RDI, developed by Dr. Steven Gutstein, is a relatively recent approach in the arena of autism treatment. RDI proposes that the core deficit in autism involves shared experience (Gutstein & Sheely, 2002). In includes many appealing activities designed to facilitate shared experience, and therefore relationship development. "Outcome" research is reported which claims RDI provides dramatic effects positively impacting not only relationship issues, but autism in an overall sense, with gross reduction of autistic symptoms. This pseudo-research once again involves retrospective chart reviews and is fraught with all the incumbent biases of selectivity of subjects, measures chosen, comparisons made, and areas focused upon. Most problematic are the breadth of the claims made (e.g., that this approach is for all individuals with autism, and that overall effectiveness has been demonstrated).

While the appealing exercises of RDI could certainly be incorporated into an ABA program focusing on advanced social skills and social relatedness areas, it would never serve as a simple substitute, as claimed, for the breadth of focus (e.g., on language, play, social, self help, cognitive areas, etc.) essential in autism treatment, nor the extent of comprehensive work necessary to produce positive results.

WHAT IS NEXT?

Surely it is likely that a new treatment will soon appear on the horizon, including attractive components, offering seemingly logical explanations for the causes of autism, and offering evidence for the dramatic results of the approach. In fact, we would be greatly surprised if this did not occur. Our advice to critically examine such claims should not be taken to mean that we do not endorse the pursuit of further understanding of the causes and treatment of autistic disorder. In fact it is our fervent hope that careful research will continue to advance the causes of prevention, treatment, and cure of autism. However, we cannot over-emphasize what is a critical responsibility for professionals and parents alike. And that is to differentiate, despite the sometimes obscuring effects of hope and desire, between the quick, simple, easy and alluring offerings that are constantly appearing on the scene, and the treatments and information that arise from careful, comprehensive, sound, and responsible professional efforts.

REFERENCES

Ayers, A.J. (1972). *Sensory integration and learning disorders.* Los Angeles: Western Psychological Services.

Bettleheim, B. (1967). *The Empty Fortress.* New York, The Free Press.

Cummins, R.A. (1991) Sensory integration and learning disabilities: Ayres' factor analysis reappraised. *Journal of Learning Disabilities, 24,* 160-168.

Dawson, G. & Osterling, J. (1997). "Early intervention in autism: Effectiveness and common elements of current approaches." In Guralnick (Ed.) *The effectiveness of early intervention: Second generation research.* (pp. 307-326) Baltimore: Brookes

Department of Health and Human Services (1999). Mental Health: A Report of the Surgeon General. Rockville, MD: Department of Health and Human Services, Substance Abuse and Mental Health Services Administration, Center for Mental Health Services, National Institute of Mental Health.

Eikeseth, S., Smith, T., Jahr, E., & Eldevik. S. (2002). "Intensive behavioral treatment at school for 4 to 7-year-old children with autism: A 1 year comparison controlled study." *Behavior Modification* **26**(1): 49-68.

Gast, D. L., Ault, M. J., Wolery, M., Doyle, P. M., & Belanger, S. (1988). Comparison of constant time delay and the system of least prompts in teaching sight word reading to students with moderate retardation. *Education and Training in Mental Retardation, 23,* 117-128.

Greenspan, S. and Wieder, S. (1997). Developmental Patterns and Outcomes in Infants and Children with Disorders in Relating and Communicating: A Chart Review of 200 Cases of Children with Autistic Spectrum Diagnoses. Journal of Developmental and Learning Disorders **1**(1) 87-141

Greenspan, S. I., & Wieder, S. (2000). A developmental approach to difficulties in relating and communicating in autism spectrum disorders and related syndromes. *Autism spectrum disorders: A transactional developmental perspective.* A. M. Wetherby, & Prizant, B.M. Baltimore, MD, Paul H Brookes Publishing: 279-306.

Gutstein, S. E., & Sheely, R.K. (2002). *Relationship Developmental Intervention with young children: Social and emotional development activities for Asperger Syndrome, autism, PDD, and NLD.* Philadelphia, PA, Jessica Kingsley Publishers.

Kane, A., Luiselli, J.K., Dearborn, S., & Young, N. (2004-2005). "Wearing a Weighted Vest as Intervention for Children with Autism/Pervasive Developmental Disorder: Behavioral Assessment of Stereotypy and Attention to Task." *Scientific Review of Mental Health Practice* 3(2): 19-24.

Leaf, J.B., Tyrell, A., McFadden, B., Sheldon, J.,. & Sherman, J.A. (2007) Comparison of Simultaneous Prompting and No-No-Prompt for teaching two-choice discrimination to three children diagnosed with autism. Paper presented at the meeting of the Association of Behavior Analysis, San Diego, CA.

Lovaas, O. I., Freitag, G., Gold, V. J., & Kassorla, I. C. (1965). Experimental studies in childhood schizophrenia: Analysis of self-destructive behavior. *Journal of Experimental Child Psychology, 2*(1), 67-84

Lovaas, O. I., & Simmons, J. Q. (1969) Manipulation of self-destruction in three retarded children. *Journal of Applied Behavior Analysis, 2*(3), 143-157

Lovaas, O.I. (1987). Behavioral Treatment and normal educational and intellectual functioning in young autistic children. *Journal of Clinical and Consulting Psychology,* **55**(1) 3-9.

Mesibov, G. B., Adams, L. W., Schopler, E. (2000). Autism: A brief History. *Psychoanalytic Inquiry,* 20, 637-647

Mesibov, G. B., Shea, V., & Schopler, E. (2005). *The TEACCH approach to autism spectrum disorder.* New York, NY, Springer Science + Business Media.

New York State Department of Health. (1999). *Clinical practice guideline: Report of the recommendations autism/pervasive developmental disorders. Assessment and intervention for young children (ages 0-3)*. Albany: Author.

Prizant, B. & Rubin, E. (1999). "Contemporary Issues in Interventions for Autism Spectrum Disorders: A Commentary." *Journal of the Association for Persons with Severe Handicaps.* **24**(3): 199-208.

Schopler, E. (2001). Treatment for autism: From science to pseudo-science or anti-science. *The research basis for autism intervention.* E. Schopler, Yirmiya, N., & Shulman, C. New York, NY, Kluwer Academic/Plenum Publishers: 9-24.

Schopler, E., Lansing, J. & Waters, L. (1983). *Individualized assessment and treatment for autistic and developmentally disabled children: Vol. 3. Teaching activities for autistic children.* Austin: TX: Pro-Ed.

Shaw, S.R. (2002). A school psychologist investigates sensory integration therapies: promise, possibility, and the art of placebo. National Association of School Psychologist Newsletter, October, 1-7.

Shaw, S.R., Powers, N.R., Abelkop, S., & Mullis, J. (2002). Sensory integration therapy: Panacea, placebo, or poison? Paper presented to the annual convention of the National Association of School Psychologists, Chicago, IL.

Smith, T. (1999). Outcome of early intervention for children with autism. *Clinical Psychology: Science and Practice, 6,* 33-49.

Soluaga, D., Leaf, J. B., Taubman, M. T., McEachin, J. J. (2005) A Comparison of Constant Time Delay Versus a Lovaas-Type Flexible Prompt Fading Procedure. Paper presented at the meeting of the <u>Association for Behavior Analysis, 2005 Annual Convention</u>, Chicago, IL.

Soulaga, D., Leaf, J.B., Taubman, M., McEachin, J, Leaf, R.B. (2008) A comparison of Constant Time Delay vs. a Lovaas-type Flexible Prompt Fading procedure. *Research in Autism Spectrum Disorders* (In Press).

Tekin, E., & Kircaali, I.G. (2002). Comparison of the effectiveness and efficiency of two response prompting procedures delivered by sibling tutors. *Education and Training in Mental Retardation and Developmental Disabilities* 37(3): 283-299.

Chapter 9

HOME VS. SCHOOL: WHICH SIDE ARE YOU ON?

By Ron Leaf

Professionals who have devoted their careers to the field of Autistic Spectrum Disorder (ASD), be it in diagnosis, etiology or treatment often have strong opinions, which unfortunately can be quite contradictory. Even those with the same philosophical belief system, such as ABA, often have incredibly diverse opinions. These disagreements often become highly contentious. It becomes a turf and ideological war. If you don't agree with my perspective then you are the enemy. If you support a parent then you must be an adversary of schools. If you support a school then you don't care about children.

Why is this? Is it possible that every situation is different and therefore the advice that fits for one student may not be the correct advice for other students? Is it possible that sometimes parents are mistaken and the correct path is something different than what a parent is asking for? If you do not agree with the parent, does that mean you are anti-parent? We know it is possible for school districts to be incorrect. If we challenge their recommendation does that mean we are anti-school?

Maybe it is not a matter of sides. We are convinced that in the majority of situations everyone truly does care about the child. Therefore we should all be on the same side. It's just a matter of different perspectives and beliefs. Getting into this turf war only intensifies an already complicated situation. We are often pigeonholed as either being "pro-parent" or "pro-school." When we advocate that a child should receive intervention at home, school districts will brand us as being "pro-parent" which they equate with "anti-school". Conversely, when we recommend that a child receive intervention at school, parents stigmatize us as "pro-school" and thus "anti-parent". We do not believe we are either anti-parent or anti-school. Putting everyone into one of these two camps creates an absurd dichotomy. Forcing people to choose sides limits options. It should not be about being on the school's or parent's side, but rather being on the child's side. Hopefully we are all "pro-child".

We must all strive to do what is in the best interest of the child and provide the program that will help him or her achieve the highest quality of life. Sometimes this may mean that a child receives services exclusively at home; sometimes it may be appropriate that intervention occurs solely at school. Often, however, a student with ASD needs services in both settings.

We think pigeonholing is extremely divisive and dangerous. It does not serve parents or schools, or most importantly, children. We must all work in collaboration to best serve the needs of children. "Autism Partnership" is the name we chose for our agency because of our conviction that working collaboratively with everyone involved in the treatment of an individual is vital to treatment success and the quality of life for all. Unfortunately, all too often such collaboration does not occur.

In a meeting with one school district, we were actually admonished for "advocating" for a child! Although everyone, **including district personnel**, agreed the services we recommended were necessary, we were branded as being adversarial because we were advocating for services that cost more than the district was used to paying. We had to remind them that everyone should be advocating for the child. Unfortunately, this is not an isolated incident. We recently received a letter from a director of Special Education who criticized us for "advocating for the family" which actually meant the child. Although everyone may have different perspectives and opinions on what would be beneficial, decisions should be based upon the child's needs and not parent or district biases or prejudices.

In another meeting, a parent pronounced that we had "sold out" because it was our opinion that it would be beneficial for her child to attend school for a small portion of the day. Applied Behavior Analysis (ABA) in schools? It is heresy! Do we not know that ABA should not occur in schools? They are the enemy! Intervention must occur exclusively at home! And if ABA has to occur in school, then it should only be after years of intervention exclusively at home and then it should be for minimal periods of time. Grudgingly, it might be possible to increase a little bit over several years.

Resistance to ABA intervention in schools is often based upon unsubstantiated opinions promoted at conferences, on the Internet, in non-research articles, misinterpretation of research and mostly folklore.

FOLKLORE

The seminal research conducted by Dr. Ivar Lovaas at UCLA is often used as the basis for using the home as the location where children receive ABA intervention (Lovaas, 1987; McEachin, Smith and Lovaas, 1993). The research is often interpreted as not supporting intervention at school. Although there may have been certain prejudices against the utilization of special education service during that era, we can say definitively there was great willingness to have the children receive education in school. We base this assertion both on the published research as well as our own direct experience as clinicians on the UCLA Young Autism Project.

One of the primary objectives of the UCLA program was to integrate children into school as soon as possible. Once children's disruptive behaviors were at manageable levels and they possessed good attending skills they were enrolled in preschools. This often occurred within the first year of intervention and sometimes even within months of the onset of treatment. But there was not a fixed time line. The timing of entry into preschool was based upon the individual needs and abilities of the child.

Although the research at UCLA is often used as justification to keep children out of school, the research is actually evidence for the importance of intervention at school. This may not be obvious from the published report because it was not particularly emphasized. However, the statement in Lovaas (1987) that,

"intervention occurred at home, in the community and at school" (page 5)

means exactly what is says: Home was not the only place where intervention occurred.

Because of our experiences at UCLA, we have found it quite surprising when our work with schools has been seen as controversial and sometimes even viewed as "anti-ABA." In reality we were taught to embrace schools as a critical component of treatment. However, for intervention in schools to be effective, district personnel must receive comprehensive and ongoing training in ABA intervention (Petursdottir & Sigurdarodttir, 2006; Smith, Parker, Taubman, & Lovaas, 1992; Smith, 2001). Much of the content of this and our other book (Leaf, Taubman, & McEachin, 2008) is aimed at promoting the availability of quality ABA in school settings. And one of the themes we will repeatedly emphasize is schools and parents must work in partnerships.

AUTISM PARTNERSHIP'S POSITION

The overall goal of intervention is to increase children's level of functioning so that they can enjoy the greatest degree of independence possible. We fully believe that the children whom we serve will only benefit from treatment if there is collaboration and consistency among all persons involved. We further believe that it is imperative that partnerships be created among all interested parties including parents, schools and any other professionals working with these children. Only then can we be assured of a coordinated effort toward helping each child to improve his or her quality of life and achieve an increased level of overall independence.

SENSE
EVEN THE BEST SCHOOL PROGRAM DOES NOT REPLACE INTERVENTION AT HOME *similarly* EVEN THE BEST HOME PROGRAM DOES NOT REPLACE INTERVENTION AT SCHOOL

It is important to understand that the benefits of an exemplary home program do not negate the need for group learning experience. Similarly, the best classroom placement does not obviate the need for intervention at home and in community settings. Comprehensive intervention requires the collaboration and integration of efforts among all individuals working with and involved in a child's life.

The goal is that children should receive intervention in the most natural and least restrictive setting possible. For children under the age of three, this would mean that the preponderance of treatment should occur in the home. Naturally, some teaching intervention would occur in the community as well (e.g., the park, a "Mommy and Me" class, McDonald's, grandparents' home, etc.).

There are circumstances, however, when school placement would not be appropriate. For example, if a child presents with severe or high rates of behavior problems such as aggression, screaming, self-stimulation, severe and persistent noncompliance or inattention, then school may not yet be an appropriate option. Additionally, children need to possess basic skills such as responding to instructions, understanding contingencies and learning from prompts and feedback. It would also be important for students to have some preparation in being able to learn in distracting environments before entering a group learning situation.

Moreover, a child should be old enough for school to make sense. Sometimes, school programs are set up for a 3-year-old to attend six hours a day, five days a week. This is not a very natural way to structure a young child's day. In our view this would actually constitute a restrictive placement.

It is best if a child's learning can be spread throughout the day and incorporate the natural rhythm of the alternation between activity and rest, and still enable them to receive several hours of intensive intervention. For example, if a child requires a nap, we want to accommodate this without reducing the amount of instruction that occurs in a day. Often this can best be accomplished within a home-based program. Another factor that may indicate home intervention as being the best alternative is if a child has a significant medical condition or other special needs that can best be met in a comfortable, familiar, "homey" environment.

The educational placement should be provided in the least restrictive setting that will enable the child to make the greatest long term gains. There is a continuum of educational placement options available and therefore it is essential to carefully evaluate which placement best serves the needs of the individual child. There are advantages and disadvantages with each potential setting and a number of factors that must be considered in making a determination. It is not necessary to automatically begin in a restrictive placement. Similarly, the team should not automatically rule out a noninclusive placement. There are times when a more restrictive setting will best meet the child's needs and will enable the child to eventually attain a higher level of independence.

All too often, placement decisions are made as though they are black or white: Either a highly restrictive setting or full inclusion. However, there is a full continuum of options that should be considered in order to best meet the needs of children.

CLASSROOM CONTINUUM

□	□	□	□	□	□
Home Bound	Self Contained	Reverse Mainstreaming	Degrees of Mainstreaming	Degrees of Inclusion	Independence

The team should consider what is projected to provide the best opportunity to rapidly advance skills in as many domains as possible. Once in a placement, there needs to be continuous evaluation to determine the earliest opportunity to successfully advance toward a less restrictive and more "typical" placement, without sacrificing the child's rate of progress. Moreover, it is not always necessary that a child move only one level at a time. For example, with outstanding progress and the right circumstances, a child could move directly from a self-contained classroom placement to full-inclusion. It is also important not to set an arbitrary time line (e.g., yearly at the IEP) for considering advancement. Sometimes the additional challenge, more stimulating environment, presence of typical peers, or increased availability of meaningful reinforcers, will enable a child to immediately be more successful in a more inclusive (although more challenging) setting. This may be true even when the child's adjustment has not been completely satisfactory in the current (less challenging and more restrictive) setting.

We often encounter tremendous resistance to children receiving ABA services in schools from parents as well as the educational community. Getting acceptance from both sides can be extremely difficult. Parents often do not see the value of their young ASD child attending school. There is often a realistic concern that agreeing to any amount of classroom time is the first step toward unraveling home-based intervention. This fear stems from mistrust. Sometimes this is based on the school not being able to provide quality education. Sometimes it is based on a misunderstanding of how school placement fits into an intensive ABA program.

Similarly, schools are often skeptical of how ABA would fit into a classroom and are mistrustful of those who advocate for this method. The skepticism is often based upon misunderstanding of the research or their negative experiences with attempts at implementing ABA. For parents and schools to work in a partnership to ensure that children receive an appropriate and meaningful education, it is important they understand the positive role schools can play in making ABA accessible to the largest number of children as well as understanding and addressing the resistance on the part of both parents and schools.

REFERENCES

Lovaas, O.I. (1987). Behavioral Treatment and normal educational and intellectual functioning in young autistic children. *Journal of Clinical and Consulting Psychology,* **55**(1), 3-9.

Leaf, R., Taubman, M., McEachin, J. (2008). *It's Time for School. Building Quality ABA Educational Programs for Children with Autism Spectrum Disorders.* NY: DRL Books

McEachin, J.J., Smith, T., & Lovaas, O.I. (1993). Long-Term outcome for children with autism who received early intensive behavioral treatment. *American Journal on Mental Retardation,* **97**(4), 359-372.

Petursdottir, A.L., & Sigurdarodttir, Z.G. (2006). Increasing the skills of children with Developmental disabilities through staff training in behavioral teaching techniques. *Education and Training in Developmental Disabilities,* **41**(3), 264-279.

Smith, T. (2001). Discrete trial training in treatment of autism. *Focus on Autism and Other Developmental Disabilities,* **16**(2), 86-92.

Smith, T., Parker, T., Taubman, M., Lovaas, I.O. (1992). Transfer of staff training from Workshop to group homes: A failure to generalize across settings. *Research in Developmental Disabilities. Special Issue: Community-based treatment programs: Some Problems and Promises,* **13**(1), 57-71.

Chapter 10

PARENTAL RESISTANCE

By Ron Leaf, John McEachin & Doris Soluaga Murtha

Since the advent of early intensive behavioral treatment, many families have come to associate meaningful progress with home-based intervention. The movement toward home as the location of services was spurred on by research such as Lovaas (1987) which demonstrated impressive outcomes from an intervention which eschewed the traditional approach to education. In many ways, home-based early intervention was a reaction against what parents perceived as inadequate programming within the school system.

Parents have every reason to be skeptical of having their child attend school. All too often, from their first exposure to professionals, parents have been given misinformation regarding issues such as diagnosis, treatment and prognosis. When parents encounter the educational system, their skepticism is often not alleviated due to lack of clear information and unconvincing plans for education. Concern about appropriate placement, teachers' skill level and educational priorities tend not to be taken seriously and parents feel forced into an adversarial position. Moreover, parents have often been told by trusted advocates that home is the optimal educational environment and therefore, attending school should be viewed with extreme caution. And when parents are told that their child is not entitled to the best education (that is, all the schools are required to provide adequate services), the natural response is anger and frustration. Resistance is understandable.

Historically, schools have not provided effective education for children with ASD. Even using the less than optimal (i.e., adequate) standard, schools have fallen short of providing meaningful educational benefit. Nevertheless, we are not willing to give up on the system, as we see definite advantages for children attending school. Just like the educational system needs to understand the benefits of home intervention, parents similarly need to recognize the potential advantages of school.

"READINESS" MODEL

The Readiness Model attempts to identify the necessary criteria for a student to be successful in a given type of placement. A child is only promoted to a less restrictive placement when it has been demonstrated that he is fully proficient in all the areas that are regarded as prerequisite skills. The intention is to only put a child in a new learning situation when there is a high level of confidence that he is developmentally ready to progress to a higher level of challenge. Unfortunately, the result of strict adherence to such a model is that students may be held back in a more restrictive level of placement longer than is necessary. This model has been promoted by some ABA providers and when parents adopt the model, they tend to cling to home-based provision even when it makes sense to begin transitioning to school.

Sometimes, professionals and parents insist on a time line. For example, a common rule of thumb is that the child must complete two years of home-based therapy before school placement is even considered. Sometimes the criterion for entering school is mastery of a myriad of skills. Although we concur that certain skills are essential, often a child is able to benefit from a school placement long before skill mastery is attained in multiple areas. Adherents to the Readiness Model generally do not come right out and say they are anti-school. There is often some reluctant acknowledgment that in the future it will be OK to spend at least some time at school. However, until a child is completely "ready," placement is not considered. Unfortunately, a student may indefinitely be deemed "not ready" for school placement.

Clearly, children will be ready to participate in school at different stages of intervention. Therefore it is important to consider behaviors and skills which are absolutely essential to have in place prior to entering a classroom. Obviously, some level of behavioral control is necessary. Children will not be successful if they exhibit severe and frequent disruptive behaviors. Such behaviors would not only be dangerous to other children but would greatly interfere with a child's availability for learning. Furthermore, disruptive behaviors may stigmatize the child and therefore reduce the social benefit that school can offer.

This does not mean that children's disruptive behaviors must be completely eliminated before they can participate in a school placement. Research has demonstrated that behavioral problems can be managed effectively in a group setting (Barrish, Saunder, & Wolf, 1969; Harris & Sherman, 1973; Taubman, Brierley, Wishner, Baker, McEachin, & Leaf, 2001).

In some cases, behavioral problems can be more effectively reduced in a group instructional format than is possible in 1:1. For example, disruptive behaviors that are attention seeking in function can be more readily ignored in a group setting where a teacher's attention can turn to other students in the class that are behaving appropriately. It is more difficult to ignore disruptive behaviors in a one-to-one format when one's mere presence can have a reinforcing effect on the behavior one is trying to extinguish.

Additionally, it is necessary that children demonstrate some basic abilities to learn in the school environment. For example, they need to be able to tolerate and process information in a moderately noisy and distracting environment. However, it is not necessary for attending skills to be perfect or that students be able to learn in group situations prior to beginning the classroom experience. It is also not necessary for a child to have extensive language or social skills to begin a school program. These are all skills that can be systematically developed at the same time you are working on school-related skills like finding your cubby-hole, waiting in line, reciting the pledge of allegiance, etc. A home intervention program needs to target the skills necessary to develop a child's ability to learn in ordinary environments and not be dependent on specially tailored settings that minimize the level of distraction.

NONSENSE
Those who are most vocal in insisting that intervention should occur exclusively at home, also insist, just as vehemently, on inclusion when children finally start attending school. They start out preaching a readiness model, but then jump to the completely opposite model. They argue for inclusion on the basis of Least Restrictive placement, but overlook the fact that being relegated to receiving education at home is even farther away from the mainstream than being placed in a setting which would allow specialized educational programming.

SENSE
There are intermediate steps that may better facilitate later success in a less restrictive setting. Being open to all options will allow selecting a plan which may ultimately result in a higher level of competence and more freedom and success in mainstream settings.

PRIORITY

All too often the predominant objective of ABA intervention is the acquisition of speech and academic skills. Social skills and behavior flexibility are not seen as priorities and not areas that are addressed in a systematic and comprehensive manner. It is often thought that social skills will emerge on their own merely through the process of exposure. The term socialization is taken to mean simply being in the vicinity of other children. Frequently, schools are not seen as the best environment for children to acquire these skills. The value of school is seen mainly as the place to get social exposure and this is viewed as a goal to be addressed further along in a child's program. School is not recognized for the opportunities it affords to make meaningful progress in academics and generalization of behavioral progress.

This perspective is quite unfortunate. First, it is important that a child's social deficits be addressed early in the treatment process. It should never be the case that social skills are placed on the "back burner." It is through the early acquisition of social skills that children develop the ability to advance socially on their own. The longer one waits, the wider the gap and the harder it is to move a child away from self-centeredness. Additionally, younger peers are often more accepting of playing with children diagnosed with ASD than later in the school experience and, therefore, can be very facilitative.

Another reason for early social exposure is that opportunities for building fluency in language are often enhanced through being around other children. Children's rate of acquisition is increased and their speech becomes more natural as a result of the additional practice provided through peer interactions.

Other advantages of early placement in school include opportunity for friendships, facilitation of natural language, and learning through social contingencies. Peer approval can become a meaningful motivator. When children become concerned about their peers, we can fade adult support and artificial contingencies.

Furthermore, school can provide children with numerous opportunities to develop skills in various learning domains (Leaf & Mountjoy, 2008). Besides academics, language, and social skills there are observational learning and group learning skills, self-help skills, independent work skills, recreational skills, and navigational skills that promote independence and integration.

BELIEF THAT SCHOOL PERSONNEL ARE INCAPABLE OF PROVIDING EFFECTIVE EDUCATION

There is no doubt that children's education has suffered because school personnel lacked proper training. It is understandable that parents might adopt the view that school personnel are incapable of providing effective education. But, it is not automatically the case that moving to home-based programs has resulted in superior education for children with ASD. In either case, effective intervention requires staff training to teach children to make meaningful progress in a variety of settings. We definitely do not think parents should give up on schools. Just as in home-based programs, with training, consultation and support we have witnessed school personnel providing exemplary education.

Classroom teachers possess many of the prerequisites which facilitate their becoming skilled ABA interventionists. First, teachers have made a professional commitment to teaching children. Second, teachers have learned many of the skills that are critical in providing effective intervention. For example, teachers have knowledge and experience in implementing academic curricula and understand experiential and hands-on teaching approaches. Finally, teachers have understanding of child development and the knowledge of which skills are to be developmentally expected at what age. These are all skill areas which can make a valuable contribution to an ABA program.

Although most teachers may not have received formal training in ABA, many of them do indeed utilize the principles of ABA even without knowing that it is ABA. Good teachers, coaches and instructors break skills into smaller parts (i.e., task analysis), work on a specific skill until it is learned (i.e., mastery), assist students as is necessary (i.e., prompting), provide multiple opportunities to practice (i.e., massed trials) and make learning fun and exciting (i.e., they are engaging and reinforcing). Because these concepts are familiar to them, they can readily identify with ABA. When they receive formal training, they can advance their skills by coming to understand the learning process in greater depth. Familiarity with the theory that underlies ABA helps them to understand why familiar teaching procedures work the way they do and helps a teacher to become more systematic. It also gives teachers effective ways to monitor students' progress through objective data collection and make ongoing programmatic refinements as needed.

BELIEF THAT CHILDREN CANNOT LEARN IN GROUPS

One-to-one instruction is the primary teaching format that Autism Partnership utilizes in the early stages of intervention. As discussed previously, it is important to move as quickly as possible toward more natural instructional formats, such as group instruction. Naturally, a degree of one-to-one may always be necessary. For example, even some college students who are having difficulty in a particular area may require individual tutoring. Adults often benefit from direct instruction as well. Private golf, dance or computer lessons may be far more effective than group instruction.

However, when it is possible to learn in a group, there are multiple benefits. Besides being more natural, learning in a group setting can be more efficient. Also, students' observational learning skills and awareness are greatly enhanced through such instruction. Since they become responsible for paying attention, even when the teacher is not directly interacting with them, they become better able to learn incidentally outside of formal instruction. Children have the opportunity to observe contingencies their peers receive, which can help their learning of appropriate behaviors. Learning while surrounded by peers helps pave the way for tolerance, interest, and interaction with peers outside of class time.

For those who need further convincing, there is extensive literature showing the efficacy of group instruction and observational learning for teaching typically developing children (Jahr & Eldevik, 2002). Additionally, there are numerous research studies demonstrating successful group learning for children with ASD (Kamps, Walker, Maher, & Rotholz, 1992; Kamps, Walker, Locke, Delquadri, & Hall, 1990; Polloway, Cronin & Patton, 1986; Handleman, Harris, Kristoff, Fuentes, & Alessandri, 1991; Schoen & Ogden, 1995; Shelton, Gast, Wolery, & Winterling, 1991).

UNDERSTANDING THE TEACHER'S PERSPECTIVE

All too often, educators' integrity and motives have been questioned. Moreover, their skills have been scrutinized and challenged. Even though they have chosen an admirable career, they are often not treated as respected professionals. If they don't possess the skills necessary to educate children with ASD, it is not out of lack of caring or wanting to do their best. Like parents, teachers have to endure a continuous onslaught of contradictory and mistaken information. On an ongoing basis, they are told they must employ a plethora of educational techniques, often with tremendous hype but not a shred of research demonstrating effectiveness.

Educators' resistance to new techniques is certainly understandable. After all, why should they believe that ABA is any different than the vast array of other procedures they have been told will produce astonishing results? And all too often, the hype surrounding ABA is not much different than any other educational strategy. Moreover, it is extremely labor intensive and overwhelming when there are many students with their own IEP's and demands. Unfortunately, teachers have received limited training in ASD or ABA. They have been indoctrinated with the belief that ASD is a very serious and life-long disorder and parents with high expectations are just in denial about the severity of their child's condition and are being completely unrealistic. Therefore, when they meet an overbearing advocate, their knee jerk reaction is one of resistance.

Teachers need the opportunity to participate in training in order to help them understand the foundations of effective education. More importantly, they need to receive ongoing training and support to help them practically employ ABA educational strategies. And we need to be sensitive to the plight of teachers and understand their resistance.

Teachers' and administrators' expectations need to be raised. It will be essential for educators to recognize the enormous capabilities of students with ASD, and that their students' outcomes will be greatly improved through their openness and willingness to employ a systematic educational approach. And, although they will surely encounter ABA fanatics (similar to zealots of other disciplines), they should not categorically reject ABA.

REFERENCES

Barrish, H.H., Saunder, M., & Wolf, M.M. (1969). Good behavior game: Effects of individual Contingencies for group consequence on disruptive behavior in a classroom. *Journal of Applied Behavior Analysis*, 2(2), 119-124.

Handleman, J.S., Harris, S.L., Kristoff, B., Fuentes, F., & Alessandri, M. (1991). A specialized program for preschool children with autism. *Language, Speech and Hearing Services in Schools, 22*, 107-110.

Harris, V.W., & Sherman, J.A. (1973). Use and analysis of the "good behavior game" to Reduce disruptive classroom behavior. *Journal of Applied Behavior Analysis, 6(3)* 405-417.

Jahr, E., & Eldevki, S. (2002). Teaching cooperative play to typical children utilizing a Behavior modeling approach: A systematic replication. *Behavioral Interventions*, 17(3), 145-157

Kamps, D.M., Walker, D., Locke, P., Delquadri, J., & Hall, R.V., (1990). A comparison of instructional arrangements for children with autism served in a public school setting. *Education and Treatment of Children, 13*, 197-215.

Kamps, D.M., Walker, D., Maher, J., & Rotholz, D. (1992). Academic and environmental effects of small group arrangements in classrooms for students with autism and other developmental disabilities. *Journal of Autism and Developmental Disorder, 22*, 277-293.

Leaf, R.B., & Mountjoy, T. (2008). Advantages of School Settings. In Leaf, R.B., Taubman, M, & McEachin, J.J. (Eds.) *It's Time For School: Building Quality ABA Educational Programs.* New York, NY: DRL Books, (2008).

Lovaas, O.I. (1987). Behavioral Treatment and normal educational and intellectual functioning in young autistic children. *Journal of Clinical and Consulting Psychology, 55*(1), 3-9.

Polloway, E.A., Cronin, M.E., & Patton, J.R. (1986). The efficacy of group versus one-to-one instruction: A review. *Remedial and Special Education, 7*, 22-30.

Schoen, S.F., & Odgen, S. (1995). Impact of time delay, observational learning, and attentional cuing upon word recognition during integrated small-group instruction. *Journal of Autism and Developmental Disorders, 25*, 503-519.

Schreibman, L., & Koegel, R.L. (1982). Multiple-cue responding in autistic children. . *Advances in Child Behavioral Analysis & Therapy, 2, 81-99.*

Shelton, B.S.,, Gast, D.L., Wolery, M., & Winterling, V. (1991). The role of small group instruction in facilitating observational and incidental learning. *Language, Speech and Hearing Services in Schools, 22*, 123-133.

Taubman, M., Brierley, S., Wishner, J., Baker, D., McEachin, J., & Leaf, R.B. (2001). The Effectivness of a group discrete trial instructional approach for preschoolers with Developmental disabilities. *Research in Developmental Disabilities, 22*(3), 205-219.

Tingstrom, D.H., Sterling-Turner, H.E., & Wilczynski, S.M. (2006). The good behavior game . *Behavior Modification, 30*(2), 225-253.

Chapter 11

EDUCATIONAL RESISTANCE

By Ron Leaf, John McEachin & Doris Soluaga Murtha

As resistant as parents may be to the notion of Applied Behavior Analysis (ABA) in schools, school districts often are equally resistant. There are a number of reasons why districts seem to reject the notion of ABA in classrooms:

1. They believe in their approach and have received training in other methods that they feel are effective.

2. They have a negative view based upon practices from the early days of ABA.

3. They have been fed a heavy dose of misinformation from prejudiced professionals and even received distorted information from ABA practitioners who are poorly qualified.

4. They view ASD as a life-long condition and therefore believe changing their educational practices will not make a difference.

Such reasons may not be directly stated. More often we hear rationales such as the following:

"WE ARE PREPARED!"

In the past, school personnel often had an extremely limited understanding about ASD. Often there existed a very pessimistic view of children's potential. The school day was often comprised of relatively meaningless tasks, with the sole purpose of keeping students occupied and therefore out of trouble. If educational programs occurred, a "traditional model" of education was primarily followed whereby children received a watered down version of the traditional curriculum.

Districts today often state that they are well versed in educating students with ASD. Although they may not utilize ABA, they contend that they are successful with their students. All too often as long as a child is not aggressive and maintains skills that they have acquired, they are pleased with the *status quo* and do not see any reason to change. Often, administrators and teachers have a definition of "meaningful" progress that is rather meager. [See **Chapter 14**, Meaningful Progress]

Even those teachers who attempt to utilize ABA instructional techniques often lack the training that is necessary to produce meaningful results. Their implementation of ABA is often incomplete and lacks the level of individualization necessary to make it an effective approach. Often they have attended limited trainings on ABA. Moreover, training may be conducted by someone who does not possess experience, let alone expertise, in ABA as it is applied to children with disabilities.

"WE'LL TAKE THE ONE-DAY PACKAGE"

We received a call from a school district requesting a one-day training for their teachers. When the director of Special Education was told the consultation fee, she was delighted. When asked why she was so happy, she responded that by only having to pay the one day fee, she would save hundreds of thousands of dollars. She went on to explain that their district was facing a number of law suits all of which exceeded $100,000 each. Therefore by participating in the **ONE**-day training, their personnel would be trained, they would be legally defensible and thus save a tremendous amount of money. She actually believed that all it would take was one day of training!

Unfortunately, this is not an isolated experience. We routinely receive calls with such requests. For example, after a week of training, will we "certify" that staff are "trained" in ABA? Can staff become "experts" in ABA after a few weeks of training? These kinds of sentiments seem to reflect a lack of understanding of just how complex ABA can be.

Training in effective teaching methods is analogous to becoming a gourmet chef or police officer, or even flying a jumbo jet. One cannot become an expert with just one day, a week or even a month of training. It takes intensive and comprehensive training with ongoing support to become an effective ABA practitioner. Implementing quality ABA requires not just an understanding of behavioral principles but supervised practice applying such methodology.

After staff have participated in a didactic workshop where they learn the foundations of ABA, often they believe they are prepared to provide ABA in their classes and do not need the hands-on workshop to practice ABA teaching techniques. The irony is that the more training they receive, the more they realize just how complicated it is to provide effective treatment.

The National Research Council (2001) suggested the following:

1.   Training in which participants receive updated information regarding the course of autism and effective educational strategies.

2.   Hands-on opportunities to practice skills.

3.   Ongoing consultation.

4.   Administrative attitudes and support are critical in improving schools.

"ABA IS NOT EFFECTIVE"

The lack of proven effectiveness is often cited as the rationale for not providing ABA. The positive outcomes from the UCLA YAP are viewed as suspect because of supposed methodological flaws. In reality, the claims about flawed methodology have been shown to be largely unfounded (Baer, 1993; Lovaas, Smith & McEachin, 1989). Furthermore, even professionals who have discussed methodological weaknesses have not denied the effectiveness of ABA treatment (Mesibov, 1993). But many educators remain steadfast in their belief that ABA has limited, if any, effectiveness. Often the following arguments will be made:

1. *"There haven't been any replications of the Lovaas research"* In fact there have been a number of partial replication studies:

    Anderson, Avery, DiPietro, Edwards, & Christian, 1987

    Birnbrauer and Leach, 1993

    Sallows & Graupner, 1999

    Sheinkoph and Siegel, 1998

    Smith, Groen and Wynn, 2000

    Cohen, Amerine-Dickens and Smith, 2006

These investigations have demonstrated the effectiveness of the UCLA model. Children made substantial gains in multiple skill areas (e.g., language, IQ, behavior, etc.). However, the results were not as impressive as the original study. This may in large part be due to far fewer hours (i.e., an average of 18-25 hours versus an average of 40 hours); reduced length of treatment and less trained staff. For a more complete discussion on generalization of findings from the UCLA Autism Project, please see **Chapter 2**.

2. *"There aren't any comprehensive studies demonstrating the effectiveness of ABA."* In fact there are a number of studies that have demonstrated the effectiveness of ABA across multiple children:

> Fenske, Zalenski Krantz and McClannahan, 1985.
>
> Handleman, Harris, Celeberti, Lilleht and Tomcheck, 1991
>
> Harris, Handleman, Gordon, Kristoff and Fuentes, 1991
>
> Harris, Handleman, Kristoff, Bass and Gordon, 1990
>
> Hoyson, Jamieson and Strain, 1984
>
> Koegel, Koegel, Shoshan and McNerney, 1998
>
> McGee, Daly and Jacobs, 1994

3. *"The evidence that ABA is effective is somewhat limited and has not withstood the test of time."* DeMyer, Hingtgen and Jackson (1981) identified over 200 studies conducted between 1970 to 1980 that demonstrated the effectiveness of ABA in the treatment of autism. Matson and his colleagues conducted a comprehensive review of the literature from 1980 to 1996 and identified more than 550 articles in peer reviewed journals that demonstrated the effectiveness of ABA in the treatment of autism (Matson, Bernavidez, Compton, Paclawskyj and Baglio, 1996).

4. *"There aren't any comparative analyses that show ABA to be more effective than any other approach"* There have indeed been a few comparative studies, primarily looking at ABA vs. an eclectic model (Lovaas 1987; Eikeseth, Smith, Jahr and Eldevik, 2002; Howard, Sparkman, Cohen, Green, and Stanislaw, 2005). Although that type of research is not abundant, there have been several large scale reviews of various procedures in an attempt to identify "best practice". Three such reviews have been con-

ducted: New York State Department of Health Early Intervention Clinical Practice Guideline Report of Recommendations, 1999; A Report of The American Surgeon General, 1999; Committee on Educational Interventions For Children With Autism: National Research Council, 2001. While these are not comparative analyses they provide strong support for ABA's effectiveness. And as we have already discussed there is a substantial body of research that demonstrates uniquely favorable outcomes for ABA treatment of ASD.

Perhaps Catherine Maurice (2002) said it best:

"Why is this topic of early intensive behavioral intervention, its value, and its ability to produce recovery in at least some children still "hotly debated" at all? How many more decades will it take for the establishment to accept the evidence that already exists? It is astonishing to me that various special educators and psychologists keep calling for more data to substantiate the value of intensive behavioral intervention and yet they themselves have produced no data to speak of that validate approaches such as play therapy, therapeutic nurseries, special education and psychotherapy. How much more debate do we have to engage in, as generations of autistic children flounder?" (Pages 4-5).

"ABA RESULTS DO NOT HOLD UP OVER TIME"

ABA is often rejected because it is viewed as a teaching strategy with limited long term benefits. The following are typical comments:

1. *"It does not generalize! Sure students may learn skills in specific situations but learning rarely transfers to more natural situations."*

2. *"You can never get rid of reinforcement, one-on-one or artificial teaching."*

3. *"Effectiveness will not last and over time regression will occur."*

4. *"The skills that are learned are robotic."*

Generalization, durability, and natural-looking behavior are largely dependent upon employing quality ABA intervention (Stokes & Baer, 1977). Skilled ABA interventionists recognize that it is critical to employ strategies that facilitate generalization by systematically utilizing a variety of instructions, materials and consequences. They understand that fading procedures is critical to facilitating independence, and that it is essential to work in a variety of natural situations, such as school.

Condemning an approach because of poor application is unjustified. It would be similar to suggesting that bypass surgery is not effective because there is a cardiac surgeon whose patients have done poorly. It is not that ABA is an ineffective method. Outcomes are dependent upon correct implementation and the skill of the practitioner. Being an effective interventionist requires expertise that comes through training, supervised practice and continuing education. As stated previously, there are hundreds of scientific articles that have appeared in peer reviewed journals demonstrating that ABA can produce excellent results with good generalization and enduring outcomes for students of all ages.

"ABA IS OUTDATED"

Over the past 30 years there have been tremendous advances in the field of ABA. There has been both an evolution in philosophy as well as refinement of treatment procedures. These changes have been responsible for substantially improving the quality of life for students with ASD. Individuals who typically faced the plight of spending their entire life in restrictive settings are now better able to enjoy a much higher quality of life. Programs now employ comprehensive behavioral strategies that are based upon positive, practical and proactive approaches. The evolution of the behavioral approach has been instrumental in the successful educational placement of students with ASD in less restrictive educational settings.

"ABA IS DISRESPECTFUL OF STUDENTS"

We often hear people that either do not understand the complexity of ABA or want to discredit it, state that it is like doing dog training with a child. They also see it as being rote in nature and mechanistic in its application. However, we have the greatest respect for the children we are teaching, and it is because of that respect that we are constantly seeking the most effective way to help them learn. Behavioral theory provides us with a road map that enables students to discover the joy of learning and to gain confidence in their ability to figure out how the world works.

"ABA IS EXPERIMENTAL"

Districts will often use the rationale that they will not support ABA because they considered it new and experimental. Furthermore, they will state that there is limited empirical evidence that demonstrates effectiveness. Although the tremendous interest in ABA is somewhat recent, ABA intervention is not a new procedure. Lovaas (1987) and McEachin, Smith and Lovaas (1993) are cited as the only two investigations that show the effectiveness of behavioral intervention with children with ASD. In fact, ABA is based upon more than 50 years of scientific investigation with individuals affected by a wide range of behavioral and developmental disorders. Since the early '60's, extensive research has proved the efficacy of behavioral intervention with children, adolescents and adults with autism.

Research has shown ABA to be effective in reducing disruptive behaviors typically observed in individuals with ASD, such as self-injury, tantrums, noncompliance and self-stimulation. ABA has also been shown to be effective in teaching commonly deficient skills such as complex communication, social, play and self-help skills. More than 30 years ago, Lovaas and his colleagues (Lovaas, Koegel, Simons & Long, 1973) published a comprehensive study demonstrating that intensive ABA could be successful in treating multiple behaviors across multiple children.

Although the work by Lovaas is the most frequently cited, there is other evidence that intensive ABA can result in substantial benefit (e.g., Anderson et. al, 1987; Birnbrauer & Leach, 1993; Fenske et al., 1985; Harris et. al 1991; Hoyson et al., 1984; Maurice, 1993; Perry, Cohen, & DeCarlo, 1995; Sheinkorpf & Siegel, 1998; Smith, 1993; Smith, Eikeseth, Klevstrand & Lovaas, 1997). Harris and Handleman (1994) reviewed several research studies which showed that more than 50% of children with ASD who participated in comprehensive preschool programs using ABA were successfully integrated into non-handicapped classrooms, with many requiring little ongoing treatment.

"ABA IS PUNITIVE"

Individuals continue to have the view that ABA intervention is an aversive approach. This sometimes appears to be based upon people's exposure in undergraduate psychology classes to films and readings from long ago. Although during the early days of treatments aversive procedures were sometimes used, even then the majority of treatment involved utilizing positive reinforcement. In the last fifteen years the vast majority of intervention has solely utilized positive practices. In fact, when we encounter the term "positive behavioral intervention" we often respond "is there any other kind?"

Hopefully in all fields there are evolutions and growth. To condemn a discipline because of the early days is unfair. For example, heart surgery 25 years ago was extremely crude by comparison with what is done today. Luckily, however, pioneers were willing to lay the foundation. We certainly would not condemn today's neurosurgeons because of past times when lobotomies were performed.

Those who continue to view ABA as punitive perhaps have had the unfortunate experience of observing behaviorists who persist in utilizing outdated procedures. Although there continue to be some "professionals" who utilize aversive procedures unnecessarily, the vast majority of professionals utilize only positive behavioral approaches.

"ABA HAS LIMITED AGE RANGE"

Critics of behavioral intervention will state that ABA is only effective with young children. Therefore, it is irrelevant for the vast majority of their students. They often cite Lovaas' research as their evidence. Lovaas's study, however, did not show that ABA is ineffective with older children. It did not even attempt to compare the use of intervention across children of different ages.

It stands to reason that the older a child is at the beginning of treatment, the harder it will be to close the developmental gap. However, there is no evidence to indicate that children older than four who receive intensive ABA intervention cannot achieve successful outcomes. Indeed, there is ample evidence that behavioral intervention can be effective at all ages. We just do not know the limits of what children can achieve at the older end of the range. In fact the majority of research on ABA has been done with older children, adolescents and adults. ABA has been shown to be effective in reducing disruptive behaviors and teaching critical skills to older students. Adolescents and adults have been able to learn communication, self-help, vocational and independent living skills through teaching procedures and intervention strategies based on ABA.

Although we do not know the exact age when achieving the "best outcome" is no longer a possibility, there is possibly a "window of opportunity" for best outcome. No one would argue against the statement that earlier treatment is better for all disorders and conditions. However, it is absurd to utilize this as a rationale not to provide intervention for adolescents and adults. Although the outcomes most likely diminish with age there is convincing evidence that ABA is effective with older populations, just not as effective with younger children (Fenske, Zalenski, Krantz, and McClannahan, 1985).

NOT REJECTION, JUST RESISTANCE

Sometimes schools do not outright reject ABA and only show resistance. Without fully embracing ABA, they see it as being partially effective. Often they will have some of the reservations discussed above, such as it is only useful for certain things, does not generalize or is not a very natural approach, but at least they do not summarily dismiss its utilization.

Often ABA is viewed as an extremely narrow approach. For example, it is all too common a belief that ABA can only be employed in one-on-one situations. Therefore, it may only occur for a limited time of the day in a classroom. Or it is believed that ABA is only effective for teaching basic conversational skills or beginning academic skills. As a result, there is the misconception that ABA is not really helpful for teaching play, social or advanced conversational skills. Sometimes the perspective on ABA is that it is only useful for students who are very impaired. Therefore, ABA is deemed inappropriate for children who are considered to be "higher" functioning.

Because of this perspective schools will often employ ABA in an extremely limited fashion. For example, a student's Individual Education Plan (IEP) will specify that ABA/DTT should be provided for one hour per day. Or the IEP may specify that it is only to occur in a one-to-one teaching format. Or that it is to be utilized only during pull out sessions, so as to reduce distractions. This narrow approach often stems from a misunderstanding of ABA, how it differs from Discrete Trial Teaching and how to most effectively utilize ABA.

A CADILLAC OR A CHEVY

Often school district administrators, as well as lawyers, will limit access to ABA intervention by saying that the law does not require them to provide the "Cadillac" program. In other words, the district is only required to provide an adequate program. There is no legal obligation to provide an optimal educational program.

As one can certainly appreciate, this is reprehensible to parents. Imagine being told that an educational program that may be instrumental in your child living a substantially higher quality of life is not a legal obligation! Differences in program quality may mean the difference of your child eventually going to college, getting married and working independently versus remaining severely involved and living in a restrictive setting. It would evoke the same anger one would feel if a health care provider informed a parent that they are only willing to provide "ordinary" surgery and therefore their child may remain substantially impaired and have a greatly compromised quality of life.

From our perspective, while the "Cadillac" is not required, the "jalopy" is not acceptable either. Besides the moral issues, looking for excuses not to provide effective services is nonsense for a number of reasons:

1. Districts spend a great deal of money in providing a smorgasbord of training. By providing concentrated training in evidence-based approaches they will most likely spend less money and develop more expertise.

2. With proper training and ongoing expert oversight, districts could utlize their existing cadre of paraprofessional staff. What is needed, however, is receptive staff and administrators as well as experienced trainers and supervisors.

3. Providing a superior program, however, could actually result in significant direct and indirect long term savings. For example:

    a. Decreased time spent in meetings with angry parents

    b. Reduced staff turnover. Trained staff work more effectively and efficiently and have greater job satisfaction.

    c. Reduced staff ratios (with training, staff learn how to provide individualized group instruction that is effective)

    d. Other expensive services may be reduced or eliminated

    e. **REDUCED COSTS OF LITIGATION AND SETTLEMENT**

Finally, the dichotomy between ordinary and high quality intervention is often bogus. All too often districts are trying to pass off their broken down jalopy as a serviceable and reliable vehicle. If they actually implemented the basic standards for Free Appropriate Public Education there would be a marked improvement. And it would not take that much more to actually provide a superior program. The difference between the "Cadillac" and "Chevy" is not so much number of hours provided, as it is quality of staff and frequency of supervision. Unfortunately, these are rarely the issues that are argued.

RESOLUTION???

We are convinced that parents and districts have the same goal: for children to be successful. However, there is often a lack of consensus on how to achieve this goal. A great deal of the problems seem to stem from differing information, semantics and poor communication. This can sometimes result in mistrust and an inability to work collaboratively. Common misconceptions of ABA seem to only further interfere with the process. Perhaps resolution can start with a common understanding of ABA.

REFERENCES

Anderson, S.R., Avery, D.L., DiPietro, E.K., Edwards, G.L., & Christian, W.P. (1987). Intensive home-based intervention with autistic children. *Education and Treatment of Children, 10,* 352-366.

Baer, D.M. (1993). Quasi-random assignment can be as convincing as random assignment. *American Journal on mental Retardation,* 97(4), 373-375.

Birnbrauer, J.S., & Leach, D.J. (1993). The Murdoch early intervention program after two years. *Behaviour Change, 10,* 63-74.

Cohen, H., Amerine-Dickens, M., & Smith, T. (2006). Early Intensive Behavioral Treatment: Replication of the UCLA Model in a Community Setting. Journal of Developmental & Behavioral Pediatrics, 27 (2), 145-155.

DeMyer, M. K., Hingtgen, J. N., Jackson, R. K. (1981). Infantile autism reviewed: A decade of research. *Schizophrenia Bulletin,* 7(3), 388-451

Department of Health and Human Services (1999). *Mental Health: A Report of the Surgeon General.* Rockville, MD: Department of Health and Human Services, Substance Abuse and Mental Health Services Administration, Center for Mental Health Services, National Institute of Mental Health.

Eikeseth, S., Smith, T., Jahr, E., & Eldevik. S. (2002). "Intensive behavioral treatment at school for 4 to 7-year-old children with autism: A 1 year comparison controlled study." *Behavior Modification* **26**(1): 49-68.

Fenske, E.C., Zalenski, S., Krantz, P.J., McClannahan, L.E. (1985). Age at intervention and treatment outcome for autistic children in a comprehensive intervention program. *Analysis and Intervention in Developmental Disabilities, 5,* 49-58.

Handleman, J.S., Harris, S.L., Celiberti, D., Lilleht, E., & Tomcheck, L. (1991). Developmental changes of preschool children with autism and normally developing peers. Infant-Toddler Intervention, 1, 137-143.

Handleman, J. S., Harris, S. L. (1984). Can summer vacation be detrimental to learning? An empirical look. *Exceptional Child, 31*(2), 151-157

Harris, S. L., Handleman, J. S., Gordon, R., Kristoff, B., & Fuentes (1991). Changes in cognitive and language functioning of preschool children with autism. *Journal of Autism and Developmental Disorders, 21*(3), 281-290]

Harris, S. L., Handleman, J. S., Kristoff, B., Bass, L. & Gordon (1990). Changes in language development among autistic and peer children in segregated and integrated preschool settings. *Journal of Autism and Developmental Disorders, 20*(1), 23-31

Hoyson, M., Jamieson, B., & Strain, P.S. (1984). Individualized group instruction of normally developing and autistic-like children: The LEAP curriculum model. *Journal of the Division of Early Childhood, 8,* 157-172.

Koegel, L. K., Koegel, R. L., Shoshan, Y., & McNerney, E. (1999). Pivotal response intervention II: Preliminary long-term outcomes data. *Journal of the Association for Persons with Severe Handicaps, 24*(3), 186-198]

Lovaas, O. I., Koegel, R., Simmons, J. Q., & Long, J. S. (1973). Some generalization and follow-up measures on autistic children in behavior therapy. *Journal of Applied Behavior Analysis, 6*(1), 131-166

Lovaas, O. I., Smith, T., & McEachin, J. J. (1989). Clarifying comments on the young autism study: Reply to Schopler, Short, and Mesibov. *Journal of Consulting and Clinical Psychology, 57*(1), 165-167

Lovaas, O.I. (1987). Behavioral Treatment and normal educational and intellectual functioning in young autistic children. Journal of Clinical and Consulting Psychology, 55(1), 3-9.

Matson, J. L., Benavidez, D. A., Compton, L. S., Paclawskyj, T., & Baglio (1996). Behavioral treatment of autistic persons: A review of research from 1980 to the present. *Research in Developmental Disabilities, 17*(6), 433-465

Maurice, C. (2002). Recovery: Debate diminishes opportunity. Association for Science in Autism Treatment Newsletter, Summer, 2002, 1-5.

Maurice, Catherine (1993). *Let me hear your voice.* A family's triumph over autism. NY: Fawcett Columbine.

McEachin, J.J., Smith, T., & Lovaas, O.I. (1993). Long-Term outcome for children with autism who received early intensive behavioral treatment. American Journal on Mental Retardation, 97(4), 359-372.

McGee, G.G., Daly, T. & Jacobs, H.A. (1994). The Walden preschool. In *Preschool Education Programs for Children with Autism,* S.L. Harris and J.S. Handleman (Eds.). Austin, TX: Pro-Ed.

By Mesibov, G. B. (1993). Treatment outcome is encouraging. *American Journal on Mental Retardation, 97*(4), 379-380

National Research Council (2001): *Educating Children with Autism,* Washington, D.C.: National Academy Press.

New York State Department of Health. (1999). *Clinical practice guideline: Report of the recommendations autism/ pervasive developmental disorders. Assessment and intervention for young children (ages 0-3).* Albany: Author.

Perry, R., Cohen, I., & DeCarlo, R. Case study: Deterioration, autism, and recovery in two siblings. *Journal of the American Academy of Child & Adolescent Psychiatry, 34*(2), 232-237

Sallows, G. O. & Graupner, T. D. (2005). Intensive behavioral treatment for children with autism: Four-year outcome and predictors. *American Journal on Mental Retardation, 110*(6), 417-438

Sheinkopf, S., & Siegel, B. (1998). Home based behavioral treatment of young children with autism. *Journal of Autism and Developmental Disorders, 28*(1), 15-23

Smith, T. (1993). Autism. In Giles, Thomas R. (Ed)., *Handbook of effective psychotherapy.* Plenum behavior therapy series. New York, NY, US: Plenum, Vol. xvii: 107-133.

Smith, T., Eikeseth, S., Klevstrand, M., & Lovaas, O. I. (1997). Intensive behavioral treatment for preschoolers with severe mental retardations and pervasive developmental disorder. *American Journal on Mental Retardation, 102*(3), 238-249

Smith, T., Groen., A., & Wynn, J.W. (2000). Randomized Trial of Intensive Early Intervention for Children with Pervasive Developmental Disorder. *American Journal on Mental Retardation, 105,* 269-285

Smith, T. (2001). Discrete trial training in treatment of autism. *Focus on Autism and Other Developmental Disabilities, 16*(2), 86-92.

Smith, T., Parker, T., Taubman, M., Lovaas, I.O. (1992). Transfer of staff training from workshop to group homes: A failure to generalize across settings. *Research in Developmental Disabilities. Special Issue: Community-based treatment programs: Some Problems and Promises, 13*(1), 57-71.

Stokes, T.F., Baer, D.M. (1977). An implicit technology of generalization. *Journal of Applied Behavior Analysis, 10*(2), 349-367.

Thompson, S. S. (1997). Special education service delivery: Perceptions and practices in intervention assistance models and traditional models. *Dissertation Abstracts International Section A: Humanities and Social Sciences, 58*(6-A), 2163

Chapter 12

WHOSE IEP IS IT ANYWAY?

By Andrea Waks

HOW IT WAS MEANT TO BE

The original concept of the IEP was very different than what we often see today. The idea was that the IEP would be developed in a collaborative meeting with parents and teachers. It was supposed to be an informal meeting with a simple discussion of the type of goals that would make sense. The goals could be jotted down on a piece of paper. It would not be a legal document but simply a road map. Not every goal to be worked on was to be included. And goals that were on the paper may not be worked on. It was to be a short and positive meeting. One that did not include tape recorders, advocates, attorneys, or administrators who did not know the child. Parents did not sit on one side and school personnel on the other. It was not school driven, parent driven or team driven. It was child driven. It was to be an enjoyable and an inspirational process.

SOMEHOW IT ENDED UP LIKE THIS

Key decision makers are unfamiliar with the child. Participants hold preconceived notions of effective treatment. Service providers act as if their intervention is the most or only important component of intervention. Recommendations are denied based on district policy. Parents make requests for multiple services that have not been scientifically validated. Placement offers are determined prior to the meeting without any opportunity for open discussion or input. Parents are treated as if they do not really understand the needs of their child. Teachers are treated as though they are incompetent and uncaring. Parents fail to demonstrate appreciation for the countless hours devoted to their child. Instructional staff are admonished from discussing or agreeing with certain aspects of a child's program. Parents insist their child should receive an optimal education. Administrators become defensive about the quality of their programs. Participants become angry and disrespectful. Administrators come in and out of meetings as if what is being discussed were unimportant. This is definitely not the IEP meeting that was envisioned by the drafters of the Individuals with Disability Education Act (IDEA).

Why would parents request services they did not truly believe their child needed? Why would a service provider make a recommendation for services they did not believe were necessary? Why would school districts make an offer of services they did not believe were appropriate? Trusting it would not be so, it is incumbent upon all members of the IEP team to understand effective strategies for the education of students with ASD, understand educational mandates, be familiar with available and offered services, and most importantly, understand the unique needs of the child. What would you be requesting if this were your child's IEP meeting?

We participate in hundreds of IEP meetings for the children we serve. Often we have well established relationships with both the family and the school district and appreciate the link between the school and home. We work with children of all ages. We work with older children for whom the majority of services occur in school. We also serve children before the age of two and therefore therapy is conducted primarily in the family's home.

When working with very young children, treatment often begins well before the school district becomes involved. We have the opportunity to work intimately with family members, helping them gain a better understanding of their role in treatment and how they can best help their child. Effective treatment includes active parental involvement and expertise as well as participation in the therapy process. This relationship with parents is inevitable and it is critical in providing effective intervention for children. We must, however, remain objective and keep our focus on what is necessary for the child. We need to consider parental input, but must also recommend what our experience and research has shown to be effective in meeting the child's needs. School districts are often wary of the relationship we have with families, questioning whether we are acting as the voice of the parents, and often not considering that we are **ALL** supposed to be the "voice" of the child!

We also work closely with many school districts in the capacity of direct service provider as well as classroom consultant. We have the opportunity to help school districts train staff, develop curriculum, and build effective school programs. We see school personnel putting tremendous time, effort, and resources into developing appropriate programs to meet the needs of the children in their districts. Parents are often suspicious of the relationships we have with school personnel, believing our recommendations are influenced by what the district wants us to say. We have even been accused of being a "shill" for school districts!

As philosophies and approaches differ, we do not expect our views and recommendations will be agreed upon by all members of an IEP team. We do, however, hope that what we share will be respectfully considered. Often our recommendations please neither the school district nor the family. They do, however, reflect what we believe to be the needs of the child. By building trusting relationships we can be heard, opening the door to productive discussion and hopefully effective education. ASD impacts the life of a child in countless ways. Fortunately, with intensive and comprehensive intervention, meaningful educational experiences are attainable. Our experience has repeatedly shown us that those children who benefit most from education are those who are fortunate enough to have dedicated teams of teachers, services providers, administrators, and parents who are working collaboratively to address their needs. Our experience has shown us that without a collaborative team progress is greatly compromised.

We walk into most IEP meetings optimistic of a favorable outcome. But it seems the perception of what constitutes a favorable outcome may be different for each member of the team. Most IEP meetings start off positively enough and, thankfully, many are completed with satisfaction and mutual agreement that the child is receiving the support he needs. Somehow, our experiences with the IEP process for children with ASD have become increasingly complicated, disharmonious, and legally convoluted. We believe it does not have to be this way. Our hope is that by sharing our experiences with the IEP process experiences, we can help members of IEP teams see other perspectives and consider how they can improve the process and therefore better meet the individual needs of the child.

This chapter is not intended to serve as a legal treatise on the IEP process, but to provoke thought in those involved in the process as to how to facilitate and create a more collaborative process.

THE IEP PROCESS

The Education for All Handicapped Children Act (EAHCA) of 1975, the federal law providing for the educational service of children with disabilities was renamed in 1990 to the Individuals with Disabilities Education Act (IDEA),[1] not coincidentally, to reflect the emphasis on the *Individual* child. Under IDEA, children with qualifying disabilities are entitled to a free appropriate public education (FAPE) comprised of special education and related services to meet the unique needs of the child. The avenue by which a free appropriate public education is to be achieved is through the development of an Individualized Education Program (IEP).[2] The IEP is a written document reflecting the educational needs of the child and the individualized special education required to meet those needs, a tool for identifying educational objectives and monitoring a child's program, and a forum for parent participation.

The goal of IDEA was to ensure that children with special education needs were provided with the educational opportunities of their non-disabled peers. The IEP is the means to educational access for children with disabilities. Preparing and creating a meaningful document is essential for assuring a child receives appropriate services. The IEP begins with a determination and statement of the child's present levels of performance, from which goals and objectives are developed to help guide teaching and monitor progress, and finally placement and services are determined that will facilitate the achievement of those goals and objectives.

Ideally, an IEP meeting is a forum for meaningful discussion by persons interested in and knowledgeable about the child.[3] Participating in a collaborative IEP meeting where the members of the team can openly share their ideas, develop an effective program based on

---

[1] Individuals with Disabilities Education Act of 1990 (IDEA), 20 U.S.C. § 1400 *et seq.*; Implementing Regulations, 34 C.F.R. 300 *et seq.* IDEA was reauthorized with revisions in 1997 by President Bill Clinton and again in 2004 by President George W. Bush (Individuals with Disabilities Education Improvement Act).

[2] 20 U.S.C. § 1401(9); 34 C.F.R. § 300.17

[3] Under 20 U.S.C. § 1414(d)(1)(B); 34 C.F.R. § 300.321(a) required parties in attendance at an IEP meeting include:
    (i) The parents of the child;
    (ii) Not less than one regular education teacher (if the child is or may be participating in the regular education environment);
    (iii) Not less than one special education teacher of the child, or where appropriate, not less than one special education provider of the child;
    (iv) A representative of the public agency who—
        (1) Is qualified to supervise the provision of specially designed instruction to meet the unique needs of children with disabilities;
        (2) Is knowledgeable about the general education curriculum; and
        (3) Is knowledgeable about the availability of resources of the public agency;
    (v) An individual who can interpret the instructional implications of evaluation results...;
    (vi) At the discretion of the parent or the agency, other individuals who have knowledge or special expertise regarding the child, including related services personnel as appropriate; and
    (vii) Whenever appropriate, the child with a disability.

the needs of the child, and can leave with a desire to work together should ideally be the outcome of all IEP meetings. Sadly, IEP meetings are too often filled with contention and mistrust, feeling more like the first step on the road to Due Process.

Given the importance and emphasis placed on the individual needs of the child, it is incumbent upon the members of the IEP team, to have an understanding of available treatments and most importantly an understanding of the needs of that particular child. Often the key decision makers have never seen the child, have responsibility for hundreds of other students, accountability to those outside the IEP meeting, and have likely sat or will sit in thousands of IEP meetings. Conversely, the parents of a child live and breathe every aspect of their child's life. They have responsibility only for their child, and will participate only in those IEP meetings involving their son or daughter. The investment in a child's education can feel easily lost in the anonymity. Obviously, the family's emotional investment in the IEP process is significantly more intense than the degree of investment of other team members.

Even large school districts with access to enormous resources can end up making poor decisions about how to conduct the IEP process. We have encountered one such district where the amount and nature of information which can be shared in either written reports or discussion at an IEP meeting is severely curtailed. Additionally, that district's policy dictates that any information submitted by a non-district service provider may be used solely for the purpose of determining present levels of performance. This district's master contract states that a non-district service provider's attendance at an IEP meeting "acting as a student's advocate" constitutes or may constitute a conflict of interest. As professionals choosing careers in education, we would hope every person attending an IEP meeting is advocating on behalf of the child. An open discussion held among persons knowledgeable about the child is the fundamental basis upon which an IEP must be developed. It is perplexing why any party acting on behalf of a child would attempt to limit the information shared among the members of the IEP team. Knowledge about the child, knowledge about autism, knowledge about available treatments, and trust are essential elements for a productive IEP.

Sitting in IEP meetings, we have often wondered whether we are talking about the same child. Present levels of performance are intended to be a foundation for the development of goals and objectives reflective of a child's needs and the reasonable expectations we hold for that child. It is difficult to come together to develop and agree upon goals and objectives when it does not seem as if the team is describing the same child. School districts accuse us of overemphasizing deficits and focusing on the child's weaknesses. Parents tend to view us as overemphasizing the child's strengths and thereby minimizing the child's needs. Always, the aim must be to present an objective and balanced view of both a child's strengths and deficits.[4]

While it is both important to celebrate the achievement of a child and required by IDEA to discuss a child's strengths, it is incumbent upon the IEP team to evaluate and recognize the areas of need if a child is going to make meaningful progress. While we agree that the atmosphere of an IEP meeting should remain as positive as possible, it is imperative that open discussions about a child's areas of need and recommendations to address those needs are not viewed as argumentative, negative, or adversarial, but rather the foundation to a meaningful program. We urge those responsible for running IEP meetings to allow for open and honest discussion.

While special education teachers must often feel the brunt of a parent's request or a recommendation for alternative placement, seeking alternative or additional services is not an accusation of instructional failure or incompetence, but rather an acknowledgment or recognition that a particular child may have educational needs (e.g., learning style, curricular needs, behavioral excesses/deficits) beyond those which can be appropriately or effectively addressed in a particular environment. The child must not be slighted in favor of the desire to appear responsible for teaching skills and addressing behavioral needs which cannot be reasonably taught or addressed in a particular situation. The focus must remain on protecting the needs of the child.

---

[4] Under 20 U.S.C. § 1414(d)(3)(A); 34 C.F.R. §300.324, IDEA 2004 recognizes the need for broad considerations in developing an IEP
  (a) Development of IEP
    (1) General. In developing each child's IEP, the IEP team must consider:
      (i) The strengths of the child;
      (ii) The concerns of the parents for enhancing the education of their child;
      (iii) The results of the initial or most recent evaluation of the child; and
      (iv) The academic, developmental, and functional needs of the child. (20 U.S.C. 1414(d)(1)(B)).

A UNIQUE PERSPECTIVE: A CLINICIAN WHO IS ALSO AN ATTORNEY

I (the author of this chapter) first began working with children with Autism Spectrum Disorder (ASD) in the late 1970's at UCLA on the Young Autism Project under the direction of Dr. Ivar Lovaas. After several years working as a behavioral consultant, I decided to attend law school. I had my first exposure to IDEA and special education law when I took an education law class and began researching a paper on mainstreaming. The name Lovaas and programs based on Lovaas' research kept coming up in my on-line searches. That is when I first realized what a hotbed of litigation this area had become. I graduated shortly thereafter and began practicing special education law, representing children with special education needs.

The vast majority of cases I represented involved children with ASD whose parents were trying to receive funding for intensive ABA-based programs. They believed the classrooms being offered were not meeting the needs of their children or they believed their children needed intensive services but were not ready for a classroom. After experiencing the frustration of seeing children denied necessary services, watching families having to fight for the educational services the met their child's needs as guaranteed under IDEA and witnessing brutal attacks on well-meaning individuals, both parents and professionals, I stopped practicing law. I returned to the clinical world and joined Autism Partnership where I believe I can have a more constructive role in meeting the needs of these children by being directly involved with their intervention in a clinical capacity.

When I returned to Autism Partnership my responsibilities included conducting assessments, helping in the design and development of programs, consulting in classrooms, providing clinical supervision, and attending IEPs. For most of the children we serve, classroom placement, as well as direct intensive ABA based intervention, are critical components of their programs. I have had the unique opportunity to be involved in programming from both the perspective of an attorney and as a clinical representative of a non-public service provider. Naively, I would not have believed the perspectives to be much different. After all, from either perspective one would think that the mission is to help the child. As I learned quickly, there is indeed a dramatic difference, which I would summarize as follows:

LAWYER	CONSULTANT
Expects child to be benefiting at that moment	Views Classroom development as a process that may take time
Not concerned about staff morale	Must build a positive relationship with staff
Highlights the deficits	Starts by emphasizing the strengths
Considers everything critical	Has to prioritize and may need to let some things go
Expects Discrete Trial Teaching implemented by the book	More concerned with making teaching effective
Mainly cares that Behavior Plan is in writing	Wants staff to understand process of analyzing behavior
Looks for reams of data	Happy with manageable amount of data that is meaningful
Not concerned about where resources will come from	Has to work with what is available

The dichotomy first became clear to me when a school district to whom we were providing classroom consultation asked me to observe the classroom of a child whose parents were requesting a home program. The first time I returned to the classroom as a consultant after practicing law full time, I walked out of the classroom wanting to call all of the parents and tell them to immediately file for due process. But...I took a couple of deep breaths and reminded myself that I was there because the school district recognized the need to change and wanted to make their program better. It took awhile for me to learn to balance both the legal perspective and the consultative perspective. The classroom teacher had just started teaching earlier in the month. She had participated in five days of hands-on training and had not yet received any follow up consultation. None of her three teaching assistants had received any formal training and two of them had no experience. My initial impression was extremely positive. The teacher was trying to implement and incorporate ABA-based strategies in all aspects of the classroom, she had created a good classroom structure, she captured teachable moments, she facilitated social interaction, and she was highly receptive and motivated. As a consultant I could not have hoped to see more from a new teacher. This was the start of a quality program.

But I then remembered that I was not there to consult to the classroom, but rather to evaluate the "defensibility" of the classroom for a particular child. The support staff was not sufficiently trained, the teacher was just beginning to develop curricula, there were no data collection systems, and there was still quite a bit of unstructured time, especially in the afternoon. I was not sure how much learning or systematic instruction was occurring throughout the school day. From a legal perspective I was thinking this family will definitely prevail, not because the instructional staff did not have the potential to become effective teachers, but because classroom development is a process and this classroom was not yet at a stage where it could meet most of the needs of its students.

About a year and a half later I had the opportunity to revisit this classroom as part of my regular consultation rotation. It was a completely different classroom. There were instructional centers, integrated data collection systems, individualized curricula and you could not tell the support staff from the teacher. Systematic instruction occurred throughout the day. It was a quality program, and therefore "defensible."

For a consultant, time is on your side. You can determine the pace of change and would normally ensure that behavior change on the part of the staff and structural change within the program is evolutionary. From a legal perspective, however, each child is entitled to an appropriate education without having to wait for evolution to occur. One cannot say to a parent or a hearing officer, "We think in about one, maybe two, years we will be getting around to some very effective teaching."

When I go into a classroom, in either capacity, I am looking for pretty much the same elements, but how I view them, how I interpret them, and how I prioritize them can be very different. As a classroom consultant my focus, at least initially, is on the instructional staff. As a lawyer, I approach a classroom with an eye towards the individual child I am representing. The primary priority is whether that particular child is benefiting from that classroom at that time. Is the child able to meet meaningful goals and objectives from the presently available instruction? While cognizant of the potential impact on the instructional staff, as a lawyer it was my responsibility to determine whether the staff were sufficiently trained and whether they were aware of and able to meet the needs of that child at that time:

- Was the classroom reasonably calculated to confer educational benefit?

- Are there meaningful mainstreaming opportunities?

- What does the data show about student progress?

- Is the teacher-to-student ratio sufficient to meet the child's needs?

■ Are there curricular and behavioral plans individualized for each child?

■ Is there instruction occurring throughout the day?

These are questions I ask both as a lawyer and as a classroom consultant. From a legal perspective, regardless of the efforts being made to develop an effective learning environment at some time in the future, the emphasis remains on that moment in time. How the deficiencies and weaknesses in the classroom are impacting a child's progress become critical evidence in a case. As a classroom consultant, the focus is on the process, therefore I know and accept that it may be a long time before many of these important elements are completely achieved.

Knowing that classroom development takes time, the initial focus of the consultation is building a relationship with the classroom staff and facilitating an atmosphere of receptivity and collaboration. Successful classroom consultation requires a great deal of effort and hard work on the part of the teacher. I consider my initial goal to be met when the staff wants us to come back. While practicing law, I did not have to worry about maintaining a constructive relationship with the teaching team. Furthermore, when I was asked to look at a classroom, it was done with the expectation that the classroom should be providing an effective teaching environment based on the needs of that one child and it should be in place today. As a consultant, I must work with what is presently available, including the number of students, the physical structure of the room, the availability of support staff and instructional aides, and the experience of the staff. The consultation plan is developed around the current stage of the classroom, building on and emphasizing the existing strengths, while working around limitations we cannot overcome.

WHAT'S THE IDEA?

Under IDEA, a child with a qualifying disability is entitled to a "free appropriate public education (FAPE)" tailored to meet the unique needs of the child. The statute itself provides little substantive guidance as to what level of education constitutes "appropriate." We know the Supreme Court[5] has determined that a school district is not required to maximize a child's potential, but is required to develop an IEP which is "reasonably calculated to enable

---

[5] Board of Education of the Hendrick Hudson Central School District v. Rowley, 102 S.Ct. 3034, 458 U.S. 176, 73 L.Ed.2d 690 (1982)

[the child] to receive educational benefits." Given the limited guidelines provided by the statute itself and the vast variability in special education needs of the children it is intended to protect, it is not surprising educators, courts, and families have been challenged to interpret the legal standard imposed by IDEA.

Both the 1997 and the 2004 amendments to IDEA reiterate the strong emphasis placed upon parent participation in the IEP process. Despite their role as equal members of the IEP team, for many parents the IEP process can be daunting, unfamiliar, and intimidating. The IEP process is guided by the substantive and procedural requirements set forth in IDEA and the implementing regulations (34 Code of Federal Regulations (C.F.R. 300) et seq.). While providing parents with a copy of the procedural safeguards in an easily understandable format is a required component of the IEP process, comprehending and applying the legal mandates can be overwhelming.

Because we work with children living in a wide geographical area, we have the opportunity to participate in IEP meetings in many different school districts. District policy, interpretation of the law, and the information shared at IEP meetings is as varied as the number of districts we serve. Some districts support intervention across settings, while other districts insist that all educational services must be provided within a classroom setting. Some districts we work with recognize there are children who need educational programming virtually 52 weeks per year. Other districts routinely attempt to limit services offered at IEP meetings to 40 weeks per year based on district policy. We work with school districts where parents are encouraged to visit several classrooms before an IEP meeting, we also work with a school district that expressly prohibits parents from making any classroom observations prior to a child's IEP meeting based on its interpretation of IDEA.

We have been asked to adjust our education and treatment recommendations so as not to exceed what the district interprets as the minimum legal requirements for FAPE. Parents and service providers are frequently reminded that the legal obligation of a school district does not entitle a student to a "Cadillac but a serviceable Chevy." The car analogy, while illustrative, does little to promote an atmosphere of caring, trust, and acting in the best interest of the child. Often district policy and/or a district's interpretation of the law are reflected in information presented as well as in an offer of placement and services. Given most families' lack of experience with IDEA, the families' reliance on this information becomes an important element of building a trusting relationship. Imposing limitations or constraints on services based on policy and interpretation, and not on the individual needs of the child, contributes to the wariness some families feel throughout the IEP process. Conversely, families' misunderstanding of the entitlements provided by IDEA can create inflated expectations and lead to requests for services which exceed any reasonable interpretation of the educational obligations set forth under the statute.

When parents are deciding whether they should bring an attorney to their IEP meeting they need to understand that increases perception that the meeting is going to be first step toward litigation and apprehension of hostility and distrust. We always hope the IEP process can be completed without the need for representation on either side. But, unfortunately, in some areas the availability of services often seems contingent upon the threat of pending litigation as opposed to the needs of the child.

We are not sure how to measure where the basic floor of opportunity ends and the maximizing of potential begins or exactly when progress is legally sufficient. But, as individuals dedicated to helping children, we hope that our mutual goal is to ensure that children are learning the skills they need to lead as happy and productive lives as possible.

ASD AND THE IEP

Autism is a qualifying disability under IDEA[6]. The defining features of ASD are impaired development in the areas of social interaction and communication and a limited repertoire of activity and interests[7]. The diagnostic criteria for ASD include deficits in the areas of behavior, communication, social interaction and play. It should follow that the educational needs of most children with ASD would involve these areas. Accordingly, goals and objectives will typically need to be developed to address behavior, socialization, communication, and play skills with services implemented to address those needs. As cognitive functioning is not part of the diagnostic criteria, it should not be surprising that for many children with ASD, the greatest deficits extend beyond academic performance.

IDEA amendments of 1997 and 2004 placed an increased emphasis on the involvement and progress of children with disabilities in the general education curriculum, *i.e.* the cur-

---

[6] Under 20 U.S.C. 1401; 34 C.F.R. §300.8 Autism is defined as:
    ©) (1) Autism means a developmental disability significantly affecting verbal and nonverbal communication and social interaction, generally evident before age 3, that adversely affects a child's educational performance. Other characteristics often associated with autism are engagement in repetitive activities and stereotyped movement, resistance to environmental change or change in daily routines, and unusual responses to sensory experiences....
[7] DSM- IVR, Autistic Disorder 299.00

riculum used with non-disabled peers. Nonetheless, a school district's responsibility does not end with goals and objectives and services designed to increase access to the general education curriculum. IDEA specifically recognizes that there are some children who have needs stemming from their disability that may not be directly related to the general education curriculum[8]. Accordingly, an IEP team is required to consider special education and related services which will enable a child to participate in extracurricular and nonacademic activities; yet goals & objectives proposed and services recommended in non-academic domains are often rejected as falling outside the purview of educational responsibility. It is incumbent upon the IEP team to consider options for placement, related services, and support to meet both sets of needs.[9]

A statement describing necessary program modifications and/or accommodations must be included in the IEP.[10] While accommodations should be considered and utilized as appropriate, they must not be used as a substitute for instruction. We have participated in numerous IEP meetings where the use of accommodations was emphasized in lieu of instruction in those areas which would have enabled the child to acquire the skills to obviate the need for the accommodations. For example, seating a child in the front of the classroom nearest to teacher may well increase the likelihood of the child attending to the teacher; similarly, facing a child away from a window may decrease the likelihood he will be distracted by actions outside the classroom. These accommodations, although potentially successful, can not take the place of teaching a child the skills he needs to access his environment in an independent manner. In the long run, goals developed and strategies designed to teach necessary skills will afford children increased independence.

---

[8] Under the definitions set forth in 20 U.S.C. 1401(29); C.F.R. §300.39
  (a)(1) Special education means specially designed instruction, at no cost to the parents, to meet the unique needs of a child with a disability, including:
    (I) Instruction conducted in the classroom, in the home, in the hospital and institutions, and in other settings....
  (b)(3) Specially designed instruction means adapting, as appropriate to the needs of an eligible child under this part, ...the content, methodology, or delivery of instruction—
    (I) To address the unique needs of the child that result from the child's disability; and
    (ii) To ensure access of the child to the general curriculum....

[9] Under 20 U.S.C. 1414(d)(1)(A); 34 C.F.R. §300.320 an IEP must include:
  (2)(i) A statement of measurable annual goals, including academic and functional goals designed to—
    (A) Meet the child's needs that result from the child's disability to enable the child to be involved in and make progress in the general education curriculum; and
    (B) Meet each of the child's other educational needs that result from the child's disability;...
  (4) A statement of special education and related services and supplementary aids and services, based on peer-reviewed research to the extent practicable, to be provided to the child, or on behalf of the child, and a statement of the program modifications or support for school personnel that will be provided to enable the child–
  (i) To advance appropriately towards attaining annual goals;
  (ii) To be involved in and make progress in the general education curriculum in accordance with paragraph (a)(1) of this section, and to participate in extracurricular and nonacademic activities; and
  (iii) To be educated and participate with other children with disabilities and nondisabled children in the activities described in this section;...

[10] 20 U.S.C. 1414 §(d)(1)(A): 34 C.F.R. §300.320(a)(6)(I)

Based on recommendations generated by the committee on Educational Interventions for children with Autism (formed at the request of the U.S. Department of Education's Office of Special Education Programs), children having ASD (from the time a diagnosis is suspected) require active engagement in intensive programming with repeated and systematic instruction for a minimum of 25 hours per week, 12 months a year (full-year programming) with sufficient individual or very small group instruction (no more than 2:1 staff ratio). Parent involvement and expertise, as well as training, are essential components to an early intervention program. A traditional school calendar may adequately address the needs of most students. However, given what is now understood about the education for students with ASD, it is not likely that the traditional educational models developed decades ago would be chosen as the standard educational model for children with autistic spectrum disorder. Nonetheless, adherence to a traditional school calendar with limited discussion for individualized extended school year services is a common source of contention at the IEP meetings we attend. It seems the National Research Council's OSEP's service recommendations should be a good starting place for the discussion of educational services for children with autism.

The growth of autism treatment has exploded. With this growth, has come a wide range of available treatment options, many of which have no empirical evidence of efficacy, as well as an abundance of service providers lacking the experience and skill to implement effective intervention. Understanding there is no one right answer to the treatment of autism, philosophical differences are inevitable. At some point in the process, IEP team members may have to agree to disagree. As providers of ABA-based intervention, we are strongly convicted in our belief of the efficacy of this approach. Philosophical differences in the treatment of ASD will guide treatment recommendations and offers. However, philosophical preferences cannot replace the need for scientific rigor and validation or overshadow the individual needs of the child. Accordingly, the 2004 reauthorization of IDEA requires special education and related services be based on peer-reviewed research, to the extent practicable.[11]

It is understandable why parents would want to investigate any and all available treatment options for their child. Given the reality of limited time, funds and resources, it remains perplexing why requests would be made for treatments that have little or no empirical support, potentially undermine the effectiveness of other treatment, and clearly seem beyond the broadest interpretations of an educational mandate. The need for intensity in

---

[11] 20 U.S.C. §1414 (d)(1)(A)(IV); 34 C.F.R.§300.320(a)(4)

services is well established, but intensity does not lie in shared numbers alone. Parents' credibility is greatly enhanced when placement and service requests are based on sound treatment methodologies reflective of the needs of their child. Districts' credibility is greatly enhanced when offers of placement and services are based on sound treatment methodologies, consistent with empirically established treatment guidelines, and reflective of the needs of the child.

The more collaborative the process, the more effective and meaningful an IEP document will be.[12] Reflecting on the many positive and productive IEP meetings we have attended, trust seems to be the constant factor in creating a collaborative atmosphere. Trust the family is seeking appropriate services for their child. Trust the parents will be committed members of the treatment team. Trust the school district is recommending and offering services based on the needs of that particular child. Trust that district personnel are trained and knowledgeable. And trust that service providers are not recommending services based on the requests of the family or the financial gains of the agency. Each time we sit at an IEP table, as parent, school representative, service provider, or legal counsel, we must remember we are all there on behalf of a child. The following, while simple, seem to be some of the elements that facilitate a trusting relationship:

1. Setting aside of district policy for the individual needs of the child (it is clear that invoking policy is a violation of IDEA)

2. Familiarity with the child

3. Understanding of autism and autism-related treatment

4. A complete IEP team

5. Open discussion

6. Supportive atmosphere

7. Requesting and offering services which have stood up to scientific rigor

8. Understanding of and procedural adherence to the law

9. Appreciation of the efforts of the instructional staff

---

[12] A special thanks to Glenda McHale for giving us the opportunity to work with the epitome of professionalism, collaboration, expertise, and love of children.

Having a conversation about learning to water ski on a summer vacation, watching a child perform in a school play, listening to a student explain why another student might be absent from class, hearing about a first visit from the tooth-fairy, seeing a child's face light up as his best friend arrives–these situations might easily be taken for granted as everyday occurrences of a six-year old. But experiencing how much work and effort it took collectively from a team of parents, teachers, behavior interventionists, and most importantly, a child, confirms our belief that with systematic, intensive intervention and skilled individuals, the possibilities can be without limit. As arduous as the IEP process has become, the results can be **astounding**. Too often we are faced with skepticism and disbelief when goals are suggested that seem unrealistic and out of reach. Fortunately, we know that with appropriate education, these goals are necessary, attainable, and address the skills that are the foundation for creating meaningful life experiences. Participating in the intervention that has successfully enabled these children to achieve these experiences and understanding the services that are needed to continue this level of progress reminds us always to keep our eyes toward the child and the **individualized** in IEP.

REFERENCES

Abelson, A. G., & Weiss, R. (1984). Mainstreaming the handicapped. The views of parents of nonhandicapped pupils. *Spectrum, 2,* 27-29.

Autism Society America (1991). Educational rights: An intro to IDEA, FERPA & section 504 of the rehabilitation act. *UCLA Evaluation Clinic,* 1-26.

B. Ammons Protection and Advocacy, I. (1999). Parents rights. *B. Ammons Protection and Advocacy, INC.,* 1-63.

Barry, A. L. (1994). Easing into inclusion classrooms. *The Inclusive School, December,* 3-6.

Blau, G. L. (1985). Autism—assessment and placement under the education for all handicapped children act: A case history. *Journal of Clinical Psychology, 41*(3), 440-447.

Block, J. S., Weinstein, J., Seitz, M., & Zager, D., Editors (2005). School and parent partnerships in the pre-school years. In D. Zager (Ed.), *Autism spectrum disorders: Identification, education, and treatment (3rd ed.).* Mahwah, NJ: Lawrence Erlbaum Associates Publishers.

Brown, W., Horn, E., Heiser, J., & Odom, S. (1996). Innovative practices project blend: An inclusive model of early intervention services. *Journal of Early Intervention, 20*(4), 364-375.

Etscheidt, S. (2003). An analysis of legal hearings and cases related to individualized education programs for children with autism. *Research and Practice for Persons with severe disabilities, 28*(2), 51-69.

Etscheidt, S. (2006). Behavioral intervention plans: Pedagogical and legal analysis of issues. *Behavioral Disorders, 31*(2), 233-243.

Gersten, R., & Woodward, J. (1990). Rethinking the regular education initiative. Focus on the classroom teacher. *Remedial and Special Education, 11*(3), 7-16.

Giangreco, M., & Broer, S. (2005). Questionable utilization of paraprofessionals in inclusive schools: Are we addressing symptoms or causes. *Focus on Autism and Other Developmental Disabilities, 20*(1), 10-26.

Hanell, G. (2006). *Identifying children with special needs: Checklists and action plans for teachers.* Thousand Oaks.

Kohler, F. W., Strain, P., Hoyson, M., & Jamieson, B. (1997). Merging naturalistic teaching and peer-based strategies to address the IEP objectives of preschoolers with autism: An examination of structural and child behavior outcomes. *Focus on Autism and Other Developmental Disorders, 12*(4), 196-206.

Larsen, L., Goodman, L., & Glean, R. (1981). Issues in the implementation of extended school year programs for handicapped students. *Exceptional Children, 47*(4), 256-263.

Mandlawitz, M. (2002). The impact of the legal system on educational programming for young children with autism spectrum disorder. *Journal of Autism and Developmental Disorders, 32*(5), 495-508.

Sallows, G. (1999). Educational interventions for children with autism in the U.K.: Comment on the Jordan et al. June 1998 final report to the DFEE. *Conference Paper,* 1-15.

Schreck, K. A. (2000). It can be done: An example of a behavioral individualized education program (IEP) for a child with autism. *Behavioral Interventions, 15*(4), 279-300.

Simpson, R. L. (1995). Individualized education programs for students with autism: Including parents in the process. *Focus on Autistic Behavior, 10*(4), 11-15.

Smith, S. W., Slattery, W. J., Knopp, T. Y. (1993). Beyond the mandate: Developing individualized education programs that work for students with autism. *Focus on Autistic Behavior, 8*(3), 1-15.

Spann, S. J., Kohler, F. W. Soenksen, D. (2003). Examining parents' involvement in and perceptions of special education services: An interview with families in a parent support group. *Focus on Autism and Other Developmental Disorders, 18*(4), 228-237.

Woods, M. (1995a). Parent-professional collaboration and the efficacy of the IEP process. In R. L. Koegel, & L, K. Koegel, (Eds.), *Teaching children with autism: Strategies for initiating positive interactions and improving learning opportunities.* Baltimore: Paul H Brookes Publishing.

Woods, M. (1995b). Parent-professional collaboration and the efficacy of the IEP process. In R. L. Koegel & L. K. Koegel (Eds.), *Teaching children with autism: Strategies for initiating positive interactions and improving learning opportunities.* Baltimore: Paul H Brookes Publishing Company.

Yell, M.L. & Drasgow, E. (2000). Litigating a free appropriate public education: The Lovaas hearings and cases. *Journal of Special Education, 33*(4), 205-214.

Zucker, S. H., Perras, C., Gartin, B., & Fidler, D. (2005). Best practices for practitioners. *Education and Training in Developmental Disabilities, 40*(3), 199-201.

Chapter 13

GOALS, GOALS, GOALS

By Ron Leaf & Toby Mountjoy

In the field of early intensive behavioral treatment for ASD there seems to be an assumption that the more skills that are included in a student's educational program, the better the outcome. There seems to be a belief that we must teach a child each and every skill that has ever been included in an autism curriculum, regardless of the sutdent's present ability or need. So detailed curriculum guides are purchased, such as *The Me Book* (Lovaas, 1981), *Behavioral Intervention for Autistic Children* (Maurice, Green, and Luce, 1996), or *A Work in Progress* (Leaf and McEachin, 1999) and **every** program contained in every book is targeted. Often this is done in a cookbook manner whereby you start at the beginning and work through each skill in the order listed. There may be little analysis of what programs are necessary for a particular child in terms of skill and behavior. There also might not be an understanding of the objectives of the particular programs. The goal is simply to be able to check off as many targets as possible, as if we were building a house brick by brick. Once we have all the bricks in place, the child will be recovered from autism.

It is quite easy and therefore not very meaningful to create thousands of goals. For example, one could identify 25 goals (and really hundreds) in teaching non-verbal imitation:

OBJECT MOVEMENT	LARGE BODY ACTION	OUT OF CHAIR	FINE BODY ACTION	CHAIN
Roll Car	Wave	Turn Off Light	Point to Nose	Stand Up & Turn Around
Throw Ball	Clap	Close Door	Point to Eyes	Touch Head & Clap
Wave Flag	Stomp Feet	Retrieve Item	Touch Elbow	Retrieve Ball & Car
Beat Drum	Touch Tummy	Throw Away Trash	Touch Ankle	Turn on TV & Sit Down
Spin Top	Touch Head	Stand Up	Point to Finger	Stand Up & Wave

Alternatively, one could identify five goals (i.e., object movement, large body, out of chair, fine body, chains, etc.) or identify just one goal: non-verbal imitation! The programs in books like *A Work in Progress* (Leaf and McEachin, 1999), *The Me Book* (Lovaas, 1981), or *Behavioral Intervention for Young Children with Autism* (Maurice, Green, & Luce, 1996) have been broken down into very small parts. It is not necessary for every child to follow the same task analysis. Some children may need a more detailed task analysis than provided in the books to learn effectively. Others may benefit from a broader approach which does not seek to teach everything in such tiny steps and looks to teach overall concepts. The teaching should be based upon the learning ability of each student.

By having too many goals, it is often impossible to run every program. Teachers simply cannot run hundreds of programs. Therefore, program non-compliance is induced! If indeed all the programs are run then there is most likely not enough concentration on any particular program to ensure enough practice of the skill to learn it. So although the child may work on hundreds of different programs the child may master very few.

NARROWING THE SCOPE

Obviously, not all the skills that a child needs to learn can be contained in a book. A child would need to absorb an entire library of books! Furthermore, it is not necessary to teach a child every conceivable curriculum target. Unfortunately, many times people act as if it is a contest in which the child who learns the most programs wins! Often, mastering numerous goals is a false indicator of success. We know many adults who have mastered all the programs contained in curriculum guides who are still seriously affected by ASD and have restrictive lives because they have not learned behavior control or cannot recognize the impact of their behavior on other people. As a result they are socially isolated and alienate people in their lives.

Because of the belief that the more goals the better, there is a tendency to load up IEP's with as many goals as possible. Being able to demonstrate mastery of scores, even hundreds, of targets makes everyone feel like the program is a big success. Goals should not be added simply because they appear on some developmental checklist. You should choose goals that will make the biggest impact on the student's ability to acquire knowledge and ultimately enhance his quality of life. As an example a child may not know the labels of fingernail and eyebrow and could certainly learn it but maybe there are other skills that might prove to be more functional and useful, such as increasing tolerance for denied requests or improving ability to express desires. By age four most students can identify shapes and colors. If a student with ASD does not know these concepts it would be tempting to include them as goals in an IEP, but you should consider seriously this area of skill deficit is impeding his development compared to other areas of delay that might be even more seriously affecting his life, such as play and social interaction. There are hundreds of pre-academic skills that could be targeted, but few of them will yield the kind of punch you get from teaching observational learning and joint attention.

USING TARGETS TO TEACH MULTIPLE SKILLS

When using a curriculum guide, there needs to be a general understanding of the various programs, the objectives they aim to accomplish, and how programs interrelate. Each program can have multiple objectives and benefits beyond the specific skills that are acquired. The activity itself is often not the main reason and certainly not the sole reason for a program to be implemented. For example, non-verbal imitation (NVI) may appear to be simply teaching a child how to copy actions, such as clapping and waving, but there are broader goals that can also be addressed within this teaching activity that can serve as building blocks for future learning:

- NVI is a simple skill which can lead to rapid success and facilitate engagement in the learning process

- NVI is the foundation upon which other important skills are based (e.g., verbalization, play, social, self-help, etc.)

- NVI establishes an effective tool for teaching many important skills

- NVI facilitates learning from prompts

- NVI facilitates attending to a teacher's actions and leads to awareness of the actions of peers

- Imitation builds awareness of the environment.

- Imitation helps develop sustained attention.

- Imitation is a task which can be used to establish or re-establish compliance and attention.

For some children the skill of NVI may be primarily selected as a means to establish the pattern of waiting to find out what the teacher wants you to do. For other children, the primary objective may be to learn to copy the actions of others. For all children working on NVI is a means of developing good learning skills (i.e. attending and compliance). Programs need to be carefully selected and reflect the child's abilities and needs. Critical objectives need to be identified and then programs should be selected to meet those goals. There has to be an understanding that there are multiple programs that can be employed to meet most objectives. For example, a child who has attending problems could develop better attending skills through NVI, matching or Communication Temptations. The programs selected, therefore, will play to the child's strengths as a means of improving deficits in skills or behavior.

THE IMPACT OF BEHAVIORS ON SELECTION OF CURRICULUM

For many children with ASD behaviors such as distractibility, self-stimulation, tantrums, noncompliance and isolation are common at the beginning of treatment. These behaviors must be dealt with first and foremost to increase children's attention and behavior control so that they can learn from teaching sessions. It is critical that curriculum choices facilitate changes in these kinds of behaviors over the short and long term. Often curriculum is chosen, however, because the child's peers know certain skills or because it is the next thing on the list or in the book. This will not bring about the most rapid improvement in a child's ability to learn. Programs should be selected according to the behavioral and learning goals which will have the most pivotal impact. Keep in mind that the ultimate goal is for the child to be able to learn in a normal manner and not require a multitude of skills to be taught using Discrete Trial Teaching.

Problematic behaviors need comprehensive functional assessment and curriculum designed to teach new replacement skills if they are to change over the long term. For example, if a child engages in high rates of self stimulation during "free time" then play skills would be a critical area of curriculum. Children who tantrum and become disruptive in order to avoid demands may need a comprehensive compliance program as well as analyzing why a child may avoid demands.

SEQUENCING

Intervention typically begins with teaching beginning skills, then proceeds to intermediate skills and, if the child progresses rapidly enough, moves into the advanced curriculum. Skills should be targeted in a systematic order, guided by what we know about developmental sequencing. However, we also need to be alert to signs of unexpected areas of strength. Probing is necessary in advanced and outlying skill areas to find pockets of strength. We must take into account the unique learning style of each student and remember that sometimes children walk before they crawl, read before they talk, or talk before they comprehend.

PIVOTAL SKILLS

Dr. Lovaas often expressed that one of his fondest hopes was that once children learned a few words they would then understand the "meaning" of language. In turn, by understanding that words have meaning, this would trigger their understanding of the world in general. In other words if the children learned some pivotal skill, such as the meaning of words then they would take off on their own. Behaviorists conceptualize this as **massive** "response generalization". That is, the learning of one behavior/skill would generalize to other skills. He analogized it to the portrayal of Helen Keller in *The Miracle Worker*. When Helen learned that the substance of water was called "water", she realized that objects, people and actions had names. This became the pivotal skill which facilitated her understanding of the world in general.

Dr. Lovaas had originally hoped that teaching language would lead to major gains in all other areas and that language would be the pivotal skill. Unfortunately, that was not the case. No one has discovered one skill or groups of skills that trigger such an epiphany. However, we believe there are many concepts that once learned will greatly speed the learning process. Therefore, the emphasis of intervention should be on learning these concepts. Specific programs, therefore should be selected as a means to learning these concepts. Here are some examples of programs that we have found can serve as springboards for accelerating progress in areas that are pivotal to overall development:

1. Understanding contingencies

2. Joint Attention

3. Observational Learning

4. The Power of Communication

5. Initiation

6. Social Interest

7. Joy of playing

If we target the right goals it will not be necessary to teach everything in the curriculum. A child will eventually be able to extrapolate and pick up information incidentally if we choose teaching strategies that maximize learning how to learn. The process is parallel to developing the skills of a chef. It would be inefficient to train him to prepare every recipe that has ever been invented. What we should be teaching are selected examples which allow us to highlight the process of cooking.

NONSENSE
1. Having too many goals 2. Blindly following a curriculum
GOOD SENSE
1. Selecting a modest number of goals that can be worked on realistically 2. Targeting skills that will yield the biggest payoff across a wide range of learning domains

Hopefully, this becomes more evident when one considers that at the time we were treating children at UCLA, we did not have a vast cookbook of programs. Fortunately it turns out that the modest library of programs that had been developed were more than sufficient. By selecting the right targets we did not need to teach hundreds concepts. The children who had the best outcomes did not need to be taught everything. They were able to acquire observational learning skills and were therefore able to learn more and more of the necessary language skills and cognitive concepts on their own.

One cannot be an effective teacher without establishing clear goals. But not just any goals will get us to our destination. We need to stick to goals that are meaningful and functional and will produce the biggest impact on the major learning domains. And remember it is not a contest to see who can master the most targets. Be ambitious but realistic.

REFERENCES

Maurice, C., Green, G. & Luce, S., Editors (1996). *Behavioral intervention for young children with autism: A manual for parents and professionals.* Austin, TX: PROED.

Koegel, R.L., Koegel, L.K., McNerney, E.K. (2001). Pivotal areas in intervention for autism. *Journal of Clinical Child Psychology, 30*(1), 19-32.

Lovaas, O. I., Ackerman, A. B., Alexander, D., Firestone, P., Perkins, J., & Young, D. (1981). *Teaching Developmentally Disabled Children: The Me Book.* Austin, TX: Pro-Ed.

Leaf, R, & McEachin, J., Editors 1999. *A Work in Progress: Behavior Management Strategies & A Curriculum for Intensive Behavioral Treatment of Autism.* NY: DRL Books

Chapter 14

MEANINGFUL PROGRESS?

By Ron Leaf, Sandy Slater, Dave Rostetter & John McEachin

EXPECTATIONS OF PROGRESS

Everyone would most likely agree that students should make meaningful progress. Teachers, parents or coaches would not be satisfied if at least adequate progress was not being achieved. And of course the more significant the progress the better everyone would feel. But our degree of satisfaction with any level of progress is dependent on our expectations. Before teaching even begins, we generally have some idea about how far we think the student might progress.

Parents' and school district personnel's views of a child's potential for progress are often quite different. Parents may believe that their child is capable of making tremendous progress and perhaps even achieve normal functioning. Therefore, if their child makes modest—but not substantial—gains, a parent may conclude that the progress was not "meaningful".

Conversely, the school may believe that most students with autism will make modest gains at best. This leads to the common conclusion that **ANY** change is meaningful. Since it is generally believed that a student with ASD will always be severely affected and will therefore require tremendous support, then as long as a student is not getting worse, he or she will be regarded as receiving educational benefit. And if a student happens to be learning a few skills then teachers are regarded as being quite successful.

WHAT THE LAW PROVIDES

Federal law guarantees that all children including those with special educational needs are entitled to receive a "**Free Appropriate Public Education**" (i.e., FAPE). The definition of FAPE is found in the federal regulations at 34 C. F. R. Part 300.313:

> As used in this part of the regulations, the term **free appropriate public education** or **FAPE** means special education and related services that:
>
> (a) Are provided at public expense, under public supervision and direction, and without charge;
>
> (b) Meet the standards of the State Education Agency, including the requirements of this part;
>
> (c) Include preschool, elementary school, or secondary school education in the State; and
>
> (d) Are provided in conformity with an individualized education program (IEP) that meets the requirements of §§300.340-300.350."
>
> (Authority: 20 U.S.C. 1401(8))

This definition is repeated virtually verbatim in every state's regulations and the State Plan filed with U. S. Department of Education required of each state as a condition of receipt of federal assistance. As such, it is the starting point for any analysis of progress or benefit in special education. The United States Supreme Court established the standard for FAPE in *Board of Education of the Hendrick Hudson Central School District vs. Rowley*, Rowley, 458 U.S. 176 (1982):

> We therefore concluded that the "basic floor of opportunity" provided by the Act (IDEA) consists of access to specialized instruction and related services which are individually designed to provide educational benefit.

Although there are many criteria used to evaluate FAPE, it often comes down to the question, did the student make "meaningful progress?" However, there is not really any definition of what constitutes meaningful progress. How many words, goals or concepts must a child achieve in order to have made meaningful progress? What new skills does a child have to learn? How do we determine if a child has received educational benefit?

Unfortunately, these questions are not easily answered. In many instances, considerable disagreement may exist among professionals and between school staff and families on whether a child has made progress as well as the amount of progress. Even when there is clear and objective evidence about the absolute level of progress (e.g., student learned four colors and six body parts) the judgment about meaningfulness is a subjective process that can be influenced by preexisting beliefs and values.

Our position is that just because a child learns, it does not necessarily mean the learning was "meaningful". What needs to be examined is the rate of acquisition in comparison to the child's capability. Some children with ASD can learn at the same rate as typically developing children. It is a matter of adapting teaching to fit their individual learning style and intensifying the teaching methodology. Learning 10 words a year, or a month, or even a week, could actually be slow progress and for some students would even be considered regression.

Minimal or trivial progress is simply not acceptable. A student keeping pace with his/her disability is simply not acceptable. In order to be appropriate, educational interventions must result in identifiable and measurable acceleration in learning.

THIS IS FAPE and GOOD SENSE

Under FAPE students are entitled to make "meaningful" progress. Although "meaningful" is difficult to define, for the vast majority of students, the *status quo* or limited progress in our opinion is unaccepable. In order for students to satisfy the legal requirement, a student's learning needs to be at an accelerated rate. Many students are capable of learning and thereby eventually reducing or eliminating services. But it will mean not accepting the *status quo*.

A teacher whom we greatly admire, John Wooden (1973), the former UCLA basketball coach, said it best:

> *"Remember this your life time through*
> *Tomorrow there will be more to do*
> *And failure waits for all who stay*
> *With some success made yesterday*
> *Tomorrow you must try once more*
> *And even harder than before"*

John R. Wooden

PATHS OF PROGRESS

Although the precise number of different trajectories is difficult to determine, we have found from the research and from clinical experience that there are four main groups which seem to follow identifiably different paths of improvement. The differences between the groups become greater over time as illustrated in the hypothetical chart below. We will describe at a very gross level how these groups may be differentiated.

TABLE 1: PATHS OF PROGRESS

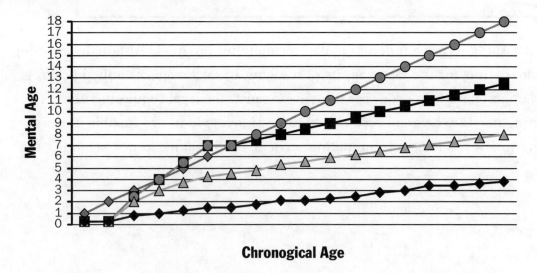

Path 1 (Diamonds): These children make minimal progress even with intensive intervention. Their learning ability is profoundly impaired and even the nonverbal skills which are an area of strength for most children come very slowly if at all. Fortunately this is a tiny proportion of those diagnoses with ASD. We estimate that only around 2% of the autistic population falls into this group (, Eikeseth, Klevstrand, & Lovaas, 1997; Lockeyer & Rutter, 1970).

Path 2 (Triangles): Children on this path make modest progress. Although they are capable of acquiring basic skills, the gaps between typical development and these children's development continue to increase. In the Lovaas studies (1987 and 1993), 2 of the 19 children who received intensive intervention followed this path. These children will have significant communication difficulty, but are able to progress in nonverbal areas of development.

Path 3 (Squares): These children make significant progress and are able to keep the developmental gap from becoming overly wide. Children that follow this path have the capabilities to learn fairly rapidly. Although they may not learn at the same pace as typically developing students they are capable of learning significant amounts of academic information. Therefore, meaningful progress is typically far above what most educators believe is possible. In the Lovaas study, 8 of the 19 children followed path 3.

Path 4 (Circles): These children not only narrow the developmental gaps with intensive early intervention, but they will eliminate the gaps. These students are capable of learning at least at the same pace as "typically" developing students and during the period of intensive treatment are actually learning at a much faster rate that typically developing children. In the Lovaas *et al.* studies (Lovaas, 1987; McEachin, Smith and Lovaas, 1993), these are the children who were in the best outcome group (i.e., 9 out of 19).

The projected differences between these groups at outcome is summarized in the following table (Table 2).

TABLE 2: STATUS AFTER TREATMENT

	HYPOTHETICAL ILLUSTRATION OF OUTCOME			
	PATH 1	PATH 2	PATH 3	PATH 4
SPOKEN WORDS	0	3	500	5,000
PROGRAMS	0	7	25	40
IQ	Untestable	30	80	110

RECOVERY?

The concept of "recovery" is quite controversial to say the least. Many parents have been told by professionals, including physicians, psychologists, educators, speech therapists and occupational therapists, that Autistic Disorder is not only an extremely serious disorder but that it is a severe life long disorder with very little hope of improvement. "Don't expect progress, you will only be disappointed." Often, they first hear about the possibility of recovery when they read Catherine Maurice's book, *Let Me Hear Your Voice: A Family's Triumph (1993)*, a book which may have been recommended to them by another parent. When they read that **both** of Catherine's children "recovered" from autism, they not only become hopeful but empowered. Both her children recovered, so parents have a reason to believe it may be a possibility that their child has a chance for recovery.

School district personnel may be much more jaded in their views. Differences in expectations are often based upon differing views about the nature of the disorder. It often comes to a head on the occasion of a child's first IEP. This is the time when parents begin to express the hope that their child can overcome his disability. These high hopes set the stage for conflict with school district staff if they do not believe it is a possibility. In fact, when they hear a parent even hint at this as being their long term desire the likely interpretation is that the parent is "in denial". Skepticism on the part of school districts can even become cynicism. Parents have heard from school districts that ABA is promoted by greedy, "money-grubbing" behaviorists who are duping parents. Although attending personnel usually do not confront the parent's "denial", it is readily apparent that there is strong disagreement. Lines are drawn in the sand, tape recorders are turned on and the unnecessary, very stressful road to litigation begins.

Many district personnel, as well as other professionals believe that "recovery" is so rare that it should not even be considered as a plausible outcome. After all, typically they have heard, just like parents, that autism is a life long disorder with very little prospect for improvement. And their experiences have often confirmed this belief, although that may be partly due to a self-fulfilling prophecy.

WHAT IS "RECOVERY"?

When we train school district personnel, we often mention that Catherine Maurice's children "recovered". Immediately, a few hands are raised. "What do you mean when you say recovery?" Before answering the question, we ask how many believe that recovery is even a remote possibility? Typically very few believe it is a possibility. It is painfully clear that school districts and parents have extremely different perspectives. And when asked what they think when a parent mentions "recovery", they express a range of emotions from anger to pity. But almost universally it is their conclusion that the parent is naive, uninformed, deluded, or "in denial". They admit when a parent mentions "recovery" it is hard not to hide their disbelief and even anger and they therefore likely respond to them in a patronizing way.

We go on to explain that the concept of recovery was first raised in Dr. Lovaas 1987 outcome study. The operational definition of recovery was that at the **conclusion** of treatment:

1. Children's IQ scores were in the normal range on standardized testing as assessed by independent psychologists.

2. Children were successful in classrooms for typically developing children, **WITHOUT SUPPORTS AND THEY WERE NOT DISTINGUISHED FROM THEIR PEERS** by independent observers who had no prior knowledge of the children's diagnosis.

Long term follow-up showed that children were indistinguishable on blind clinical interviews and several clinical measures including intelligence testing, adaptive behavior scales, and personality testing. We explain that under optimal treatment conditions (i.e., early, intensive and comprehensive treatment) nine out of the 19 children achieved "best outcome" (i.e., "recovery"). Although the majority of children under these best conditions did not achieve this outcome, parents are hoping that their child will beat the odds. We are careful not to over-encourage parents, just as Lovaas did not suggest that children are "cured". We simply do not know what happens in the child's brain and we do no want to imply that the child's brain has been repaired. We just acknowledge that with intensive and quality treatment, it is possible for children to make outstanding progress and some can even become indistinguishable from their peers.

School personnel often will continue to disagree with the concept of "recovery" and will offer these rejoinders:

1. *"These children improved so much they must not have been truly autistic"*

Having a diagnosis of Autistic Disorder does not imply that someone could not improve. The extremely poor prognosis that has been associated with ASD was documented at a time when effective treatment was not available. Outcomes are clearly different now that we know more about how to treat ASD. Critics cannot reject the validity of a diagnosis merely because there was a good outcome. Consider a stroke victim who after receiving intensive speech, occupational and physical therapy returns to normal functioning. Does that mean they did not have a stroke? In other words, just because someone improves and even improves significantly, it does not mean they were originally diagnosed incorrectly. It is necessary to examine the validity of the diagnoses from the YAP on its own merits.

The children in the UCLA Young Autism Project (YAP) were diagnosed by highly trained professionals who were totally independent of YAP. Also, YAP existed during the early 1970's when there were more stringent diagnostic criteria and therefore children were more "classically" autistic. In other words, there were not so many "high functioning" children who were being diagnosed as autistic. At that time if a child exhibited any social abilities or social interest or if they had advanced language skills, they were less likely to be diagnosed with autism. So the children treated in the study met stringent criteria for diagnosis and were very likely to have had a poor outcome if they had not received intensive treatment.

2. *"Perhaps they don't present as autistic anymore, but their symptoms are hidden"*

Who cares? Even if this is true, does it really matter? If they are able to achieve such a high quality of life we are not really concerned about the label. It certainly does not refute the effectiveness or necessity of treatment.

Catherine Maurice (1999) provided insight as a parent of two children who "recovered":

> My son, now almost twelve years old, is in the sixth grade. Similarly
> to his sister, his latest school reports show significant academic
> strength and good social interaction. How normal are they? The
> question, after a while, becomes absurd. How normal are any of us?
> The fact is that they no longer display any of the behaviors associated
> with autism, they are aware of their history, they are empathetic and
> engaging children. The questions frustrate as well because, in the
> past few years, it becomes apparent to me that no amount of data,
> school reports, or follow up evaluations will convince those who are
> determined not to be convinced."

3. *"Well, you selected children who would have favorable outcomes"*

This is a very common rationale for rejecting the results of the Lovaas research. However, there are many reasons why this is not true and would have actually been impossible. First, children were assigned to the intensive treatment or control group prior to meeting them. Second, as mentioned earlier, the diagnostic criteria were quite narrow at the time of YAP, and thus the majority of children would today be considered as "classically autistic". Third, analysis has shown that they were a representative sample and therefore would not be considered as "high functioning" (Lovaas, Smith & McEachin, 1989). And finally, we did not have a clue as to what were favorable indicators of success. This was groundbreaking research and we did not have any idea how much progress the children would make from the intervention, let alone what would have been predictive of favorable outcome.

While it appears that, given our current knowledge about how to treat ASD, the majority of children are not going to completely recover, it is also fair to say that the majority are going to make considerable progress. Our goal should be to uncover what is the true potential of each child and set goals that will enable them to achieve at their level of capability.

PROGNOSTIC INDICATORS

It is difficult to determine in advance which children will respond most favorably to treatment. This difficulty may be due to a few factors. First, lack of cooperation can mask their abilities. Additionally, their poor functioning may not necessarily indicate cognitive impairment. It may be that poor observational learning has hindered their acquisition of knowledge and skills. The observational learning deficits may be amenable to treatment and the intellectual impairment that is suggested by I.Q. tests would not necessarily provide an accurate prediction of outcome.

Although there are not many research findings, presence of communication skills and overall degree of cognitive ability prior to treatment is correlated with outcome. However, the best predictor appears to be rate of learning once a child begins intensive, comprehensive and quality intervention. One study (Leaf, 1982) examined the implications of rate of learning with the children in YAP and found a strong relationship between a faster rate of learning during the first three months of treatment and a child's overall likelihood for a better outcome (Leaf, 1982). It turned out that all of the children who acquired a minimum of 10 nonverbal imitations, 10 verbal imitations and 10 receptive instructions within the first three months of treatment achieved best outcome status (Leaf, 1982). Smith, Groen and Wynn (2000) utilized a similar measure and also found the acquisition of verbal imitation and expressive labeling within the first three months of intervention "appeared to be more strongly associated with outcome than were any of the standardized tests" (page 282). After 12 months of treatment there is an even more reliable indication of which path of progress a child is going to follow. Our experience suggests that progress over one year's time with quality intervention is predictive of rate of progress for the next year.

We believe that the following are indicators of more favorable outcomes. However, we want to be clear that this is not based upon an experimental analysis but based upon over 30 years of clinical experience. Second, these indicators are certainly not accurate for all children. That is, there are children who may have positive indicators but who do not fare well and there are those who possess few of the indicators who end up with much better outcomes.

PRE-TREATMENT FACTORS ASSOCIATED WITH BETTER OUTCOME

1. <u>Level of communication</u>. Although any attempt to communicate is a positive sign, the presence of speech is quite favorable. For example, in the research conducted by Ivar Lovaas (1987), most children who achieved "best outcome" status had some degree of communication skills (verbal or nonverbal) prior to treatment.

2. <u>Social interest</u>. Children who demonstrate an awareness of others, are responsive to social interactions or even attempt to interact have a distinct advantage.

3. <u>Lack of passivity</u>. Perhaps surprisingly, children who exhibit acting out behaviors (e.g., crying, tantrums, non-compliance, aggression, etc.) often achieve a more favorable outcome. Children with disruptive behaviors clearly are attempting to alter the environment and are responding to environmental factors. They care about what happens to them and are therefore more motivated. Thus, it is a matter of teaching them the appropriate behaviors and skills to meet their desires.

4. <u>Involvement with Self Stimulatory Behaviors</u>. Children who are more easily directed away from repetitive and ritualistic behavior will progress better with treatment. Although they may be highly interested in self stimulatory activity and may become highly distressed when others interfere, as long they can be shaped away from such activity they will in time learn to be reinforced by more conventional types of stimulation like that which controls the social and play behavior of typically developing children.

POSITIVE FACTORS AFTER THE ONSET OF TREATMENT

1. <u>Skill acquisition</u>. Children's rate of learning skills early in treatment is highly indicative of how well they will respond to intervention and therefore their eventual outcome. Conversely, children whose learning is quite slow often do not achieve the same degree of success.

2. <u>Overall learning</u>. Children who achieve a favorable outcome demonstrate a good overall response to treatment in a number of areas including communication, social, play, and self-help skills once treatment begins.

It is important to emphasize once again that the pre-treatment factors and positive factors during the early stages of treatment have not yet been well researched. But preliminary findings and anecdotal evidence suggest that these factors are likely indicators of a child's rate of progress.

WHAT IS REALISTIC?

There is no consensus on what type of outcome is realistic to expect. When children are first diagnosed, it is clear that most are far behind typically developing children in terms of various developmental areas including intellectual, cognitive, communication, play, social and self-help (Volkmar, Sparrow, Goudreau, & Cicchetti, 1987; Carpentieri & Morgan, 1996; Van Meter, Fein, Morris, Waterhouse, & Allen, 1997). It is not surprising that there is a tremendous gap. Typically, these children have been withdrawn, uninterested and not observant of the world around them except in a very limited way.

But we know from the literature that children with Autistic Disorder are capable of making considerable progress if they receive sufficiently intensive intervention (e.g., Fenske, Zalenski Krantz & McClannahan, 1985; Handleman, Harris, Celiberti, Lilleht & Tomcheck, 1991; Harris, Handleman, Kristoff, Bass & Gordon, R., 1990; Hoyson, Jamieson & Strain, 1984; Koegel, Koegel, Shoshan & McNerney, 1999; Lovaas, 1987; McEachin, Smith & Lovaas, 1993). Naturally there will be tremendous variation among children (Lovaas, Koegel, Simmons & Long, 1973; Lovaas, 1987; Harris & Handleman, 2000). We do know, however, that children with Autistic Disorder are generally far more capable than most educators and other professionals believe. Therefore education should be designed to teach children as many skills as possible so as to minimize the developmental gaps.

CONSTRUCT OF MEANINGFUL PROGRESS

As one can see from the depiction of possible paths of progress, there are widely varying possible outcomes. It would be very helpful to identify which path a child should be on so that we know what to aim for. Perhaps we can formulate an individual definition of meaningful progress based upon prognostic indicators and more importantly how a student responds to quality education. Obviously, we will need to periodically evaluate the prediction based upon most recent performance and adjust our expectations accordingly. We believe that progress can only be considered meaningful if it meets or exceeds what we have judged to be the student's potential. Here are some proposed criteria that may be useful in defining meaningful progress:

Path 1: The criteria for meaningful progress for a child on Path 1 would be quite limited. They may not be able to acquire any functional vocabulary, even after several years. Gains in other areas will occur extremely slowly. Self-stimulatory behavior interferes substantially with the development of adaptive skills. Meaningful progress will need to be measured in extremely small steps over an extended period of time. These students will fall farther and farther behind compared to Paths 2, 3 and 4.

Path 2: Meaningful progress for a child on Path 2 would see moderate gains in nonverbal skills such as matching and imitation. Although communication skills will emerge slowly, they are capable of learning basic concepts, especially if presented in a visual modality. These students will progress faster that Path 1, but will continue to fall far behind on the developmental curve. School Districts too often conclude that the rate of progress that these students demonstrate is the expectation that should apply to most students with ASD. However, outcome studies from intensive behavioral treatment indicate Path 2 should only comprise approximately 10% of students with ASD (e.g., Lovaas, 1987; Sallows and Graupner, 2005).

Path 3: Meaningful progress would consist of a much more rapid rate of learning for a child on Path 3. They should be learning more than 100 words per year with a corresponding rate of acquisition of concepts and general knowledge. The developmental gap is still widening but is not nearly as great compare to students on Path 1 and 2. Students on Path 3 should be successfully learning academic skills.

Path 4: A child on Path 4 should be significantly closing the developmental gap (e.g., in 1 year of treatment they have gained 1.5 to 2 years developmental growth on psychometric measures) and the rate of learning needs to continue at a similar pace to be considered as having made "meaningful" progress. For example, a student would need to be learning more than 1,000 words per year to achieve meaningful progress. This would appear as a steeply ascending curve on a chart of developmental progress.

EXTENDED SCHOOL YEAR (ESY)

The degree of developmental gap that exists for children with ASD is affected by rate of progress. Faster progress means less of a gap. Our educational journey is actually a race against time. In order to achieve our definition of "meaningful progress" it is usually necessary that a student receive services throughout the year. Extended breaks are like taking our foot off the accelerator pedal. If we are going to be successful in this race, we need to keep our foot pressed firmly to the floor. The National Research Council (2001) recommended that children receive services for 52 weeks a year. They recognized that autism does not take vacations! Taking a six week break or even longer results in lost opportunity that can never be recouped. Even if regression as measured on an absolute scale did not occur, extended breaks mean falling behind compared to what the student could be achieving with continuation of services.

Many school districts set up extended school year solely to prevent regression and do not aim to advance student skills over the long summer break. Some amount of regression even for typically developing children is common, but it is expected that most children can recoup their losses within a short period of time. If students simply maintain their skill level from June until September, then the legal requirement for FAPE is deemed to be fulfilled. However, as we have previously discussed, standing still for a child with ASD is tantamount to regression because during this time their typical peers continue to progress at an accelerated pace. That is the nature of ASD and that is why intensive intervention is necessary. Without year round services the developmental gap will widen and the student will farther behind. That is not our definition of meaningful progress.

ARBITRARY BENCHMARKS

A measure of progress that is commonly used consists of calculating the percentage of goals that have been achieved in the annual IEP. Although this may seem clear enough, if one considers the process of setting goals it becomes evident that such a measure is totally arbitrary. It is just as much related to the ambitiousness of the goals as it is a function of how much the student learned. At the IEP everyone makes a somewhat educated guess as to how much the child will learn in the upcoming year. Will she learn 5 words, 10 words or 100 in the next year? Some participants may feel 5 is reasonable while others argue for 100. What percent reduction of aggression can be expected: 10%? 25%? 50%? If you have low expectations (e.g., 5 words and 10% reduction of aggression) and the child accomplishes them, does that mean she has made meaningful progress? If however, you had high expectations and she did not accomplish the goals does that mean she failed to make meaningful progress? If we accept percent of goals met as the measure of outcome, then there is inherent temptation to set goals low. It would be foolish to set them high and run the risk of not meeting the goals. No one can really complain because it is only a guess, after all.

However, goals need to be much more than a guess. They should be based upon objective observation and data examining a child's rate of progress during a period of quality intervention. By quality we mean systematic and intensive instruction undertaken with the presumption that the student is highly capable and that every minute in school should be an opportunity to learn. Typically, initial IEP goals are determined in a 30-day evaluation period. This may not be enough time. In order to make projections 12 months into the future, it often takes three to six months to adequately assess a child's skill level and likely rate of progress. This will enable educators, practitioners, and parents to come closer to set more realistic and ambitious goals. And once there are sound goals, the definition of meaningful progress becomes easier to ascertain.

THE INDIVIDUALIZED DECISION MAKING PROCESS

For many students with disabilities, the IEP process has become routine, and largely ineffective. Its intent to individualize and result in "specialized instruction to meet the unique needs of the child", is rarely achieved. The process is too often done as a formality and is far too casual to resemble a thoughtful statement about a student's education. While this is certainly a problem for the 85% of the nation's special education population who are "mildly disabled" or mainly need help with articulation or reading problems, students who struggle with more pervasive and severe disabilities are profoundly affected when the IEP process does not live up to its ideal. Students with ASD desperately need individualized programming aimed at producing meaningful progress with clear criteria for evaluating outcomes so that interventions can be modified as necessary. For these students, the words of the Supreme Court really do ring true: ". . . access to specialized instruction and related services which are individually designed to provide educational benefit."

The obligation to ensure that the Court's standard is met lies squarely with school districts. The principal failure of school districts and state education agencies has been to refuse to grapple with defining benefit *before* the lawsuit. Apparently, as long as the District is not in some imminent danger of legal action, it is preferable to avoid the problem. Those of us who have seen the result of this failure are utterly committed to helping avoid it. The costs in money, resources and good will is enormous. One such case can cost a District hundreds of thousands of dollars, frequently exceeding half a million dollars in legal and expert fees alone.

Here are some thing that families and school districts can do to improve the process and outcomes for students:

- Become knowledgeable about the real possibilities for students. Read the literature and rely on external expertise that has a track record of performance.

- Avoid any programs or professionals claiming there is a single comprehensive approach that absolutely works.

- Avoid the "emotion of the big gain" event when the student is first introduced to a systematic intervention and shows remarkable growth.

- Celebrate success.

- Use the IEP process to actually establish present levels of performance that address all the necessary areas and truly reflect the student's current performance.

- Discuss expectations and work hard to determine what are reasonable outcomes from instruction.

- Do not ever destroy a family's dreams, but always help to achieve the programs that move the student in those directions.

- Allow teachers the discretion to teach and intervene in a wide variety of ways.

- Take data consistently as a part of instruction and use it to inform instructional decisions.

- Assess and report progress consistently and regularly.

- Define and write what constitutes meaningful progress for a student and explain it fully to all parties.

GOOD SENSE
USE THE IEP PROCESS TO COMMUNICATE AND PLAN AS THE SUPREME COURT EXPLAINED IT

The explanations of benefit and progress in this chapter will hopefully assist school districts and families in coming to grips with benefit and meaningful progress in an atmosphere of trust born of knowledge and real understanding. This is entirely possible, and is absolutely in everyone's interest, particularly the child. Once people are willing to recognize that autism is a far more treatable condition than previously thought possible, more opportunities will be created and children will attain much more positive outcomes. Many, many children can exceed the slow rate of progress that people have been willing to settle for. We need to be aiming higher.

REFERENCES

Board of Education of the Hendrick Hudson Central School District vs. Rowley, Rowley, 458 U.S. 176 (1982).

Carpentieri, S. & Morgan, S. B. (1996). Adaptive and intellectual functioning in autistic and nonautistic retarded children. Journal of Autism and Developmental Disorders, 26(6), 611-620.

Federal regulations at 34 C. F. R. Part 300.313: (Authority: 20 U.S.C. 1401(8)).

Fenske, E.C., Zalenski, S., Krantz, P.J., & McClannahan, L.E. (1985). Age at intervention and treatment outcome for autistic children in a comprehensive intervention program. Analysis and Intervention in Developmental Disabilities, 5, 49-58.

Handleman, J.S., Harris, S.L., Celiberti, D., Lilleht, E., & Tomcheck, L. (1991). Developmental changes of preschool children with autism and normally developing peers. *Infant-Toddler Intervention*, 1, 137-143.

Harris, S., Handleman, J.S., Kristoff, B., Bass, L., & Gordon, R. (1990). Changes in language development among autistic and peer children in segregated and integrated preschool settings. *Journal of Autism and Developmental Disabilities*, 20, 23-31.

Harris, S. L. & Handleman, J. S. (2000). Age and IQ at intake as predictors of placement for young children with autism: A four- to six-year follow-up. Journal of Autism and Developmental Disorders, 30(2), 137-142.

Hoyson, M., Jamieson, B., & Strain, P.S. (1984). Individualized group instruction of normally developing and autistic-like children: The LEAP curriculum model. Journal of the Division of Early Childhood, 8, 157-172.

Koegel, L. K., Koegel, R. L., Shoshan, Y., & McNerney, E. (1999). Pivotal response intervention II: Preliminary long-term outcomes data. *Journal of the Association for Persons with Severe Handicaps, 24*(3), 186-198].

Leaf, R. B. (1982). Outcome and predictive measures. Paper presented at the annual meeting of the American Psychological Association, Washington, DC.

Lockyer, L. & Rutter, M. (1970). A five- to fifteen-year follow-up study of infantile psychosis: IV. Patterns of cognitive ability. British Journal of Social & Clinical Psychology, 9(2), 152-163.]

Lovaas, O.I. (1987). Behavioral Treatment and normal educational and intellectual functioning in young autistic children. Journal of Clinical and Consulting Psychology, 55(1), 3-9.

Lovaas, O. I., Koegel, R., Simmons, J. Q., & Long, J. S. (1973). Some generalization and follow-up measures on autistic children in behavior therapy.Journal of Applied Behavior Analysis, 6(1), 131-166.

Lovaas, O. I., Smith, T., & McEachin, J. J. (1989). Clarifying comments on the young autism study: Reply to Schopler, Short, and Mesibov. *Journal of Consulting and Clinical Psychology, 57*(1), 165-167.

Maurice, Catherine (1993). Let me hear your voice. A family's triumph over autism. NY: Fawcett Columbine.

Maurice, Catherine (1999). "ABA and us: One parent's reflections on partnership and persuasion." Address to Cambridge Center for Behavioral Studies Annual Board Meeting, Palm Beach, Florida, November, 1999.

McEachin, J.J., Smith, T., & Lovaas, O.I. (1993). Long-Term outcome for children with autism who received early intensive behavioral treatment. American Journal on Mental Retardation, 97(4), 359-372.

National Research Council (2001): Educating Children with Autism, Washington, D.C., National Academy Press.

Sallows, G. O. & Graupner, T. D. (2005). Intensive behavioral treatment for children with autism: Four-year outcome and predictors.American Journal on Mental Retardation, 110(6), 417-438.

Smith, T., Eikeseth, S., Klevstrand, M., & Lovaas, O. I. (1997). Intensive behavioral treatment for preschoolers with severe mental retardations and pervasive developmental disorder. American Journal on Mental Retardation, 102(3), 238-249.

Smith, T., Groen., A., & Wynn, J.W. (2000). Randomized Trial of Intensive Early Intervention for Children with Pervasive Developmental Disorder. American Journal on Mental Retardation, 105, 269-285.

VanMeter, L., Fein, D., Morris, R., Waterhouse, L., & Allen, D. (1997). Delay versus deviance in autistic social behavior. Journal of Autism and Developmental Disorders, Vol 27(5), 557-569.

Volkmar, F. R., Sparrow, S. S., Goudreau, D., Cicchetti, D. V., et al. (1987). Social deficits in autism: An operational approach using the Vineland Adaptive Behavior Scales. Journal of the American Academy of Child & Adolescent Psychiatry. 1987 Mar Vol 26(2) 156-161.

Wooden, J. R. (1973). The Wooden Style. *Time*, February 12.

Chapter 15

INCLUSION - SENSE AND NONSENSE

By Ron Leaf, Tracee Parker & John McEachin

INTRODUCTION

A number of different terms and definitions have been used over the years to describe the movements, concepts, approaches and the process itself of including children with disabilities within the general population of regular education students (Fuchs & Fuchs, 1994). To date, there is no one universally accepted definition of "inclusion" (Harrower, 1999; Fuchs & Fuchs, 1994; Havey, 1998). Additionally, the applications of inclusion range from students with mild learning disabilities to those with only behavioral challenges to ALL students with disabilities. The scope has included at a minimum the elimination of segregated schools, but often extended to elimination of ALL segregated classrooms. There is wide variation in the type of strategies or models that are proposed to promote successful inclusion. Commonly these approaches or models appear based on one's affiliation with a particular movement, culture or subculture. Similar to the definition, there is no established standard or practice with regard to how this model is implemented or its effectiveness evaluated. (Harrower, 1999; Fuchs & Fuchs, 1994).

For the purposes of clarity within this chapter, the following terms and definitions will be utilized:

Inclusion or Full Inclusion: Refers to the practice, philosophy and approach of integrating ALL students (including those with ASD) into school settings where they share the same resources and opportunities with regular education students, on a FULL time basis.

Integration: Refers to the practice, philosophy and approach of educating students part of the time in less restrictive settings including but not limited to the general education classroom. This practice has also been referred to as "mainstreaming". Students can be integrated by varying degrees according the student's particular needs and abilities. The degree of inclusion is characterized not only by the amount of time spent outside the special education class, but also by the nature and location of services provided. In addition to the regular education class, this may include resource or special education classrooms which vary in intensity and structure, "pull out" (providing special services outside of the classroom), "push in" (providing services within the regular classroom context), reverse mainstreaming (more-abled students coming into the special education setting), and peer tutors or aides.

INCLUSION AS A REACTION AGAINST THE EVIL OF SEGREGATION

Historically, children with developmental delays were often removed from the community at a very young age and placed in residential institutions. In the first half of the 20th century, children who we now recognize as having ASD would have been regarded as schizophrenic or mentally retarded and not capable of learning. They could be found amongst the multitude of intellectually impaired and behaviorally "unmanageable" who, regardless of whether they were living at home or in state hospitals, had little chance of receiving an education because it was generally believed that they could not benefit from teaching. In the second half of the 20th century students with ASD were beginning to be recognized as a distinct diagnostic group. People gradually began to realize that institutionalization was not a good option. However, segregation still existed within the school system. All too often, by the mere fact of their diagnosis, students with ASD (even in its mildest forms) were placed in highly restrictive settings. They failed to acquire new skills and their disruptive behaviors often increased in both frequency and intensity within segregated classrooms. Indeed, they were not going forward, they were actually regressing.

Inclusion came about as a reaction against children receiving poor education in special education classrooms for far too long. It was first described, and applied to students with physical disabilities possessing normal intelligence. Because their handicaps made it difficult to envision these students managing in a typical classroom setting they were removed from the mainstream and placed with other students who were also excluded for a variety of reasons. This resulted in students who were academically capable being placed in restrictive settings with students who had significant learning difficulties and/or behavioral challenges. Eventually there was an uprising against the injustice. Not surprisingly, when accommodations were made for their physical disability, students were more effectively educated in typical placements. Additionally there was a positive impact socially and non-disabled students became more accepting of individuals who are different.

Inspired by the success with physically disabled children, educators subsequently applied this approach to students with other types of disabilities including those with learning disabilities (Simmons, Kameenui & Chard, 1998; Waldron & McLeskey, 1998), developmental disabilities (Hurley-Geffner, 1995), and behavior problems/disorders (Falk, Dunlap & Kern, 1996; Locke & Fuchs, 1995). Fueled by factors including de-institutionalization and normalization (Bachrach, 1986; Wolfensberger, 1972;) and general dissatisfaction with special education, the "inclusion model" gained greater momentum in its application to students with increasingly difficult challenges, including many with severe disabilities (Downing, Eichinger & Williams, 1997; Giangreco, 1993; Hilton & Liberty, 1992; Hunt & Goetz, 1997; Janney & Snell, 1997; Kennedy, Cushing, Itkonen, 1997); and eventually to those identified within the continuum of ASD (Harrower & Dunlap, 2001; Gaylord-Ross & Pitts-Conway, 1984; Kamps, Barbetta, Leonard, Delquadri, 1994; Kamps, et al., 1995; Kohler, Strain & Shearer, 1996; Pierce & Schreibman, 1997; Russo & Koegel, 1977; Strain, 1983)

Self-contained placements do not necessarily offer the teaching of meaningful skills. Students may spend a great deal of time in activities that are not functional for them and therefore will not help them achieve greater degrees of independence and more importantly obtain a higher quality of life. The day is all too often spent doing "busy work." Although most everyone is well intentioned and creating a pleasant atmosphere, spending the majority of time doing arts and crafts, listening to songs, completing repetitive tasks or "playing independently" will not be helpful to the student in acquiring essential skills. As students get older, it becomes all too clear that their future is bleak. A parent's dreams are shattered as they come to realize that their child is making limited progress and will always have to be in a restrictive setting.

Inclusion would appear to be a wonderful solution! First, their child would not be exposed to other children who exhibit disruptive behaviors, thereby reducing the likelihood of their imitating and learning such behaviors. Moreover, children in inclusion would seem to provide good modeling of appropriate language, play and social skills. Additionally, a typical education classroom may afford students with disabilities, including ASD, the opportunity to participate in more mainstream and varied social and educational experiences that may not be offered in segregated placements (Harrower, 1999). And, having a child in inclusion where they are exposed to an academic curriculum is naturally a welcomed relief!

Differences in expectations can also have a dramatic impact. If one believes a student will be successful, there is a greater likelihood that will be the outcome, not only because of attitude but because of the increased effort that naturally come along with positive expectations. When inclusion programs are implemented there is generally an allocation of manpower and resources which also help ensure students will be successful, advance to the next grade level and eventually graduate.

Conversely, low expectations, commonly found in self-contained classrooms, become a self-fulfilling prophecy. The traditional perspective has that students will learn a little but they will always be limited by their disability. A day would be considered "good" or "great" primarily based on the absence or low rate of disruptive behaviors, and not so much the degree to which new skills are acquired. Naturally the best way to prevent disruptive behaviors is provide a lot of "support" and make very few demands.

As we previously discussed, the historical belief that students with ASD will make minimal gains at best became a self-fulfilling prophecy. Indeed, most children who were in special education were NOT very successful, thus there was little incentive to put in place an optimal educational program. However, without good programming, long term failure is guaranteed. All too often special education is infiltrated with doom and gloom!

THE PENDULUM SWINGS TOO FAR: INSISTING ON FULL INCLUSION FOR EVERYONE

Unfortunately, many professionals have indiscriminately extended the concept of inclusion to ALL students with disabilities, including those with ASD (Stainback & Stainback, 1996; Fuchs & Fuchs, 1994). All too often, students are misplaced in full-time "nonrestrictive" settings, regardless of their educational needs and despite the fact that some students demonstrate severely disruptive behaviors and skill deficits that could more effectively be addressed in a more intensive instructional setting.

Jerry Newport, an adult with ASD, has recounted his experience being included in regular education. Here is what he said in a speech entitled "THE MYTH OF INCLUSION" (Newport, 2002)

> Inclusion is another oversold concept. I write both as a victim and beneficiary. The
> myth about inclusion is that if your child is in a normal class, that normalcy will

magically rub off on your child. The truth is far different.

After twelve years of inclusion, I stood at center stage in the gym on graduation day and delivered my salutatory address on "The Relative Unimportance of Grooming." I probably had my fly open but the gown concealed that and was too long for me to try picking my butt in public.

My main benefit from inclusion was that I have never felt as if society can deny any basic rights to me because I am different. So while I am more happy than not that I was fully included, I wish it had been more of a mix. I strongly suggest that for most of my peers in autism, more challenged in youth than I was, that total inclusion is not the way to go at first, if at all.

You have to remember too, whose needs are at stake. Toss out your ego. The goal is not to have your child included, at any cost, so you can say, "He's fine now. He's in a normal class just like your brat." If that means four German Shepherds and a private SWAT team for assistance, that is not inclusion. That is delusion and a waste of taxpayers' money. (Page 2)

Inclusion was a response to serious flaws in the educational system and a reaction against discriminatory practices. Unfortunately, some inclusion proponents have taken a very sound ideal to ridiculous extremes. Bernard Rimland in an editorial for Autism Research Review International has referred to such extremists as "advozealots" (Rimland, 1993). It is important to note that many supporters of inclusion are not zealots. But the extremists have commanded a significant audience and when people blindly follow the crusade students can be harmed despite the good intentions.

The ideal classroom placement should be based upon the student's strengths and deficits. In order to meet the widely varying needs of individual students there has to be a continuum of placement opportunities. The job of the IEP team is to achieve the best balance between meeting the needs of the student and keeping him as close to the mainstream as possible. Students should not have to begin their education in a restrictive environment and work their way to the least restrictive setting. If a student could be in a less restrictive setting, even if he requires special support to be successful, then he is entitled to that support. If a restrictive setting is being considered, the burden of proof is on the school district to show that mainstream placement is NOT appropriate, rather than parents having to justify the request for mainstream placement. We must be guided by data and what is in the best interest of the child and not by ideology, dogma or economics.

The desired outcome is for a student to develop a high level of competence and independence and have access to the full range of opportunities that exist in the community. This goal is similar to the goal for a patient with a serious medical condition. For a patient who is gravely ill, going into the Intensive Care Unit (ICU) is equivalent to a segregated special education classroom. It is the setting which most effectively allows the patient to return to health and be free from the restrictions caused by his condition. You could say that spending time in a restrictive setting is the best way to have long term success, and ironically denying the patient access to this specialized setting could result in less independence over the long term.

Naturally, if a student is capable of achieving success in a general education setting, from the outset, that is where he should be. However, many students need to acquire foundational skills in a setting where the level of demands and the level of proficiency required is something they can attain. Just like spending time in the minor leagues where the pitches are a little slower, which allows a batter to sharpen his eye. Full inclusion may not offer the type of teaching necessary to enable such students to actually learn new skills. Many students with ASD do not start out with the behavioral control, requisite skills or learning style to be able to benefit from full inclusion. Some would argue all that would be needed is to provide accommodations and supports. However, if the setting is not appropriate, accommodations only serve to mask the lack of progress.

FINDING THE MIDDLE GROUND

Perhaps in an effort to incite strong action against the evils of segregation, people in the "FULL inclusion" camp have adopted an extreme ethic which has evolved into a very exclusive, "all or none" view of inclusion. Within the educational and research arenas, people are often pigeonholed as either pro- or anti-inclusion. However, educational placement should not be a black or white decision.

When considering the range of placement options, what truly constitutes "restrictiveness" must be determined according to the needs of the specific child. It should NOT be a matter of whether inclusion is good or bad. It should be based on what placement or combination of placements would provide the student the best learning opportunities to maximize his potential.

NONSENSE
EXTREMISTS WHO, ALTHOUGH RIGHT TO RAIL AGAINST SEGREGATION, ZEALOUSLY PROMOTE A ONE-SIZE FITS ALL SOLUTION TO MEETING THE VARIED NEEDS OF INDIVIDUAL STUDENTS.
SENSE
WE SHOULD ALL FIGHT HARD TO PREVENT SEGREGATION BUT WE MUST NOT ELIMINATE CHOICES FOR STUDENTS WHO NEED SPECIALZED PLACEMENTS.

There are indeed students who are in restrictive placements who would be more appropriately placed in more integrated settings. What the inclusion zealots insist on can be right for many students, but they are not justified in bypassing the decision making process and taking away options for students who need them. Full inclusion should be the outcome of a careful decision process, not the starting point. Placement should only be determined after development of meaningful instructional objectives and consideration of the most effective approach for teaching the agreed upon skills. Too often this is not the basis or methodology for deciding on placement or programmatic focus.

LEAST RESTRICTIVE ENVIRONMENT

Often parents, educators and attorneys use Least Restrictive Environment (LRE) as justification that students should be placed in inclusion. It is their interpretation that it is actually mandatory that all children be initially placed in inclusion. If they should demonstrate significant problems, then they may be placed in a more restrictive setting.

However, this is a misinterpretation of the law. What the law actually says is that children with disabilities shall be educated with non-disabled children to the maximum extent appropriate EXCEPT when education in the regular environment with supplemental aides and service CANNOT BE ACHIEVED SATISFACTORILY.

It does not say that a child, regardless of skills or behaviors, must be first placed in inclusion! Yes, inclusion needs to be seriously considered. However, if there is evidence that inclusion would result in a student not achieving satisfactory results, then there is no prohibition on a more restrictive educational placement.

More importantly, legal issues aside, this approach would mandate a vast number of students to fail before a configuration of individualized and appropriate educational services and placements are designed. When this "legal rationale" is used to strong-arm the maintenance of an inappropriate and detrimental placement, the student may, and often does, undergo an extended period of failure before effective intervention is provided. In the long run, students who could have been integrated to varying degrees much sooner, are often restricted from these options for longer periods due to the problematic history that has been established. This history is often both behavioral (behaviors that have been shaped in these settings) as well as social (the negative reputation that has now been created with their peers).

DELUSIONS ABOUT INCLUSION

To say there has been tremendous interest in inclusion would be an understatement! Surprisingly, there is very little research to demonstrate that inclusion is clearly more advantageous than alternative placements that have been deemed restrictive. Inclusion zealots rarely discuss the disadvantages. Moreover, there are some tremendous fallacies. The following are just some of the most critical and troublesome delusions about inclusion.

DELUSION 1: EXPOSURE IS SUFFICIENT

There is often the myth that if a child is placed in an inclusion setting, desirable and meaningful changes will occur. That is, not only will their behaviors conform to social norms but they will readily acquire communication and social skills. Moreover, they will pick up valuable school readiness skills, as well as develop in areas of cognition and academic skills. The truth, however, is that for most children with ASD exposure alone is not sufficient for learning to occur. Research has shown that exposure and inclusion <u>ALONE</u> are insufficient for children with Autistic Disorder in achieving an appropriate education (Hunt & Goetz, 1997; Kohler, Strain, & Shearer, 1996). If exposure was sufficient then most likely the child would not be showing the deficits associated with ASD. Actually, if exposure was sufficient, then anyone who wants to become a professional athlete would just need to spend a lot of time in the locker room. Or we should all hang out on the Harvard campus, and be brilliant, just through association.

All too often children with ASD have not acquired or generalized the requisite skills to enable them to learn from incidental social exposure and traditional instructional methods alone. Often children have not established foundational skills such as observational learning, concentration and attentional skills necessary for learning in typical group instructional settings. Research has shown that direct instruction is often necessary for effective and meaningful learning to take place (Callahan & Rademacher, 1999; Davis, Brady, Hamilton, McEvoy & Williams, 1994; Dunlap, Dunlap, Koegel & Koegel, 1991; Goldstein & Cisar, 1992; Hunt, Farron-Davis, Wrenn, Hirose-Hatae & Goetz, 1997; McGee, Morrier & Daly, 1999; Pierce & Schreibman, 1997; Smith & Camarata, 1999).

Consequently, it is highly unlikely that the child will pick up information in a casual, less direct manner. It is ironic that many of the zealots who believe children with ASD are unable to learn observationally, and insist on exclusive one-to-one instruction in distraction free environments, are often the same individuals who push <u>FULL</u> inclusion.

NONSENSE
THE BELIEF THAT EXPOSURE TO TYPCIALLY DEVELOPING CHILDREN IS ALL IT TAKES TO REMEDY SOCIAL SKILLS DEFICITS.   IF A CHILD COULD EASILY ASSIMILATE THE SKILLS OF OTHERS THEN THOSE DEFICITS WOULD NEVER HAVE OCCURRED IN THE FIRST PLACE AND THE CHILD CERTAINLY WOULD NOT HAVE ENDED UP WITH ASD.

DELUSION 2: INCLUSION FACILITATES BEHAVIORAL CONTROL

One of the benefits of inclusion that teachers and parents often describe is significant reduction in disruptive behaviors. Children's aggression, crying and noncompliance will seemingly dissolve when they enter the regular education setting. There are a number of factors that may contribute to this change:

1. It may be that the student was previously bored in a more restrictive placement and therefore the inclusion placement is sufficiently challenging to the child.

2. Another explanation may be that the peers are serving as good models of appropriate behavior.

3. A third possibility is that the student is influenced by peers. That is, they may fear the embarrassment and repercussions if they engage in disruptive behaviors.

4. It may be that the school's staff maintains higher expectations and intolerance for disruptive behaviors.

Although the above explanations may all be reasons for the reduction of disruptive behaviors, there may be alternative explanations as well. If any of the following factors are operating, then seeming behavioral improvement as a result of inclusion is really just a facade.

5. The child is receiving extensive attention from the instructional staff.

6. The child is receiving continuous prompting and is therefore guaranteed success.

7. There are tremendous accommodations made in curriculum, rules and expectations.

8. The child is permitted to do what they want, e.g., avoid tasks or engage in self-stimulation.

Even more damaging than the facade, is that the child may be learning exactly the opposite of what we want him to learn, e.g., others will do things for you, it is okay NOT to follow the rules, you do not have to do your work, and that odd or inappropriate behavior is socially acceptable in natural and socially integrated settings.

DELUSION 3: INCLUSION GUARANTEES FRIENDSHIPS

Inclusion has often been viewed as a tremendous advantage because of the social benefit it can afford. It is argued, that by being around typically developing children, students with autism will be able to acquire the social skills necessary to develop friendships. As discussed previously, one of the flaws with this thinking is the belief that children can acquire these skills merely through exposure. Unfortunately, most children with ASD require systematic, comprehensive intervention to learn these skills.

Proponents of inclusion, both professionals and parents, justify inclusion because of the "appearance" of friendships. During the early school years, comments are often made about how caring and interested the other children are. Peers will often make sure to include students with ASD in their games, while providing the necessary support and care to facilitate success. However, one must ask whether they are developing true friendships? Or are the other children simply being friendly because of the student's disability?

Are children being asked to birthday parties or play dates because their peers really want them as their "buddy" or because they are trying to do the kind thing? "Friendships", by definition, involve reciprocity. It is <u>mutually</u> beneficial and there is equity in the give and take with one another. A true friendship is not based solely upon the feeling of responsibility or kindness, at least in the case of healthy relationships. When this balance is missing, we often refer to the relationship as "co-dependent".

Additionally, it should be noted that friendships are typically developed based upon mutual interests and similarities. In theory, it may be idyllic if everyone had friends regardless of cognitive ability, interests or other diversities. However, it simply is not our culture's reality. It is imperative that we teach children with ASD the necessary skills so they can develop true lifelong friendships based upon mutual interests, needs and desires, AND the skills to sustain such relationships.

Fortunately, when children are of preschool, kindergarten or early elementary school age, they are typically very accepting. However, by the first grade it is more often the girls who are interested in playing with our children. Perhaps it is because girls are more nurturing and patient and typically will stay longer with activities. In the next few years the girls will have generally formed their own cliques. Because the social skills of many of our children, predominantly boys, have become increasingly disparate from those of their peers, they are included less and less. In general, as typical children become older, they often become less patient, more intolerant and sometimes even cruel. Students with ASD are sometimes faced with the harsh reality that these peers were not actually their friends. And this can be absolutely devastating. It is not uncommon that this results in tremendous confusion, sadness and even depression. This confusion and frustration is fueled by the fact that for so long, they were "accepted" for behaving in the same ways that they are now being ostracized for. And these maladaptive behaviors are now more ingrained and generalized, due to the long history of "acceptance".

From a social learning standpoint, consider this: In their efforts to be kind and please their teachers and parents, peers often succumb, accept and reinforce inappropriate behaviors, which they would never tolerate from a typical peer or friend. Over time, the student with ASD "learns" that these are acceptable and adaptive ways to interact with their "friends". Later on, when these students are referred to us for therapy, the undoing of these "social/behavioral lessons" will require extensive time and intervention.

DELUSION 4: DISRUPTIVE BEHAVIORS WILL BE LEARNED IF A STUDENT IS IN SPECIAL EDUCATION

Although it is certainly possible for a child in a special education classroom to pick up the undesirable behaviors of classmates, it does not have to occur. A quality special education program will employ effective programs to teach discrimination of which behaviors are okay to imitate and teach them **NOT** to imitate unacceptable behaviors, regardless of whether they are modeled by typical or "non-typical" peers. It is essential that they learn which behaviors to model and which ones to ignore. Throughout their life they will be exposed to situations and behaviors which should not be emulated.

Teachers will need to systematically expose students to situations where appropriate behavior is being modeled and provide reinforcement for imitation of those behaviors. There also needs to be deliberate, but controlled exposure to inappropriate behaviors and reinforcement then only occurs for refraining from imitation. If a child imitates an inappropriate behavior there needs to be corrective feedback and additional opportunities to practice making the right choice. Such "lessons" will require systematic application into more natural and varied settings in order to establish these skills as functional and generalized.

DELUSION 5: MODELLING MUST COME FROM TYPICALLY DEVELOPING CHILDREN

It seems to be accepted that the best peer is a "typically developing" peer. Why? If peers are operating at a far superior level, it may actually not be optimal. Such a vast disparity in abilities may require teaching skills far beyond the level one should reasonably expect. Is a novice playing golf with Tiger Woods the best learning opportunity? Tiger is so superior that emulating him would seem impossible and discouraging. In fact, if a peer has vastly superior skills, it is likely the standard is so high that learning may become excessively difficult and in fact, quite frustrating. And, not only for the "target" child, but the typical peer as well. Certainly having a model that possesses skills from which we can learn is crucial, but perhaps not skills so advanced that it becomes intimidating and discourages effort.

An unfortunate belief is that typically developing children are the best models for children with autism and that, conversely, children with disabilities are poor models. There is actually little scientific evidence showing that children with ASD actually benefit significantly from merely being exposed to typically developing children or inclusion.

Why cannot a child with a disability be an equally ideal peer? There is certainly consensus that the optimal models are children who possess higher skill levels in areas such as communication, play and socialization as well as exhibit behavioral control. This does not mean that it should or must be a child without any deficits. Is it not better that the model be someone who performs at a moderately higher level, particularly one who has strengths in areas that the target child does not, AND weaknesses in skills that the "target" child can perform well? This reciprocity and mutual benefit might actually create the foundation of a friendship. In our many years of clinical experience, we have certainly found this to be the case.

Another consideration is the emotional impact on children who have some awareness that they are different. The message to them may be: "The only <u>acceptable</u> peers and friends are those who are typical." This may imply to our children that, "there is something wrong or inadequate with kids who have disabilities". The underlying message is, "this includes you". How does this message impact the development of self-esteem and self confidence over the long term? "Regardless of what you do or achieve, kids like you are never good enough." Certainly something to consider.

DELUSION 6: SINCE THE STUDENT IS PROGRESSING OR AT LEAST MAINTAINING, IT IS AN APPROPRIATE PLACEMENT

First, although a child may be progressing, it may be quite possible that the student may be able to learn at even a faster rate and more independently, in a more "restrictive" placement. With increased structure, individualized attention and more specially trained staff the student may do even better, in the short and long term.

Second, a child may seem to fare well in the earlier years of school because they already know many of the concepts being taught. Also the nature of the curriculum is relatively concrete and this is where children with ASD often excel. However, with increasing age and grade level, the concepts and skills necessary for learning become far more abstract. It may be appropriate to maintain a child in the mainstream for the first couple of years, but the team should be prepared to make changes as the nature of the learning becomes more and more verbally based and there is less reliance on hands-on learning. Performance and progress during the earlier years, may give a false sense of security.

Third, as discussed previously, it has been our overwhelming experience that as children age, the acceptance and "friendships" by their peers, diminishes. Even though it may feel as though a child's placement is ideal because of the development of friendships, one must evaluate whether the friendships are genuine or if peers are just being kind, bossy, friendly or co-dependent.

Fourth, when there are extensive accommodations it can appear as though the student is learning and progressing. However, the continuous support the child receives can obscure significant learning deficits which will only become more pronounced without intensive instruction. Quite often, instructional assistants are providing supports that even they are unaware of. Although the student may receive a passing grade, the requirements may be far less than the standard "norms". Many instructional assistants view their responsibilities to be that of ensuring the student's work is completed (never mind who is actually doing the thinking) and ensure that the student does not disrupt the class, is not a burden to the teacher, arrives at and remains where they are supposed to be and other housekeeping duties. This is commonly accomplished through continuous assistance and reminders to the point that the student rarely achieves any real degree of independent success. Additionally, such students are often not afforded the opportunities to "take risks" or overcome minor failures or challenges. And while the required class work and assignments may be getting done, the more essential skills for long term success and INDEPENDENCE, in both educational and "real life" settings may actually be neglected and regressing, e.g., independently attending to, remaining on and returning to task; problem solving; identification of need for assistance and requesting; self-monitoring and evaluation; self-regulation and other coping skills.

Finally, it is not uncommon that what is primarily achieved is behavioral maintenance. If indeed the student has achieved behavioral independence, this is a significant accomplishment, but at what price? Students who have the capability for significant academic progress but have only achieved staying under the behavioral radar are not really meeting their needs. And the greater number of students for whom this apparent "behavioral control" is only a façade is being done an even graver injustice. In fact, accommodations and reduced expectations <u>could</u> be an acceptable and effective initial step, if the goal were independent success and gradually increasing requirements. But unfortunately, this is rarely the case. We should be aiming not just for being present and inconspicuous, but for meaningful participation, social development, actual learning of new skills and the ability to function adaptively, successfully and independently, across a variety of natural settings.

DELUSION 7: JUST BECAUSE A STUDENT IS IN AN INCLUSIVE SETTING, CAN WE ASSUME IT REALLY IS INCLUSION?

Although a student may be in an inclusive setting, inclusion may merely be an illusion. Just because a student is in a typical classroom for the entire day, does this truly constitute inclusion? When one can identify the "included" student immediately, then the inclusion facade is somewhat shattered. Often disruptive behaviors are a clear indicator of the child's disorder. More commonly, however, the ever-present aide is the sure give away. Yes, support is an appropriate strategy, but only if it is coupled with systematic and intensive efforts to build independent responding and to fade prompts. Otherwise the presence of the aide becomes an obstacle to inclusion rather than a stepping stone.

When it is mostly the aide who is giving directions to the student, it undermines the role of the teacher and perpetuates the dependence on 1:1 instruction. Even worse is when the aide becomes the "repeater" for the teacher, that is after each time the teacher gives information to the class, the aide repeats the information for the student as often as is necessary until the student responds. This only teaches the student that the teacher is not an important person and in effect he has his own personal teacher. This is hardly what inclusion should be.

Another common problem that violates the spirit of inclusion is engaging the student in activities that only he is doing and that are not connected in any way with the instruction going on for all the other students. This becomes even more of a farce when the student is geographically isolated from the other students in the class.

Being included means having the same role and responsibility as every other member of the class and being a contributor. It means having your desk alongside everyone else and doing work that is closely related to what the others are learning. It means having no greater share of the aide's guidance than any other student. It means a whole lot more than simply residing in the same physical space as other students.

DELUSION 8: SIGNIFICANT AND ONGOING ACCOMMODATION IS AN EFFECTIVE AND APPROPRIATE LONG TERM STRATEGY FOR INCLUSION

One has to question whether it really is meaningful participation when tremendous modifications are necessary. These modifications or accommodations often include: classroom rules and behavioral expectations, expectations and demands, organization of work assignments and homework, quantity and quality of work, etc. While such modifications are appropriate in the short term, they are counterproductive in the long run. If the skill deficits that require these accommodations are not addressed and taught proactively, particularly those related to the processes of learning and functioning independently, the student becomes progressively less capable of succeeding and functioning in the real world. Thus, while everyone, including the student, is operating under the illusion that the student is progressing, s/he is actually regressing.

As an example of curriculum modification, in one classroom there was a discussion regarding Napoleon. The modification was for the ASD student to match the letter "N." If the task or skill the student is working on is so unrelated and disassociated from the rest of the class, the student is not attending to, interacting or participating within the actual group activity, what is the point? In actuality, the child is learning to ignore the other students, teacher and environmental events pertaining to the group activity. And thus, decreasing and discouraging social awareness in general.

Another common and related problem is the priority often placed on task or work completion, in lieu of focus on acquiring the <u>processes</u> necessary for independent learning. In place of opportunities to acquire independent learning skills, are often excessive accommodations and support, the focus and goal of which is to ensure that there is a completed work product. And while there is essentially no INDEPENDENT work where the student actually figures it out for himself, people congratulate themselves that entire pages of work are getting done and translate that into successful inclusion.

<u>"Best" (Worst) case scenario</u>: A student goes through the school system from elementary to high school with all the necessary supports and accommodations to be successfully and fully included. He graduates high school with "good" grades and is now embarking on the next leg of the journey into adulthood. The student has acquired limited skills in coping, socialization, communication and independence. Why? We have insulated him from the realities of functioning in society. We have accommodated his shortcomings and behavioral challenges, "protected" him from failures, thereby denying him the opportunity to learn from his mistakes. We have given him a false impression of how the "real world" operates. Worst of all, we have robbed him of the years of opportunity to acquire these critical life skills that could have occurred through sensible educational practices. But we can all celebrate and pat ourselves on the back because he has successfully "graduated."

> **NONSENSE**
>
> THE PRACTICES MOST FREQUENTLY ADOPTED IN
> EDUCATIONAL SETTINGS FOR INCLUDING STUDENTS ARE
> DIAMETRICALLY OPPOSED TO THE PROCEDURES THAT
> COULD MORE EFFECTIVELY TEACH AND DEVELOP THE
> SKILLS NECESSARY FOR TRULY SUCCESSFUL INCLUSION.

Does this mean that until students have acquired all of these requisite or "readiness" skills, they should not be integrated? Absolutely not. It means that we have a "road map" to utilize in gauging how a student is progressing in the skill areas that are essential for true success. It outlines the areas of need that must be addressed to promote long term independent gains. And it guides our journey which may include accommodations in the short run but also signals us to ensure that these skill deficits are actively addressed and acquired and accommodations eliminated before moving on to the next level or phases of integration.

THE "ROAD MAP" TO SUCCESSFUL INTEGRATION

Following are the areas that we have found important to concentrate on when preparing students for successful inclusion:

1. BEHAVIORAL CONTROL

Are the student's disruptive behaviors at a low enough frequency and intensity so that they are effectively and readily addressed in a naturalistic setting? Obviously, this is important so the student does not pose a risk or danger to themselves or others. Additionally, it is critical that they have sufficient behavioral control so they do not interfere in the education of other students.

Moreover, a much overlooked factor is the potential stigmatization that may occur if a student exhibits significant behavior disturbance, thereby reducing the likelihood of social interaction and the development of actual friendships in the future.

And finally, disruptive behaviors can directly interfere with the ability to learn. Mild to moderate levels of disruptive behavior can be tolerated as long as the necessary and appropriate behavioral treatment strategies can be implemented effectively and unobtrusively. If the behaviors are too severe this will be a serious impediment to learning within a group setting.

2. PROFICIENCY TO LEARN IN GROUPS

Students need to be able to learn in group formats. A great deal of instruction in the classroom is presented through group instruction. If a student is unable to attend or process in a group, then a great deal of the teaching opportunities will be missed and wasted. If a student has only been exposed to and taught primarily in a 1:1 setting, they generally have not acquired this ability. And if they are subsequently placed solely in a typical classroom, they will likely not be afforded the opportunity of "learning how to learn" in a group setting.

3. ATTENDING SKILLS

In order for a child to be able to process information and therefore learn, it is essential that the student possess good attending skills at least within a small group setting. If frequent prompting, direct instruction and consequences are necessary to facilitate the child's paying attention, a more restrictive placement may be appropriate for at least a portion of the school day in order to teach these skills. As discussed previously, a more structured environment may result in a quicker acquisition of attending skills, thereby allowing the child to receive more rapid and meaningful benefits from an inclusion placement. Additionally, a structured classroom could afford opportunities to systematically teach independent attending skills across gradually increasing group size (e.g., 1:2, 1:4, etc), which may not be feasible in an inclusive setting.

Another consideration is that most students' attending skills are variable. That is, a given student may be able to attend in some situations but not others, based on interests, group size, duration of presentation, teaching style, setting, etc. Thus, there may be particular subjects, activities, or settings into which a student could be successfully integrated. However, during less suitable activities, the time could be better used away from the large group to address these needs in a more intensive and structured setting, with the goal of teaching and generalizing the skills necessary for a regular education placement in the future.

4. ABILITY TO LEARN OBSERVATIONALLY

A student's capacity to learn observationally is also essential to success in the typical classroom. "Observational Learning" skills are comprised of a variety of sub-skills which, for students with ASD, generally need to be systematically targeted and reinforced. Some of these include: ability to filter irrelevant information; ability to process and recall information provided by multiple sources including peers and teacher; ability to discriminate correct vs. incorrect responses of others based on teacher feedback; and ability to make inferences based on information provided.

While this skill area is related to attending skills as discussed above, there are also some important differences. For example, a student may be relatively skilled at attending to the teacher in a group format, but may not be actually processing the information that is provided. Additionally, it is not sufficient only to attend to the teacher. A vast majority of students' learning is based upon their ability to obtain information through observation of peers. Therefore, it is necessary that a student can learn independently in this manner. If a student requires one-to-one instruction from an adult to acquire all or most new information, the benefits of inclusion are greatly reduced.

5. SKILLS COMMENSURATE WITH PEERS

If a student requires excessive curriculum modification, then full inclusion does not really make sense. In essence, if extensive accommodations and adjustments are required, if the child is not participating in the majority of classroom activities, and the student is primarily receiving instruction through their instructional assistant, is it really inclusion? Not only is the child not accessing or benefiting from the classroom curriculum; they are not really part of the classroom.

Having a student integrated during the activities in which they are most proficient would seem to make the most sense. This does not necessarily require that the student be able to perform at the same level as their peers. What it does require is that the student has adequate abilities to benefit from and acquire skills that are commensurate with the educational opportunity provided. For example: The student may not fully understand the specific content of the lesson, but they have sufficient attending skills to orient and model peers. If the goal is to increase their observational learning skills, this could be an effective inclusion setting for acquisition or generalization of these skills. Prior exposure to the main content of the lesson would allow the student to gain confidence in their ability to listen and pick up information that is being presented in a discussion format. However, it is important to ensure that the school staff members are clear that at this stage the goal is not academic achievement nor task completion, but rather improving performance in particular skill areas of observational learning (i.e., peer modeling). There also must be a substantial portion of the day where other important learning goals are being addressed in a more directly effective format.

6. INTEREST IN PEERS

More often than touting academic benefit, inclusion purports to provide great social opportunities. For a child to benefit from these social opportunities, however, it is important that the child has some degree of social interest. Naturally, this interest may need to be facilitated and nurtured. However, if there is minimal interest in peers, developing this in an inclusive setting may not be the optimal situation. A child's indifference, intolerance or avoidance toward other children will create a difficult environment to successfully teach and establish interest in peers. Even worse, however, the student may develop a reputation which will be difficult to overcome in the future.

Finally, if the student has very limited interest toward peers, the student will likely direct most if not all interactions and attention to the instructional assistant. In this case, the student is actually learning to ignore peers, making them even less interesting and important to the student.

7. BASIC SOCIAL SKILLS

While it is not necessary for a child to possess highly developed or sophisticated social skills in order to benefit and fit into an inclusive setting, some rudimentary skills are essential. If a student lacks the awareness and concern that picking his nose, passing gas, or having food on his face, is not socially acceptable, he may unwittingly repel classmates. Additionally, if he cannot wait his turn, stand in line, or refrain from unrelated verbal comments during class discussion, his peers may come to view him as odd or annoying, even though these social skill deficits are not significantly disruptive to the classroom.

As with other fundamental skills mentioned, these skills can be and need to be taught. However, in regular education classes the opportunity for teaching these incidental social skills occurs mainly "in the moment", which often does not provide sufficient repetition to remediate such deficits, and it will soon be too late to salvage the student's damaged reputation.

8. IMPACT ON THE CLASSROOM

As much as we are deeply concerned and interested in the education of our children, it is imperative to consider the needs of all of the students in the classroom. Our children can have a wonderful impact on their peers! Learning about differences and becoming increasingly sensitive can be a life altering experience. However, we must also consider the potentially negative impact.

Clearly, if a child's behavior poses a threat to the other students then inclusion is not the best alternative until those behaviors are sufficiently reduced. Additionally, if a child's behaviors or intervention strategies severely disrupt or interfere with the education of the other students then a more restrictive placement may be necessary at least for a portion of the school day. And of course if the student is having a negative impact on the class, it is unlikely that friendships will be developed.

9. PRIORITIZING CONTENT AND PROCESS: A BALANCING ACT

One of the greatest challenges we have encountered is obtaining a team consensus on prioritizing and balancing the focus on achievement of content and teaching the complex processes required to learn, adapt and function in the natural environment. That is, often school staff and parents tend to focus on academic achievement in inclusive settings. Of course, this is understandable; given "school" is the primary context in which academics are taught. Furthermore, recent educational edicts such as No Child Left Behind (Public Law 107-110) have created increased pressure for school districts to render academic success a high priority.

Unfortunately, this has often resulted in de-emphasis of the importance of teaching the learning "process" skills. Often the strategies implemented to ensure completion of content, serve to undermine acquisition of primary skills necessary for teaching and learning the processes. Since the reason regular education students are in the class is to learn the subject matter teachers are not prepared to stop the academic lesson to address the needs of a particular student who is not able to effectively utilize learning processes.

Additionally, as the classroom is a socialized setting, the skills necessary to be successfully included and socially accepted are based on social competencies. Once again, this is not the primary need of the general education student population. And in turn, teachers do not have the luxury of putting the rest of the class "on hold" just to deal with these socialization deficits and certainly could not do so at the rate that would be necessary to obtain improvement.

This challenge would not in itself preclude successful integration/inclusion, given that the time required to address these needs was allocated within the ASD student's daily school schedule. However, there often exists the unrealistic expectation that our children can be included for the <u>entire</u> school day, and still somehow gain these critical skills, even though they are not being specifically or systematically taught.

Another contributing factor is a similar focus on academics in IEP goals and objectives. As this is what drives the placement, the goals are predominantly academic. Given the educational and legal pressure to achieve these goals, once again school professionals often feel compelled to make academic "success" their main focus.

However, when one examines the diagnostic criteria for Autism Spectrum Disorders, one must note that academic abilities are <u>NOT</u> included. **WHY?** Because cognitive impairments are not the most significant challenges that our students face. In fact, many will excel in cognitive development, as compared to their typical peers. The deficits and needs that are inherent to ASD are: communication, social, and emotional/behavioral, as well as the awareness, ability, interest and motivation to process the relevant information that is necessary to learn from environmental events.

Without disrupting the overall classroom and calling attention to the student with ASD, these skills can not be taught in a fully included daily schedule. And yet, that is often the unrealistic expectation.

Gilliam and McConnel (1997) published Scales for Predicting Successful Inclusion (SPSI). This assessment tool can be used to predict which students have the requisite behaviors and skills and are, therefore, most likely to be truly successful in inclusion. This measure can also be quite helpful in identifying target behaviors and skills that require attention and intervention to facilitate success. Examples of the skills that they found to be predictive of successful inclusion include following classroom rules, paying attention during class discussions, and initiating activities with others. From our experience, it is clear that the majority of students who are included would not fare well on this assessment. Fortunately the skill areas that are commonly lacking can all be translated into teaching objectives and can be readily achieved for many students, if one takes an open-minded approach to where and how to teach.

One of the most problematic results of inclusion is the tremendous dependency the child develops. The student often cannot make a move without the aide either intervening or at least being right on top of the student. Although there is often the "illusion" that a child is independent, the aide is close by to provide support and assistance. The aide may provide obvious prompts or even subtle gestures and glances, but often the child in reality is highly dependent. In our experience, it is extremely common to observe aides providing subtle prompts, which they are often unaware of, thereby making it even more difficult to fade. Even if the aide is not providing direct guidance, their mere presence can be a degree of prompting and support.

As an alternative, let us say that the assignment is 20 math problems and the child could reasonably complete 5 of these independently. Instead of providing ongoing assistance, the quantity of work required could initially be reduced, establishing the expectation of <u>independent</u> completion with quality performance. Over time, the amount of work expected could be gradually increased.

Unfortunately, it has been our experience that when these issues are pointed out, aides will often state, "But when I back off or reduce assistance, he acts out, stops working, or can't pay attention". The typical response to this difficulty in fading is for the aide to provide increased assistance and attention in order to get the child back on track. This in turn, will likely reinforce these dependent behaviors, thereby continuing the vicious cycle of shaping higher and higher degrees of dependency over time.

PHILOSOPHICAL & EMOTIONAL MOVEMENT

As discussed earlier, every few years in the field of autism and developmental disabilities there is a new philosophical movement, or treatment approach, that becomes "fashionable". These movements are usually responses to problems and dissatisfaction with the current or conventional approach (Hallahan, 1998). Although they have at times led to important advances in the field, they unfortunately can also foster adverse effects as well. Because they are often over-reactions, there quickly develops total contempt for approaches which have had value. Instead of identifying and remedying specific problems, there is total disregard for **ALL** aspects of the now "outdated" approach (Fuchs & Fuchs, 1994).

Perhaps most distressing of all is that despite a paucity of definitive sound research, these "reform" movements then become politically and socially fashionable crusades that are sufficient to drive policy priorities, whereby yesterday's "golden boy" is today's "black sheep".

Many of these movements remain in fashion well beyond their "hey-day", although they may not be considered as "high fashion". The rage of the early '90's was unfounded medical and pharmacological treatments. The campaign for the late '90's was intensive ABA programming to occur **exclusively** at home. A currently fashionable crusade is "Inclusion". As with many other philosophical movements, inclusion is a reaction to ineffective education and treatment historically provided in special education classrooms.

At times, it appears the primary motivation is that it looks and feels good to have children with ASD in the presence of typically developing children. Strong proponents will assert that anything short of this is "discrimination" and inherently "degrading to the child". There is no consideration given to whether this approach is realistic, effective, or actually meets the student's needs. Furthermore, there is the **assumption** that the full inclusion approach will always be effective, and the individual will continue to learn and develop, over the long run. However, there is no scientific evidence that this contention is valid, or that this approach is, in truth, the most effective.

In fact, the preponderance of data suggests that it may be **less** effective (Bruder & Staff, 1998; Cole, Mills, Dale & Jenkins, 1991; Harrower, J.K., 1999; Zigmond & Baker, 1995). The zealots who insist all children should be fully included often succumb to what feels right rather objective analysis of scientific studies. Some of what they assert defies even common sense. Consider the case of a diabetic child. If extremists had their way, anyone proposing a restricted diet would be accused of discrimination because they would be treating the diabetic child differently than non-diabetic children. Or might they suggest that a hearing impaired child should play in the band or a child in a wheelchair should be playing soccer during regular education PE classes? And that the student should do so, regardless of how frustrated or inadequate this experience may make the child feel.

Inclusion is a reactionary movement that arose because there were serious problems identified in special education. Supporters correctly pointed out that some individuals were continually denied access to less restrictive settings because they were not considered "ready" and there was no anticipation that they would ever become "ready". Proponents blamed the **"readiness concept"** as the culprit for children remaining stuck in restrictive educational placements indefinitely. They have now gone overboard and reject any notion of evaluating to what extent a student would be able to benefit from full inclusion. "Of course, every student can benefit from inclusion so what is there to consider?" Regardless of a student's degree of disruptive behaviors or skill level he gets placed full time in classrooms for typically developing children.

Inclusion met with immediate approval for a number of reasons:

1. It addressed some inadequacies of traditional services

2. It has tremendous emotional appeal

3. It has a great deal of parental and political support

4. It has a relative degree of economic support

There are many good reasons why Inclusion should be the first option considered for a student:

1. Many children who should have been in less restrictive placements are enjoying the benefits of inclusion

2. Programs that were stuck in the morass of sub par educational practices have been forced to revise their philosophy & intervention strategies

3. Typical students have gained insight and sensitivity through their interaction with students with ASD and other disabilities

4. Some regular education teachers have acquired new skills, competency, confidence, and pride in their ability to work with and integrate students with ASD and other disabilities

Inclusion, however, is not the panacea that the advocates would like one to believe. Traditional special education services certainly have been plagued by tremendous problems that have resulted in ineffective educational treatment. In response, the zealots determined the whole system was "bad" rather than drawing the more sensible conclusion that there were abuses that needed to be corrected. It would be far more beneficial to the field to identify and correct the inadequacies rather than **throwing the baby out with the bath water**. For example, even today, the "readiness" model continues to be cited as justification to maintain placement in a self-contained classroom, when a student is not "ready" to be integrated. This lack of readiness may continue to be stated over the course of years, with little or no movement or progress towards increased integration. Additionally, there is rarely a solid plan or "roadmap" that is designed or implemented to address the specific needs and deficits that are hindering participation in more integrated settings.

SENSE
EVERY STUDENT SHOULD BE EDUCATED IN THE LEAST RESTRICTIVE ENVIRONMENT WHICH CAN MEET THEIR NEEDS. UNNECESSARILY RESTRICTIVE PLACEMENTS, BE THAT EDUCATIONAL OR RESIDENTIAL, CAN HAVE AN EXTREMELY NEGATIVE IMPACT ON STUDENTS. NEVERTHELESS, WE BELIEVE THERE ARE STUDENTS WHO DO NOT TRULY BENEFIT FROM BEING IN GENERAL EDUCATION. A "RESTRICTIVE" PLACEMENT SUCH AS A SELF-CONTAINED SPECIAL EDUCATION CLASS CAN HAVE TREMENDOUS BENEFITS FOR SUCH STUDENTS AND CAN LEAD TO GREATLY ENHANCED QUALITY OF LIFE.

Integration is not an "all or none" process. While many children may not be ready to be fully included, they may in fact be ready for some integration. Continually holding a student back because he cannot sufficiently benefit from full time inclusion is unnecessary and is a primary reason that parents and proponents of inclusion eventually get fed up and reject special education placement altogether.

The way to avoid this unfortunate outcome is to get the process started early and design a sensible plan for gradually increasing integration. It is not necessary to make grand promises. Too often those promises go unfulfilled and the child is blamed because of "inability" or lack of "readiness". If the student cannot meaningfully participate and benefit from inclusion, then the plan needs to spell out how to increase requisite group learning skills.

Meanwhile periods of the day when inclusion can be beneficial should be identified. 99% of the time that we have been involved in this process, parents not only support it, but become strong advocates for this approach. Our goal is to be able to do this from the outset rather than waiting until both special education placement and full inclusion have failed and a great amount of time has been lost.

RESEARCH

One would think that there would be a great deal of research demonstrating that inclusion is superior to more restrictive educational placements. We were simply amazed when we conducted a literature review and found extremely limited empirical evidence that suggested full inclusion to be more effective than special education.

A number of experts have commented on the absence of scientific investigations. For example, Hunt & Goetz (1997) noted that few studies have been done evaluating academic outcomes related to placement for ASD students. Cole, Mills, Dale, Jenkins (1991) stated:

"Although a belief in the educational developmental benefits of integration may provide the foundation for other rationales for integration, there is little evidence that these potential benefits actually occur." (Page 36)

Harrower (1999) noted:

"Because of the primarily philosophical nature of the debate and the paucity of the empirical evidence clearly supporting either side it appears that full inclusion will continue to be intensely debated into the future." (Page 215)

The few studies that have asserted the superiority of inclusion have not conducted a comparative analysis utilizing random assignment (e.g., Hallahan, 1998, Hunt & Goetz, 1997; Stainback & Stainback, 1996). In fact, the limited number of comparative studies that have been conducted show special education to be a more effective approach (e.g., Budoff & Gottlieb, 1976; Goldstein, Moss & Jordon, 1965).

There are studies that indicate that inclusion may actually be ineffective for students with disabilities (Gerber, 1995; Zigmond & Baker, 1995). Investigations have demonstrated that exposure does not result in improvements (e.g., Hanson, Gutierrez, Morgan, Brennan & Zercher, 1997; Hunt & Goetz, 1997; Jenkins et. al, 1985; Kellegrew, 1995; Kohler et. al, 1996). A great deal of research has shown that there is limited or no difference in developmental, language or academic progress in inclusion compared to those students in more restrictive classroom placements (e.g., Bruder & Staff, 1998; Cooke, Ruskus, Apolloni & Peck, 1981; Harris et al., 1990; Ispa & Matz, 1978; Jenkins, Jewel, Leicester, Jenkins & Troutner, 1991; Jenkins, Odom & Speltz, 1989; Jenkins, Speltz & Odom, 1985; Odom & McEvoy, 1988).

There have been studies that have indicated that students with ASD are on the receiving end of relationships and that this becomes more pronounced as the school years progress. In other words, it is not a reciprocal relationship and does not result in the development of actual friendships (Evans et. al, 1992; Hunt et. al, 1994).

A number of studies have shown that the degree of disability is related to the effectiveness of inclusion. Children with milder ASD can do well in inclusive placements, whereas children with more extreme behavior issues and skill deficits receive better educational benefit from more restrictive placements (Cole et al., 1991; Galloway & Chandler, 1978; Guralnick, 1980).

The vast majority of research that does exist demonstrates that a student's success in inclusion can be substantially improved by adding a number of behaviorally based and re-search derived procedures:

<u>Antecedent procedures</u>: (Hall, McClannahan & Krantz, 1995; Taylor & Levin, 1998; Zanolli, Daggett & Adams, 1996);

<u>Systematic fading of prompts</u>: (Sainato, Strain, Lefebvre & Rapp, 1987; Taylor & Levin, 1998);

<u>Shifting control to teachers</u>: (Smith & Camarata, 1999);

<u>Peer mediated intervention</u>: (DuPaul & Henningson, 1993; Fuchs et al., 1997; Goldstein et al., 1992; Kamps et al., 1994; Locke & Fuchs, 1995; Odom & Strain, 1986);

<u>Self-management strategies</u>: (Koegel et al., 1992; Pierce & Schreibman, 1994; Sainato, Strain, Lefebvre & Rapp, 1990; Strain, et al., 1994).

We find it absolutely shocking that so many school districts have adopted FULL inclusion as their standard educational "model", and even made it a policy. First, there is no compelling scientific evidence demonstrating inclusion to be a more effective approach. It is hard to fathom a medical approach being adopted with such limited empirical evidence of its effectiveness. Second, adopting any standard policy absolutely usurps the notion of individualization, the very foundation of IDEA. The problem here is not the philosophy that full inclusion be a primary goal. Rather, it is the way in which this ideology is often implemented. That is, full inclusion for ALL, regardless of the individual's needs.

A HIGHLY EMOTIONAL ISSUE

Although, overall research does not substantiate the superiority of inclusion vs. more restrictive options, it is clear that in many circumstances inclusion may be a far better option. As discussed previously, if a child has behavior control, attending, and other requisite skills, then full or "mostly full" inclusion may be the appropriate option. Additionally, if a quality special education program is not available then inclusion may be the better choice.

What we are advocating is that such a critical decision be made based on considerations of objective assessment and most importantly what configuration of programming, services and placement best meets the individual needs of the student, both in the short and long term. It should NOT be politically determined, dictated by policy nor based primarily on emotion. But it is a topic that generates passion and there are times when passion obscures reason. People have misinterpreted our stance as being anti-inclusion because they do not see us as fully embracing what they consider to be a fundamental issue of human rights. No one believes more strongly than we do in children's right to be part of society. Where we have chosen to concentrate our efforts is on developing skills so that children with ASD can fit in to a world that does not always make accommodations for people who are differently abled.

It has to be said: Our children deserve education and treatment that will afford them the best opportunity to achieve the highest quality of life, and not "treatment" that simply feels good.

REFERENCES

Bachrach, L. L., (1986). Deinstitutionalization: What do the numbers mean? *Hospital and Community Psychiatry, 37,* 118-121.

Bruder, M. B., & Staff, I. (1998). A comparison of the effects of the type of classroom and service characteristics on toddlers with disabilities. *Topics in Early Childhood Special Education, 18,* 26-37.

Budoff, M., & Gottlieb, J. (1976). Special class EMR children mainstreamed: A study of an aptitude (learning potential) x treatment interaction. *American Journal of Mental Deficiency, 81,* 1-11.

Callahan, K., & Rademacher, J. A. (1999). Using self-management strategies to increase the on-task behavior of a student with autism. *Journal of Positive Behavior Interventions, 1,* 117-122.

Cole, K. N., Mills, P. E., Dale, P. S., & Jenkins, J. R. (1991). Effects of preschool integration for children with disabilities. *Exceptional Children, 58,* 36-45.

Cooke, T., Ruskus, J., Apolloni, T., & Peck, C. (1981). Handicapped preschool children in the mainstream: Background, outcomes & clinical suggestions. *Topics in Early Childhood Special Education, 1,* 73-83.

Davis, C. A., Brady, M. P., Hamilton, R., McEvoy, M. A., & Williams, R. E. (1994). Effects of high probability requests on the social interactions of young children with severe disabilities. *Journal of Applied Behavior Analysis, 27,* 619-637.

Downing, J. E., Eichinger, J., & Williams, L. J. (1997). Inclusive education for children with severe disabilities: Comparative reviews of principals and educators at different level of implementation. *Remedial and Special Education, 18,* 133-142.

Dunlap, L. K., Dunlap, G., Koegel, L. K., & Koegel, R. L. (1991). Using self-monitoring to increase independence. *Teaching Exceptional Children, 23,* 17-22.

DuPaul, G. J., & Henningson, P. N. (1993). Peer tutoring effects on the classroom performance of children with attention deficit hyperactivity disorder. *School Psychology Review, 22,* 134-143.

Evans, L. M., Salisbury, C. L., Palombaro, M. M., Berryman, J., & Hollywood, T. M. (1992). Peer interactions and social acceptance of elementary-age children with severe disabilities in an inclusive school. *Journal of the Association for Persons with Severe Handicaps, 17,* 205-212.

Falk, G. D., Dunlap, G., & Kern, L. (1996). An analysis of self-evaluation and video-tape feedback for improving the peer interactions of students with externalizing and internalizing behavioral problems. *Behavioral Disorders, 21,* 261-276.

Fuchs, D., & Fuchs, L. S. (1994). Inclusive school movements and the radicalization of special education reform. *Exceptional Children, 60,* 294-309.

Fuchs, D., Fuchs, L. S., Mathes, P. G., & Simmons, D. C. (1997). Peer-assisted learning strategies: Making classrooms more responsive to diversity. *American Educational Research Journal, 34,* 174-206.

Galloway, C., & Chandler, P. (1978). The marriage of special and early education services. In M. Guralnick (Ed.), *Early intervention and the integration of handicapped and non-handicapped children* (pp. 261-287). Baltimore: University Park Press.

Gaylord-Ross, R., & Pitts-Conway, V. (1984). Social behavior development in integrated secondary autistic programs. In N. Certo, N. Haring, & R. York (Eds.), *Public school integration of severely handicapped students: Rational issues and progressive alternatives* (pp. 197-219). Baltimore: Brookes.

Gerber, M. M. (1995). Inclusion at the high water mark? Some thoughts on Zigmond and Baker's case studies of inclusive educational programs. *The Journal of Special Education, 29,* 181-191.

Giangreco, M. F. (1993). Using creative problem-solving methods to include students with severe disabilities in general education classroom activities. *Journal of Educational and Psychological Consultation, 4,* 113-135.

Gilliam, J. & McConnell, K. (1997). Scales for Predicting Successful Inclusion. Austin, TX: Pro-Ed.

Goldstein, H., & Cisar, C. L. (1992). Promoting interaction during sociodramatic play: Teaching scripts to typical preschoolers and classmates with disabilities. *Journal of Applied Behavior Analysis, 25,* 265-280.

Goldstein, H., Kaczmarek, L., Pennington, R., & Shafer, K. (1992). Peer-mediated intervention: Attending to, commenting on, and acknowledging the behavior of preschoolers with autism. *Journal of Applied Behavior Analysis, 25,* 289-305.

Goldstein, H., Moss, J., & Jordon, L. J. (1965). *The efficacy of special class training on the development of mentally retarded children.* Urbana: University of Illinois Press.

Guralnick, M. (1980). Social interaction among preschool handicapped children. *Exceptional Children, 46,* 248-253.

Hall, L. J., McClannahan, L. E., & Krantz, P. J. (1995). Promoting independence in integrated classrooms by teaching aides to use activity schedules and decreased prompts. *Education and Training in Mental Retardation, 30,* 208-217.

Hallahan, D. P. (1998). Sounds bytes from special education reform rhetoric. *Remedial and Special Education, 19,* 67-69.

Hanson, M. J., Gutierrez, S., Morgan, M., Brennan, E. L., & Zercher, C. (1997). Language, culture, and disability: Interacting influences on preschool inclusion. *Topics in Early Childhood Special Education, 17,* 307-336.

Harris, S. L., Handleman, J. S., Kristoff, B., Bass, L., & Gordon, R. (1990). Changes in language development among autistic and peer children in segregated and integrated preschool settings. *Journal of Autism and Developmental Disorders, 20,* 23-31.

Harrower, J. K. (1999). Educational inclusion of children with severe disabilities. *Journal of Positive Behavior Interventions, 1,* 215-230.

Harrower, J. K., & Dunlap, G. (2001). Including children with autism in general education classrooms. *Behavior Modification, 25,* 762-784.

Havey, J. M. (1998). Inclusion, the law and placement decisions: Implications for school psychologists. *Psychology in the Schools, 35,* 145-152.

Hilton, A., & Liberty, K. (1992). The challenge of insuring educational gains for students with severe disabilities. *Education and Training in Mental Retardation, 27,* 167-175.

Hunt, P., Farron-Davis, F., Wrenn, M., Hirose-Hatae, A., & Goetz, L. (1997). Promoting interactive partnerships in inclusive educational settings. *Journal of the Association for Persons with Severe Handicaps, 22,* 127-137.

Hunt, P., & Goetz, L. (1997). Research on inclusive educational programs, practices and outcomes for students with severe disabilities. *The Journal of Special Education, 31,* 3-29.

Hunt, P., Staub, D., Alwell, M., & Goetz, L. (1994). Achievement by all students within the context of cooperative learning groups. *Journal of the Association for Persons with Severe Handicaps, 19,* 290-301.

Hurley-Geffner, C. M. (1995). Friendships between children with and without developmental disabilities. In R. L. Koegel & L. K. Koegel (Eds.), *Teaching children with autism: Strategies for initiating positive interactions and improving learning opportunities* (pp. 105-125). Baltimore: Brookes.

Ispa, J., & Matz, R. (1978). Integrating handicapped and preschool children within a cognitively oriented program. In M. Guralnick (Ed.), *Early intervention and the integration of handicapped and non-handicapped children* (pp. 167-190). Baltimore: University Park Press.

Janney, R. E., & Snell, M. E. (1997). How teachers include students with moderate and severe disabilities in elementary classes: The means and the meaning of inclusion. *Journal of the Association for Persons with Severe Handicaps, 22,* 159-169.

Jenkins, J. R., Jewel, M., Leicester, N., Jenkins, L., & Troutner, N. M. (1991). Development of school building model for educating students with handicaps and at-risk students in general education classrooms. *Journal of Learning Disabilities, 24,* 311-320.

Jenkins, J. R., Odom, S. L., & Speltz, M. L. (1989). Effects of social integration on preschool children with handicaps. *Exceptional Children, 55,* 420-428.

Jenkins, J. R., Speltz, M. L., & Odom, S. L. (1985). Integrating normal and handicapped preschoolers: Effects on child development and social interaction. *Exceptional Children, 52,* 7-17.

Kamps, D. M., Barbetta, P. M., Leonard, B. R., & Delquadri, J. (1994). Classwide peer tutoring: An integration strategy to improve reading skills and promote peer interactions among students with autism and general education peers. *Journal of Applied Behavior Analysis, 27,* 49-61.

Kamps, D. M., Leonard, B., Potucek, J., & Garrison-Harrell, L. (1995). Cooperative learning groups in reading: An integration strategy for students with autism and general classroom peers. *Behavioral Disorders, 21,* 89-109.

Kellegrew, D. H. (1995). Integrated school placements for children with disabilities. In R. L. Koegel & L. K. Koegel (Eds.), *Teaching children with autism: Strategies for initiating positive interactions and improving learning opportunities* (pp. 127-146). Baltimore: Brookes.

Kennedy, C. H., Cushing, L. S., & Itkonen, T. (1997). General education participation improves the social contacts and friendship networks of students with severe disabilities. *Journal of Behavioral Education, 7,* 167-189.

Koegel, L. K., Koegel, R. L., Hurley, C., & Frea, W. D. (1992). Improving social skills and disruptive behavior in children with autism through self management. *Journal of Applied Behavior Analysis, 25,* 341-353.

Kohler, F. W., Strain, P. S., & Shearer, D. D. (1996). Examining levels of social inclusion within an integrated preschool for children with autism. In L. K. Koegel, R. L. Koegel, and G. Dunlap (Eds.), *Positive behavioral support: Including people with difficult behavior in the community* (pp. 305-332). Baltimore: Brookes.

Locke, W. R., & Fuchs, L. S. (1995). Effects of peer-mediated reading instruction on the on-task behavior and social interaction of children with behavior disorders. *Journal of Emotional and Behavioral Disorders, 3,* 92-99.

McGee, G. G., Morrier, M. J., & Daly, T. (1999). An incidental teaching approach to early intervention for toddlers with autism. *Journal of the Association for Persons with Severe Handicaps, 24,* 133-146.

Newport, J. (2002). The Myth of Inclusion. *Feat of Arizona Newsletter,* Spring, 2(3).

Odom, S., & McEvoy, M. (1988). Integration of young handicapped children and normally developing children. In S. Odom & M. Karnes (Eds.), *Early intervention for infants and children with handicaps: An empirical base* (pp. 241-267). Baltimore: Paul H. Brookes.

Odom, S. L., & Strain, P. S. (1986). A comparison of peer-initiation and teacher antecedent interventions for promoting reciprocal social interactions of autistic preschoolers. *Journal of Applied Behavior Analysis, 19,* 59-71.

Pierce, K., & Schreibman, L. (1994). Teaching daily living skills to children with autism in unsupervised settings through pictorial self-management. *Journal of Applied Behavior Analysis, 27,* 471-481.

Pierce, K., & Schreibman, L. (1997). Multiple peer use of pivotal response training to increase social behaviors of classmates with autism: Results from trained and untrained peers. *Journal of Applied Behavior Analysis, 30,* 157-160.

Russo, D. C., & Koegel, R. L. (1977). A method of integrating an autistic child into a normal public-school classroom. *Journal of Applied Behavior Analysis, 10,* 579-590.

Sainato, D. M., Strain, P. S., Lefebvre, D., & Rapp, N. (1987). Facilitating transition times with handicapped preschool children: A comparison between peer-mediated and antecedent prompt procedures. *Journal of Applied Behavior Analysis, 20,* 285-291.

Sainato, D. M., Strain, P. S., Lefebvre, D., & Rapp, N. (1990). Effects of self-evaluation on the independent work skills of preschool children with disabilities. *Exceptional Children, 56,* 540-549.

Simmons, D. C., Kameenui, E. J., & Chard, D. J. (1998). General education teachers' assumptions about learning and students with learning disabilities: Design of instruction analysis. *Learning Disability Quarterly, 21,* 6-21.

Smith, A. E., & Camarata, S. (1999). Using teacher implemented instruction to increase the language intelligibility of children with autism. *Journal of Positive Behavior Interventions, 1,* 141-151.

Strain, P. S. (1983). Generalization of autistic children's social behavior change: Effects of developmentally integrated and segregated settings. *Analysis and Interventions in Developmental Disabilities, 3,* 23-34.

Strain, P. S., Kohler, F. W., Storey, K., & Danko, C. D. (1994). Teaching preschoolers with autism to self-monitor their social interactions: An analysis of results in home and school settings. *Journal of Emotional and Behavioral Disorders, 2,* 78-88.

Stainback, W., & Stainback, S. (1996). Collaboration, support, networking, and community building. In S. Stainback & W. Stainback (Eds.), *Inclusion: A guide for educators* (pp. 193-199). Baltimore: Brookes.

Taylor, B. A., & Levin, L. (1998). Teaching a student with autism to make verbal initiations: Effects of tactile prompt. *Journal of Applied Behavior Analysis, 31,* 651-654.

Waldron, N. L., & McLeskey, J. (1998). The effects of an inclusive school program on students with mild and severe learning disabilities. *Exceptional Children, 64,* 395-405.

Wolfensberger, W. (1972). *The principle of normalization in human services.* Toronto: National Institute on Mental Retardation.

Zanolli, K., Daggett, J., & Adams, T. (1996). Teaching preschool age autistic children to make spontaneous initiations to peers using priming. *Journal of Autism and Developmental Disorders, 26,* 407-421.

Zigmond, N., & Baker, J. M. (1995). Concluding comments: Current and future practices in inclusive schooling. *The Journal of Special Education, 29,* 245-250.